Colonial Tropes and Postcolonial Tricks

Liverpool Latin American Studies

Series Editors: John Fisher, *University of Liverpool,*
and Steve Rubenstein, *University of Liverpool*

Liverpool Latin American Studies, New Series 10

Colonial Tropes and Postcolonial Tricks

Rewriting the Tropics
in the *novela de la selva*

Lesley Wylie

LIVERPOOL UNIVERSITY PRESS

First published 2009 by
Liverpool University Press
4 Cambridge Street
Liverpool
L69 7ZU

British Library Cataloguing-in-Publication Data
A British Library CIP Record is available

ISBN 978-1-84631-195-6

Typeset in Plantin by Koinonia, Bury
Printed in Great Britain by the MPG Books Group, Bodmin and King's Lynn

For my mother,
Dorothy Wylie

Contents

Acknowledgements

I would like to thank the Arts and Humanities Research Board and the Master and Fellows of Emmanuel College, Cambridge, for supporting the doctoral research on which this book is based. I would also like to thank the Department of Literature, Film, and Theatre Studies at the University of Essex for appointing me to a research post, during which I completed the book.

Many people helped me in the writing of this book. Steven Boldy was a generous, dedicated, and insightful doctoral supervisor to whom I wish to express my considerable gratitude. Geoffrey Kantaris and Catherine Davies examined this book as a PhD thesis. They offered helpful advice, and posed some incisive and important questions. Ciaran Cosgrove, Peter Hulme, Lúcia Sá, Erica Segre, Alison Sinclair, and Ross Wilson all offered invaluable advice at different stages of the book's development. Above all, I would like to thank my family and my husband for their unwavering support and encouragement.

Some sections of the book have been published in an earlier form. I would like to thank *Romance Studies* and Maney Publishing (www.maney.co.uk/journals/romance; http://www.ingentaconnect.com/content/maney/ros) for granting me permission to reproduce parts of 'Hearts of Darkness: The Celebration of Otherness in the Latin American *novela de la selva*', *Romance Studies*, 23.2 (2005), 105–16. I would also like to thank *The Modern Language Review* and The Modern Humanities Research Association for allowing me to reproduce 'Colonial Tropes and Postcolonial Tricks: Rewriting the Tropics in the *novela de la selva*', *Modern Language Review*, 101 (2006), 728–42.

Introduction

In *Keywords* Raymond Williams observed that 'nature' and 'nation' derive from the same Latin root, *nasci*, 'to be born'.[1] In the context of Spanish-American literature the coincidence between nature and the nation transcends merely a shared etymology. Throughout the founding fictions of the nineteenth and early twentieth centuries Spanish-American authors enshrined nature, especially the tropical rainforest, as a source of literary identity. While prior to independence South America's landscape and people had largely been represented by outsiders, the *novela de la selva* – the Spanish-American Jungle Novel – turned to the rainforest, and the indigenous communities who lived there, in order to construct a distinctively American literature. Through parodic reworkings of European perceptions of the tropics in literature and anthropology the *novela de la selva* transformed the burdensome texts of the colonial era into enabling stories of cultural and narrative self-determination, inaugurating a home-grown tradition of tropical nature writing, which resonates in Latin American literature to the present day.

The *novela de la selva* has often been viewed as a minor offshoot of the *novela de la tierra*, and has been discussed alongside classic novels of this genre such as Rómulo Gallegos's *Doña Bárbara* and Ricardo Güiraldes's *Don Segundo Sombra*, ignoring the environmental specificity of the genre.[2] This book examines the *novela de la selva* in the context of writing about tropical South America, particularly the dense forests surrounding the Amazon and Orinoco Rivers. In European literature, from the colonial *cartas de relación* to Romantic novels by François René Chateaubriand and Jacques-Henri Bernardin de Saint Pierre, the tropics was often conceived, paradoxically, as a space of danger and wonder, terror and adventure. This ambivalence towards the tropics continued well into the twentieth century in sensational travel accounts such as F. W. Up de Graff's *Head Hunters of the Amazon; Seven Years of Exploration and Adventure* [1923] and Julian Duguid's *Green Hell: Adventures in the Mysterious Jungles of Eastern Bolivia* [1931].

The *novela de la selva* developed alongside these accounts of the tropics, often locating their action in the very same jungles that had been written about for centuries by explorers, missionaries, naturalists, and European novelists. Despite a superficial correspondence between the *novela de la selva* and European writing on the tropics, it would be a mistake to regard these narratives as being part of a shared tradition. Rather, the *novela de la selva* parodies European discourses of the tropics and initiates a new way of writing about tropical space, celebrating the perceived Otherness of the jungle and its native inhabitants as the foundation for a distinctive Spanish-American literary identity.[3] Mary Louise Pratt has credited Alexander von Humboldt with being 'the single most influential interlocutor in the process of reimagining and redefining that coincided with Spanish America's independence from Spain'.[4] Although echoes of Humboldt's writings on the South American tropics can be discerned throughout the *novela de la selva*, particularly in José Eustasio Rivera's *La vorágine* and Alejo Carpentier's *Los pasos perdidos*, these allusions are often ironic. While Humboldt's descriptions of landscape in his *Personal Narrative* and *Views of Nature* did, undoubtedly, contribute to the development of a new idiom for describing tropical South America, his writings were firmly grounded in European aesthetic categories such as the sublime – a trope of European travel writing on the tropics that is rejected throughout the *novela de la selva*. While Pratt has stressed the importance of Humboldt's 'reinvention of America', my study is more concerned to illustrate the next step, which was the reinvention of Humboldt, among others, in the *novela de la selva*.[5]

The *novela de la selva* can be seen as the literary coming of age of a tropical stylistics that had been initiated in the first years after independence. By the time the *novela de la selva* came into vogue in the 1920s and 30s, geographical writing was a well-established genre in Latin America. The imperative to inscribe space began in the immediate aftermath of the wars of independence, when various Latin American republics began to map their territories and commission lengthy and detailed descriptions of their terrain – for example, Agustín Codazzi's *Jeografía física y política de las provincias de la Nueva Granada*, which outlined the findings of the Colombian Chorography Commission.[6] A more popular manifestation of this desire to map the nation was fulfilled by the *costumbrista* sketch, which recorded local and regional traditions. Literary expressions of 'tropicality' can be seen as early as the 1820s, when the Venezuelan poet and statesman Andrés Bello published *Silva a la agricultura en la zona tórrida* [1826] – often described as an American rewriting of Virgil's *Georgics* – in which he catalogued and eulogized the characteristic products of the South American tropics. Later on in the nineteenth century, inspired by the writings of Humboldt and European Romanticism, the tropics became source material for works such as Jorge Isaacs's *María* (Colombia) or Juan León Mera's *Cumandá* (Ecuador), although both of these novels remain steeped in the influence of European writers such as Chateaubriand and Bernardin.

While, then, the imperative to describe national landscapes was strong in the early years after independence, the *novela de la selva* did not reach the peak of its popularity until the 1920s and 30s. Although *Green Mansions* [1904] by the Anglo-Argentine writer W. H. Hudson can retrospectively be classified as a *novela de la selva*, the genre did not come into its own until the publication of the Colombian novel *La vorágine* [1924] by José Eustasio Rivera, followed by *Toá* [1933] by the Colombian writer César Uribe Piedrahita, and *Canaima* [1935] by the Venezuelan novelist and statesman, Rómulo Gallegos. In the same period the Uruguayan writer Horacio Quiroga's *Cuentos de la selva* [1918] and *Los desterrados* [1926] form an important analogue to the *novela de la selva* in the short story form.[7]

In this study, *Los pasos perdidos* [1953] by the Cuban author Alejo Carpentier will be taken to mark the outer limits of the *novela de la selva* genre. Its meditation on not only European inscriptions of the tropics but also on their reformulation in the earlier *novelas de la selva* makes this a suitably self-reflexive climax to a genre which has at its heart the rewriting of texts. Although many novels of the Boom and post-Boom eras feature the jungle as a mise en scène (for example, Gabriel García Márquez's *Cien años de soledad* [1967] and Mario Vargas Llosa's *La casa verde* [1965] and *El hablador* [1987]) there are significant differences between these and the earlier novels.

A rich tradition of writing on Amazonia can also be found, unsurprisingly, in Brazilian literature from the mid-nineteenth century onward, including Inglez de Souza's *O Missionário* [1888], Alberto Rangel's *Inferno Verde* [1907], and Mario de Andrade's *Macunaíma* [1928]. Although there are many parallels between the representation of the rainforest in literature from Brazil and, more widely, from Spanish America, this book focuses exclusively on the latter. While Brazilian literature on Amazonia has been the focus of a number of studies, most recently Pedro Maligo's *Land of Metaphorical Desires: The Representation of Amazonia in Brazilian Literature* [1998] and Lúcia Sá's *Rain Forest Literatures: Amazonian Texts and Latin American Culture* [2005], the Amazonian content of novels from Spanish America has been less well explored. Although this book will not discuss specific engagements with the Amazon in post-independence Lusophone literature, many of the motifs in the *novela de la selva*, such as the image of the jungle as a green hell, can be seen to have derived from the Brazilian tradition.

So, what are the defining features of the *novela de la selva*? Why consider some novels set in the jungle to be *novelas de la selva* and others not? Throughout this study I will use the term *novela de la selva* to denote novels from Spanish America which are distinguished by their recourse to the jungle not only as a physical space but also as a symbol for the limits of European writing on the tropics. Salient characteristics of the genre include the use of ironic narrators, a distrust of conventional aesthetic categories, and mock-heroic interludes. Unlike the protagonists of European travel writing on the tropics, the experience of the postcolonial traveller in the *novela de la selva* might well be summarized as 'I came, I saw, I *was* conquered'.

This book will focus on the four emblematic novels of the genre – W. H. Hudson's *Green Mansions*, José Eustasio Rivera's *La vorágine*, Rómulo Gallegos's *Canaima*, and Alejo Carpentier's *Los pasos perdidos*. While the fifty-year period which separates Hudson's and Carpentier's novels leads to certain stylistic shifts, the plot and themes of all of the novels to be examined here are remarkably similar. They all centre on the journeys of urban Latin Americans to the jungle – journeys which are highly symbolic quests into not only the geographical but also the moral hinterlands beyond the city. Although written in English, *Green Mansions* is paradigmatic within the *novela de la selva* genre. Hudson's parents were among the first North American settlers in La Plata in Argentina and he was born in a ranch on the pampas in 1841, where he lived until he moved to England in 1874.[8] While Hudson's literary output has been in English, thematically his novels correspond to the Spanish-American telluric tradition. In *The Purple Land, El Ombú*, and his autobiographical *Far Away and Long Ago* W. H. Hudson – or, as he is more often referred to in Latin America, Guillermo Enrique Hudson – has established his legacy as an Argentine writer. Indeed, Hudson's use of English is in some ways no less problematic than, say, Rivera's use of Spanish to write about Amerindian culture or a rampant natural space that constantly defies language per se.

As the poet Nicomedes Suárez-Araúz has argued, the *novela de la selva* should not be conflated with 'Amazonian writing'.[9] Although Sá's important recent study has shown that many twentieth-century Brazilian and Spanish-American novels on the rainforest were derived from indigenous Amazonian sources, these are novels on and not of the jungle, written by Creole writers, many of whom had spent little time in a tropical forest.[10] Hudson, for instance, had never visited Venezuela, even though *Green Mansions* is set in the rainforests around the Orinoco, and Carpentier, Rivera, and Gallegos had spent only brief periods in the jungle before writing their novels. In fact, until recently, most of these novels were regarded not as 'Amazonian' but 'regional', a term tainted by its associations with primitive literary techniques, and rural rather than metropolitan concerns.[11] In the case of *La vorágine*, for instance, the use of regional dialects, the denunciation of Peruvian and Venezuelan rubber traders in Colombia's southern borderlands, and the inclusion of long geographical descriptions, all contribute to the novel's standing as a national narrative of Colombia. Likewise, *Canaima*, alongside Gallegos's *Doña Bárbara*, has been regarded as a quintessentially Venezuelan novel. Although these novels are, for sure, concerned with regional and national questions such as border disputes between Colombia and Peru, or education in Venezuela, the authors of the *novela de la selva* were also clearly contributing to a broader movement of Spanish-American literature, which transcended the national identities of the authors. While the specific concerns of the *novela de la selva* changed from decade to decade and from country to country, the genre's overriding attention to the renovation of literary form and to the development of an authentic, recognizable tropical aesthetic provided a degree of continuity that is rarely seen in a narrative tradition spanning half a century.

Although the four novels central to this book are considered 'classics' of Latin American narrative, as a genre the *novela de la selva* has received very little critical attention. Lydia de León Hazera's 1971 study is the only full-length treatment of the novels.[12] In her opening paragraph, she correctly acknowledges the centrality of the *novela de la selva* to the search for identity in Spanish America:

> Nace la Novela de la Selva como un producto del anhelo americanista del siglo XIX que buscaba crear una literatura autóctona, y nada podía ser más autóctono que las selvas inexploradas de América, en particular aquéllas de la cuenca del Amazonas.[13]

Nevertheless, the focus of León Hazera is on the internal development of the *novela de la selva* as a genre, rather than on the important intersections between nature and literary identity which form the main theme here. More recently the *novela de la selva* has been discussed by Sá, who argues that the authors of the Spanish-American and, in particular, Brazilian jungle novel drew extensively upon indigenous source texts from the Amazon.[14] The continuities identified by Sá between an indigenous mythical tradition and writing on and from the Amazon in the nineteenth and twentieth centuries is an important step in recognizing that the authors of the *novela de la selva* were engaging not only with European writing but also with texts indigenous to Central and South America.

This book will build upon interpretations of the *novela de la selva* by León Hazera and Sá, and pose many new questions. Why did the tropical forest become a key place for the re-imagination of South America in the 1920s and 30s? What is the difference between the representation of the jungle and Amerindian tribes in these novels and in European accounts of the tropics? And, in particular, how did the *novela de la selva* contribute to a postcolonial literary identity in Spanish America?

The question of whether the *novela de la selva* can be considered 'postcolonial' is really twofold. Firstly, it involves accepting that Latin America itself can be discussed within the framework of postcolonial theory. The debate as to Latin America's status vis-à-vis postcolonial studies has lasted well over a decade, largely sparked off by an essay by the anthropologist J. Jorge Klor de Alva, who questioned whether an error is 'being committed when scholars apply tools and categories of analysis developed in the twentieth century for understanding British colonialism, especially in India and Africa, to make sense of the experiences of sixteenth- to eighteenth-century Latin America?'[15] Many of those opposed to the application of postcolonial theory to Latin America have repeatedly denounced it as just another form of colonialism which attempts to explain local conditions using foreign models.[16] They also have criticized its ahistorical tendencies, which, for example, permit the use of the same terms of analysis when discussing British colonialism in Africa and neocolonialism in Latin America.

Despite these objections a consensus has developed over the past decade or so in favour of 'including America' (the title of an important 1995 essay on the debate by Peter Hulme) in postcolonial studies.[17] However, even those who have accepted this inclusion are sometimes still troubled by a lack of attention to the particularity of Latin American 'experience' within postcolonial studies.

Hulme has noted, for example, that Edward Said's *Orientalism* and *Culture and Imperialism* 'have concerned themselves almost exclusively with the "Old World"'.[18] There is also a fear that Latin American theorists such as José Carlos Mariátegui, Angel Rama, or Fernando Ortiz might be all too readily assimilated into 'postcolonial' paradigms, thereby losing their regional and historical specificity. In an essay on Mariátegui in Robin Fiddian's landmark collection of essays, *Postcolonial Perspectives on the Cultures of Latin America and Lusophone Africa* (2000), Patricia D'Allemand has admitted to being suspicious of certain tendencies within postcolonial studies:

> Amongst my concerns [...] are the danger of dehistoricization of Latin American discourses, the dilution of their particular traits and multiplicity of meanings, and the consequent loss of sight of local traditions of thought, as well as the silencing of local debates.[19]

Despite these misgivings, however, D'Allemand's essay – and the Fiddian collection as a whole – shows precisely how, when used self-critically, postcolonial theory need not engulf local traditions, but can add an extra critical dimension to them.

The second part of the question posed above – whether the *novela de la selva* can be considered 'postcolonial' – relates to the genre itself. Although Latin America has been at the margins of the postcolonial debate over the past two decades, many of the more general observations about colonial and postcolonial identity made by Said, Homi K. Bhabha, and others can help to explain certain cultural manifestations such as the *novela de la selva*. In fact, little objection has been made to the designation of one of the writers included in this book, Alejo Carpentier, as a 'postcolonial artist',[20] or to considering him alongside other authors often considered 'postcolonial', such as Frantz Fanon, Edouard Glissant, or Wilson Harris.[21] This book will show that the textual strategies used by Carpentier in *Los pasos perdidos* (unreliable narration, parody, inter-textual allusion, self-referentiality) – all recognized as common techniques of the modern (even postmodern) novel and of postcolonial writers worldwide – were also a feature of the much earlier *novela de la selva*. There is a common misconception in Latin American literary criticism that *La vorágine* or *Canaima* were unsophisticated tributes or even contributions to a colonial discourse of the tropics which stretched back to the days of the conquest. This is quickly discounted when one positions these texts not at the end of a European literary tradition of tropical nature aesthetics and ethnography, but at the forefront of a new way of writing about the South American rainforest.

Despite this, the term 'postcolonial' has never, to my knowledge, been applied to the *novela de la selva*. Indeed, given the relatively recent emergence of the 'postcolonial' as a critical discipline, it may seem somewhat anachronistic to apply the term to the cultural production of Latin American writers in the early twentieth century, especially when so many of their countries of origin had achieved independence over a century before. There are, however, many reasons to consider the *novela de la selva* 'postcolonial'. Although the

genre did not emerge in the immediate aftermath of independence, it did come
to prominence at the end of a decade of continent-wide festivities marking a
century of independence from colonial rule. The ten years from 1910 to 1920
were characterized by nostalgia and self-introspection in Spanish America,
particularly among intellectuals and writers who were engaging in the search
for cultural identity with renewed vigour.[22] As Carlos Alonso has observed:

> The commemoration of this historical moment – a moment that was recon-
> structed and refashioned as much as it was celebrated in 1910 – posited also the
> return of the possibilities that the event had supposedly afforded when seen as
> the beginning of cultural time.[23]

The emergence of the *novela de la selva* also coincided with a period of heightened interference in South America by the United States. The discourse of
Pan-Americanism which emerged from the United States at the end of the
nineteenth century, espousing a vision of common geographic, historical, and
economic systems across North and South America, angered and frustrated
many Latin Americans and led to a wave of protest literature, including José
Enrique Rodó's *Ariel* [1900].

Martin Stabb has described the cultural production of Latin Americans in
the first decades of the twentieth century as the 'rediscovery' of America.[24] It
was during this period that writers throughout South America began to weigh
up the appropriateness of using inherited European landscape aesthetics to
represent natural spaces unknown in Europe, such as the tropical rainforest
or the Argentine pampas. The *novela de la selva* was at the forefront of this
move to reclaim ideologically its American landscape. Said has identified
this desire to repossess geography, both physical and literary, as fundamental
to postcolonial writing: 'imperialism [...] is an act of geographical violence
through which virtually every space in the world is explored, charted, and
finally brought under control. [...] Its geographical identity must thereafter be
searched for and somehow restored.'[25] Although almost all of South America
had achieved independence by the time the *novela de la selva* first appeared,
there remained many throwbacks to the period of European control. As is the
case with many so-called postcolonial nations, the 'post' in Latin America's
colonial experience has often been rather tenuous. Even after independence
the tropical rainforests around the Amazon and Orinoco rivers, and the indigenous communities who lived there, continued to be exploited by foreigners,
especially through extractive industries such as rubber or petroleum.[26] The
South American tropics also continued to be a powerful imaginative construct
in the pages of European travel writing and adventure novels, where the
verdant and labyrinthine forest harbouring all kinds of danger was used time
and again as an exotic backdrop for the white traveller.

The reinvention of tropical landscape aesthetics in the *novela de la selva*
was, therefore, crucial to the Spanish-American writer's desire to contest and
to supplant disabling cultural stereotypes. Adumbrating a now longstanding
tradition of postcolonial nature writing, the authors of the *novela de la selva*

founded this new tradition not by turning their backs on the ever-growing body of European writing on the tropics, but by rewriting it.

★ ★ ★

The aim of this book is to explore how colonial tropes of the tropics were contested in the *novela de la selva*. While chapters 2–5 of the book discuss the *novela de la selva*'s engagement with particular tropes, Chapter 1 explores the act of literary appropriation itself, affirming that the rewriting of colonial narratives in the *novela de la selva* is consistent with patterns in postcolonial writing more generally. One of the principal ways that this reinvention was achieved was through parody, where the repetition of colonial tropes in a postcolonial context denatured them and revealed their complicity with European expansionist discourse. Although Bhabha's definition of 'colonial mimicry' intersects usefully with my discussions of parody, these terms are not completely synonymous. Throughout the book I use a number of different terms, including 'colonial mimicry', 'narrative irony', and 'mock-heroic', to describe the particular nuances of parody being employed in the novels. Margaret A. Rose has defined parody as a 'device which is able, because of its peculiar dual structure, to have an ambivalent, or ambiguous, relationship to its "target"':

> Despite the fact that parodies may be *both* critical of *and* sympathetic to their 'targets', many critics have continued to describe parody as being *only* critical, or *only* sympathetic, or playful, or agitatory, or engagé, or blasphemous, or ironic, or imitative, or counter-imitative, and so on. [...] parody is able to be used to demonstrate several of the above characteristics at once, if, or when, an author chooses.[27]

Thus, parody in the *novela de la selva* is very difficult to define. Not only are there frequent shifts of tone between and within the novels but the object of ridicule is also in constant flux. In the opening chapter I am particularly concerned with the question of narrative irony, which is produced primarily through contradictions in the narratives of the urban protagonists of the *novela de la selva*. While three of the four novels central to this study purport to be 'true-life' South American travelogues, such a claim is contradicted not only by their patent literary allusions (to Humboldt's *Personal Narrative*, Shelley's *Alastor*, Lady Morgan's *The Missionary*, *Don Quijote*, and *King Lear*, to mention but a few inter-textual echoes) but also by their insistent self-reflexivity. Intertextuality is a fundamental part of the *novela de la selva*. These novels allude not only to European travel writing on the tropics but also to their own literary constructions of tropical nature. Such metatextual proclivities, especially the preponderance of self-reflexive narrators, not only bear out Roberto González Echevarría's theory of Latin American narrative as an archive but also disrupt notions of literary 'consumption'.[28] As Doris Sommer has discussed in a study of 'particularist' fiction in Latin America, texts which resist being consumed are often concerned with the establishment of peripheral identities and with the rupturing of master narratives. In the *novela de la selva* the urge for literary consumption is initiated among authors (who 'cannibalize' travel writing on the tropics) rather than readers.[29] The latter's desire for an easily digestible read is thwarted, as I will show in chapters 2 and 3, by the unknowability of the jungle and of native American culture, both of which refuse to be contained in European literary forms.

The opening chapter of this book suggests that the imperial past – specifically the legacy of European writing on the tropics – not only impelled a desire among Latin American writers to redraft topographical and anthropological texts but also afforded them the literary tools with which to formulate such a disputation. Chapters 2 and 3 will explore two particular areas of rewriting: landscape aesthetics and anthropology.

In Chapter 2 I show how the rewriting of European landscape aesthetics was pivotal to the postcolonial re-imagination of tropical nature. The pre-Copernican ideal of the observing subject being at the centre of the universe is upset throughout the *novela de la selva* by the phenomenological and aesthetic peculiarities of the forest, which, more than any other environmental space obstructs man's gaze and, as a consequence, his ability to distinguish between the landscape and himself. One by one the distinctions which validate imperial landscape aesthetics are disavowed: human/telluric, there/here, Self/Other. It is shown that this breakdown in the borders of selfhood leads to a moment of crisis in each of the novels, when the urban travellers begin to merge with nature, not in the idealistic way proposed by, say, the American Transcendentalists, but through relentless bombardment of the senses. Contrary to European travel narratives, in the *novela de la selva* landscape ceases to be a source of self-edification for the traveller. This is made most explicit by the novels' rewriting of the trope of the sublime, which is invoked in the *novela de la selva* only to show its incompatibility with a postcolonial view of the tropics as unreservedly rebarbative and unknowable. Far from confirming man's supersensible rationality over nature, the jungle insistently overwhelms the traveller and his ability either to comprehend or to describe the tropics. The replacing of conventional categories of European landscape aesthetics such as the sublime with a poetics of the ugly and the unrepresentable ironically draws upon the imperial trope of Otherness, so often ascribed to the South American tropics by Europeans. Far from endorsing colonial tropes, however, the *novela de la selva* draws upon the concept of Otherness counter-hegemonically, in order to stress the inassimilable difference of the tropical landscape, and its resistance to conventional European landscape aesthetics.

Chapter 3 also explores the ironic recourse to Otherness in the *novela de la selva*, this time in relation to the representation of Amerindian culture. European views of native populations in travel writing and anthropology have tended to the extremes of demonization and idealization, and much of this chapter shows how the repetition of these tropes in a postcolonial context instantiates the novelists' use of 'colonial mimicry', where re-articulation leads to an evacuation rather than to an affirmation of meaning. Like the *novela de la selva*'s ironic engagement with European landscape aesthetics, ethnographical categories are not completely discounted, however. James Clifford's assessment of ethnography as both implicated in imperial discourse and as 'potentially counter-hegemonic' is borne out in these novels through 'inverse-ethnography' – a process by which the perspective of subject and object is reversed, and where the Amerindian becomes the initiator, rather than the object, of an anthropological encounter.[30] Inverse-ethnography often leads to farce in the novels, which is one of the lighter forms of irony in the *novela de la selva*, but no less incisive. Other postcolonial 'tricks' which disrupt the narrators' desire for a seamless inscription of native customs include the incorporation of indigenous myths and unglossed Amerindian words, both of which produce textual lacunae and thus call into question the concept of textual authority more broadly.

After demonstrating how the formerly disabling trope of Otherness is appropriated and re-semanticized in the *novela de la selva*, chapters 4 and 5 turn to the character confronted by this insistent unknowability – the urban traveller, who, in three of the four novels central to this book is also the first-person narrator of what aspires (but always fails) to be a prototypical travel narrative about a sojourn in the tropics. Despite being Latin Americans, the perspective of the urban travellers in the *novela de la selva* differs very little from that of the other European and North American characters in the novels, or from fictional and factual travellers to the tropics in European writing. Renato Rosaldo's concept of 'imperialist nostalgia' helps to explain the protagonists' anachronistic comportment in the jungle, especially their view of wild nature as a quasi-Edenic space where they can escape the ills of modern society and enjoy a more authentic or adventurous way of life.[31] The main focus in Chapter 4 is on how the *novela de la selva* engages with idealized notions of 'going primitive' in the tropics in order to debunk the commodification of nature in European literature. Firstly the parody of the Romantic hero, particularly his view of wild nature as a pretext for protracted self-analysis, is explored. This belated recourse to Romantic images of nature and of the 'Noble Savage' merely draws attention to the discrepancies between external, literary views of forests and the reality of living in them. Chapter 4 then examines how the figure of the indomitable masculine traveller, a stock ingredient of the British imperial romance, is demystified in the *novela de la selva* as an absurd colonial throwback. The protagonists' repetition of literary topoi of the forest as a space of poetic inspiration or of unimpeded adventure registers as belated and at times comically misguided in the chaotic and inhospitable jungle.

Chapter 5 carries on from the last by examining how, far from being pleasurable, a stay in the forest can precipitate madness and savagery in travellers. Although this tendency would seem to uphold stereotypes of the tropics as a space of degeneration, it is shown that the *novela de la selva* depicts the uncurbed atavism of travellers in the forest in order to debunk European discourses of tropical pathology and disease. Throughout these novels, the colonial trope of Otherness is not only harnessed as an enabling motif for postcolonial self-expression but is also refracted back onto the urban traveller. In this way the Self/Other binary, which underpins much imperial discourse, is reversed, and the urban narrator, not the native Amerindian, becomes the referent of savagery and Otherness. This slip into atavism is made manifest in several ways, including through the traveller's physical disarray, his transgression of dietary taboos, and his penchant for cruelty and self-mutilation. The easy slip of the urban traveller into savagery beyond the regulations of the city will be shown to conform to a Freudian model of the psyche, which, as Hayden White has shown, conceives of wildness and barbarism as 'potentialities lurking in the heart of every individual'.[32] The jungle thus threatens not only the aesthetic models of travel writing on the tropics but also the Western ideal of 'civilization', which is revealed to be much less diffuse than its antonym 'barbarism' and, for the writers of the tropical *novela de la selva*, much less enabling for the postcolonial re-inscription of the nation.

Notes

1   Raymond Williams, *Keywords: A Vocabulary of Culture and Society*, rev. edn (London: Fontana Press, 1988), p. 219.

2   This is the case, for instance, in Carlos J. Alonso, *The Spanish American Regional Novel: Modernity and Autochthony* (Cambridge: Cambridge University Press, 1991).

3   Peter Beardsell, *Europe and Latin America: Returning the Gaze* (Manchester: Manchester University Press, 2000), has shown how the idea of Otherness was ideologically appropriated by postcolonial writers in Latin America.

4   Mary Louise Pratt, *Imperial Eye: Travel Writing and Transculturation* (London: Routledge, 1992), p. 111.

5   Pratt, *Imperial Eyes*, pp. 111–43.

6   See Margarita Serje, *El revés de la nación: territorios salvajes, fronteras y tierras de nadie* (Bogotá: Ediciones Uniandes, 2005), pp. 88–103, for a discussion of the relationship between cartography and national identity in Colombia.

7   For a more detailed account of the history of the genre, see Lydia de León Hazera's *La novela de la selva hispanoamericana: nacimiento, desarrollo y transformación* (Bogotá: Instituto Caro y Cuervo, 1971).

8   For an account of Hudson's life see Morley Roberts, *W. H. Hudson: A Portrait* (London: Eveleigh Nash & Grayson, 1924), and Ruth Tomlinson, *W. H. Hudson: A Biography* (London: Faber and Faber, 1982).

9   Nicomedes Suárez-Araúz, *Literary Amazonia: Modern Writing by Amazonian Authors* (Gainesville: University Press of Florida, 2004), p. 2.

10   Lúcia Sá, *Rain Forest Literatures: Amazonian Texts and Latin American Culture* (Minneapolis: University of Minnesota Press, 2004).

11   Alonso, *Regional Novel*, and Doris Sommer, *Foundational Fictions: The National Romances of Latin America* (Berkeley: University of California Press, 1991), have both offered timely reassessments of the regional novel.

12   A number of articles have been published on the *novela de la selva* over the past three decades, which suggests a turn in the genre's fortunes. They include: Tieko Yamaguchi Miyazaki, 'Canaima no Contexto dos Romances sobre a Selva', *Revista de Letras*, 20 (1980), pp. 75–87; Ileana Rodríguez, 'Naturaleza/nación: lo salvaje civil. Escribiendo Amazonía', *Revista de Crítica Literaria Latinoamericana*, 45 (1997), pp. 27–42; and Jorge

Marcone, 'De retorno a lo natural: *La serpiente de oro*, la "novela de la selva" y la crítica ecológica', *Hispania*, 18 (1998), pp. 299–308. All of these discuss, on some level, the consonance between writing and identity in Latin American literature on the tropics. See also Lesley Wylie, 'Hearts of Darkness: The Celebration of Otherness in the Latin American *novela de la selva*', *Romance Studies*, 23.2 (2005), pp. 105–16, and 'Colonial Tropes and Postcolonial Tricks: Rewriting the Tropics in the *novela de la selva*', *Modern Language Review*, 10.3 (2006), pp. 728–42.

13 León Hazera, *Novela de la selva*, p. 11.

14 Sá, *Rain Forest Literatures*.

15 J. Jorge Klor de Alva, 'The Postcolonization of the (Latin) American Experience: a Reconsideration of "Colonialism," "Postcolonialism," and "Mestizaje"', in Gyan Prakash (ed.), *After Colonialism: Imperial Histories and Postcolonial Displacements* (Princeton: Princeton University Press, 1995), pp. 241–75 (p. 264). For a discussion of Klor de Alva's polemical essay see Robin Fiddian, 'Locating the Object, Mapping the Field: the Place of the Cultures of Latin America and Lusophone Africa in Postcolonial Studies', in Fiddian (ed.), *Postcolonial Perspectives on the Cultures of Latin America and Lusophone Africa* (Liverpool: Liverpool University Press, 2000), pp. 1–26 (1–4).

16 See, for instance, Gustavo Pérez Firmat, *The Cuban Condition: Translation and Identity in Modern Cuban Literature* (Cambridge: Cambridge University Press, 1989), p. 31. A 1991 review article by Patricia Seed, 'Colonial and Postcolonial Discourse', *Latin American Research Review*, 26.3 (1991), pp. 181–200, raised important questions about postcolonial theory's paradoxical position between the 'First and Third Worlds', and sparked off a debate about cultural dependence in Latin America. This was subsequently taken up by critics such as Hernán Vidal in 'The Concept of Colonial and Postcolonial Discourse. A Perspective from Literary Criticism', *Latin American Research Review*, 28. 3 (1993), pp. 113–19, and Walter D. Mignolo, in 'Colonial and Postcolonial Discourse: Cultural Critique or Academic Colonialism', *Latin American Research Review*, 28.3 (1993), pp. 120–34.

17 Peter Hulme, 'Including America', *ARIEL: A Review of International English Literature*, 26.1 (1995), pp. 117–23.

18 Hulme, 'Including America', p. 118.

19 Patricia D'Allemand, 'José Carlos Mariátegui: Culture and the Nation', in Fiddian (ed.), *Postcolonial Perspectives*, pp. 79–102 (p. 79).

20 This is a term used by Steve Wakefield in *Carpentier's Baroque Fiction: Returning Medusa's Gaze* (Woodbridge: Tamesis, 2004), in which he examines Carpentier's reworking of the European baroque as 'a weapon for a postcolonial reinterpretation of his continent's history' (p. 101).

21 See, for instance, Stephen Henighan, 'Caribbean Masks: Frantz Fanon and Alejo Carpentier', in Fiddian (ed.), *Postcolonial Perspectives*, pp. 169–90, and Barbara J. Webb, *Myth and History in Caribbean Fiction: Alejo Carpentier, Wilson Harris, and Edouard Glissant* (Amherst: University of Massachusetts Press, 1992).

22 See Alonso, *Regional Novel*, pp. 50–52, for a fuller discussion of Pan-Americanism.

23 Carlos J. Alonso, 'The *Criollista* Novel', in Roberto González Echevarría and Enrique Pupo-Walker (eds.), *The Cambridge History of Latin American Literature*, 3 vols (Cambridge: Cambridge University Press, 1996), II, pp. 195–211 (p. 200).

24 Martin Stabb, *In Quest of Identity: Patterns in the Spanish American Essay of Ideas, 1898–1960* (Chapel Hill, NC: University of North Carolina Press, 1967), pp. 58–101.

25 Edward Said, *Culture and Imperialism* (London: Vintage, 1994), p. 271.

26 Many critics have questioned the use of the term 'postcolonial'. In the Introduction to Bill Ashcroft, Gareth Griffiths, and Helen Tiffin (eds), *The Post-Colonial Studies Reader* (London: Routledge, 1995), pp. 1–4, the editors have defended their use of the hyphen

in 'post-colonial', which stands for 'both the material effects of colonisation and the huge diversity of everyday and sometimes hidden responses to it throughout the world' (p. 3).

27 Margaret A. Rose, *Parody: Ancient, Modern, and Post-Modern* (Cambridge: Cambridge University Press, 1993), p. 47.

28 Roberto González Echevarría, *Myth and Archive: A Theory of Latin American Narrative* (Cambridge: Cambridge University Press, 1990).

29 Doris Sommer, *Proceed with Caution, when Engaged by Minority Writing in the Americas* (Cambridge, MA: Harvard University Press, 1999). In Chapter 1 I discuss the parallels between the 'cannibalism' of tropes of the tropics in the *novela de la selva* and the *Antropofagia* movement in 1920s Brazil.

30 James Clifford, 'Introduction: Partial Truths', in James Clifford and George E. Marcus (eds.), *Writing Culture: The Poetics and Politics of Ethnography* (Berkeley: University of California Press, 1986), pp. 1–26 (p. 9).

31 Renato Rosaldo, *Culture and Truth: The Remaking of Social Analysis* (London: Routledge, 1993), pp. 68–87.

32 Hayden White, *Tropics of Discourse: Essays in Cultural Criticism* (Baltimore: Johns Hopkins University Press, 1978), p. 179.

CHAPTER ONE

Colonial Tropes and Postcolonial Tricks

> Divina Poesía, [...]
> tiempo es que dejes ya la culta Europa,
> que tu nativa rustiquez desama,
> y dirijas el vuelo adonde te abre
> el mundo de Colón su grande escena.
>
> Andrés Bello, 'Alocución a la Poesía'[1]

This apostrophe, composed by Bello in 1823, instantiates a classic colonial encounter between the Latin American writer and the chequered legacy of the imperial past. Although Bello's poem could be read as arguing benignly that the innate rusticity of poetry, and its proclivity for pastoral and Romantic themes, might be better served by the luxuriant nature of the Americas, it also lends itself to a much more radical interpretation. The eponymous 'Alocución' is not only an entreaty for poetry to forsake 'la culta Europa' in favour of 'el mundo de Colón' but also an appeal to the American writer to appropriate European literary models, and to infuse into them a uniquely American flavour. Indeed, Bello's poem might be regarded as an exemplum of this mode of literary syncretism, for while it appears to conform structurally to traditional European versification, it is splintered between a rather formulaic recourse to classical imagery and awestruck descriptions of a marvellous and unknowable tropical nature. Although Bello does not explicitly reject European poetics, the insistent alterity of South America, which is defined as 'otro cielo, [...] otro mundo [...], otras gentes', abundantly reveals the necessity for the literary models of the Old World to be adapted to the physical realities of the New.[2] European stylistics might suffice as a springboard for the first generations of Latin American writers, but these would have to be intensified and refined to match the wonders of the American landscape.

The founding vision of South American nature in Bello's 'Alocución a la Poesía' is a fitting starting point for a discussion of the *novela de la selva*, a genre which flourished almost a century after this poem, but which perpetuated, nevertheless, its discourse of tropical superabundance and Otherness. An important coincidence between Bello and the authors of the *novela de la selva* is that they all exploit European stylistics in order to create a peculiarly tropical aesthetic. Criticism of the Spanish-American *novela de la tierra*, to which the *novela de la selva* is related, has tended to dwell upon its derivative propensities, particularly its relationship to European topography, ethnography, and travel writing. Carlos Fuentes has described the genre as 'más cercana a la geografía que a la literatura',[3] and Mario Vargas Llosa has deemed it 'a census, a matter of geographical data, a description of customs and usages, an ethnological document'.[4] While the descriptions of flora, fauna, and indigenous customs in the *novela de la selva* ostensibly betray some anxiety of influence from the period of occupation, the genre's allusions to European discourses of the tropics are far from deferential. Rather, the imitative proclivities of the *novela de la selva* are parodic, instantiating the novelists' desire to reclaim their environmental and narrative terrain, and to reinscribe them from a South American perspective.

Paul Connerton has argued that every experience of the present is filtered through society's knowledge of the past: 'All beginnings contain an element of recollection. This is particularly so when a social group makes a concerted effort to begin with a wholly new start.'[5] This chapter will show that the legacy of colonial travel writing in Latin America was not suppressed but became a catalyst for the self-imaginings of the postcolonial writer. As the authors of the *novela de la selva* exemplify through their selective redrafting of European travel writing, remembering the past is not just a practice of cerebral recollection; remembering or re-*membering* entails a process of re-assemblage and of radical re-fashioning.

Postcolonial Parody

In the introduction to this study I argued for a critical reappraisal of the *novela de la selva* as a postcolonial genre. The *novela de la selva*'s emergence during the lead-up to and in the aftermath of the *Centenario* movement throughout South America attests to its preoccupation with questions of political and cultural independence and with literary roots. In fact, despite what Djelal Kadir has characterized as the quest for a new start in writing from post-independent South America, the authors of the *novela de la selva* were unable – or unwilling – to extirpate themselves from the colonial past.[6] Instead they turned to European accounts of the tropics, particularly in travel writing, as a starting point from which to reimagine the postcolonial landscape. This recourse to the canon of European travel writing on the tropics was not just a case of garnering literary niceties. As Said has shown, the interrogation of colonial narratives is a linchpin of all postcolonial writing:

> Many of the most interesting post-colonial writers bear their past within them – as scars of humiliating wounds, [...] as potentially revised visions of the past tending towards a new future, as urgently reinterpretable and redeployable experience, in which the formerly silent native speaks and acts on territory taken back from the empire.[7]

This reformulation of tropes of the tropics in the *novela de la selva* is consistent not only with tendencies in postcolonial writing, but with American fiction more broadly. As Lois Parkinson Zamora has shown, the American writer's 'anxiety about origins' pushes him or her 'to search *for* precursors [...] rather than escape *from* them [...]; to connect *to* traditions and histories (in the name of a usable past) rather than dissociate *from* them (in the name of originality)'.[8] As such, European accounts of tropical South America, from the journals of early modern travellers such as Alvar Núñez Cabeza de Vaca to the scientific writing of eighteenth-century naturalists such as Alexander von Humboldt, provided the authors of the *novela de la selva* with the stock epithets of 'tropicality' upon which they could build their postcolonial vision of a heady and fecund natural environment.

Nevertheless, European discourses of the tropics were a double-edged sword for the authors of the *novela de la selva*, for while they afforded them a ready-made descriptive vocabulary for the luxuriance of the tropical landscape, they were also burdened with tropes of telluric and indigenous barbarism. How could the *novela de la selva* engage with representations of the tropics as a space of disease, degeneration, and savagery, or, inversely, of escape, solitude, or adventure, without merely compounding European stereotypes? The answer was through parody – an important narrative strategy of postcolonial writers worldwide and fundamental to the *novela de la selva*'s rewriting of tropical South America.

Parody is a critical term notoriously difficult to define.[9] Throughout its critical history it has been regarded, variously, as parasitic, comic, serious, subversive, and nihilistic; it can be both sympathetic and derisory, or even both at the same time.[10] More recently it has come to be associated with the counter-hegemonic strategies of postcolonial writing.[11] The ambivalent relationship between the postcolonial parodist and his or her target text means that even critical parody, as we have in the *novela de la selva*, can function not only as a weapon against the original narrative but also 'at the same time refunction the target's work for a new and positive purpose within the parody'.[12] Through parody, postcolonial writers not only perform a sort of close reading on the imperial text but also produce new and enabling works of literature.[13]

In Latin America the postcolonial writer's appropriation of inherited European literary forms has most often been characterized as 'cannibalization' – a process closely related to parody. This metaphor was introduced in the 1920s by a group of Brazilian modernists led by Oswald de Andrade, who adopted the metaphor of anthropophagy, long associated with the native Tupi in imperial discourse, to describe their process of artistic production. In 1928 they produced the darkly ironic 'Anthropophagous Manifesto', which enjoined the American writer to cannibalize European literature in order to subsume its virtues and commute the 'taboo into a totem'. Years later, the art critic Andrea Giunta rearticulated this war cry, encouraging the contemporary artist to 'devour, mix, appropriate and reappropriate, invert, fragment and join, take central discourse, penetrate and cut through it until it becomes a useful tool for the search for and creation [...] of our own subversive discourse'.[14] Neil Larsen has also revisited the metaphor of cannibalism in his paradigm of oppositional culture, which he divides into the 'Transcultural' and the 'Anthropophagous'. The first of these models (drawing upon the terminology of the anthropologist Fernando Ortiz, later applied to narrative by Angel Rama, and most recently adapted by Mary Louise Pratt) proposes that Latin American narrative 'avoids the double bind in which one either settles for a direct imitation of metropolitan imports or seeks to expunge all "foreign" cultural influences'.[15] The Anthropophagous model entails direct appropriation of colonial cultural forms.

This ironic appeal to 'cannibalism' is deeply revealing of the Latin American writer's pragmatic view of the past, and of the possibility of 'recycling, creolizing, [or] parodying' imperial tropes to produce the founding fictions of the postcolonial nation.[16] Such cultural strategies resemble techniques in postcolonial writing from outside the Americas. Bhabha, for instance, has argued that colonial documents are often 'rich in the traditions of *trompe-l'oeil*, irony, mimicry and repetition'.[17] Bhabha's description of mimicry as 'at once resemblance and menace' in his essay 'Of Mimicry and Man: The Ambivalence of Colonial Discourse' comes close to my understanding of how parody functions in the *novela de la selva*.[18] Mimicry is, for Bhabha, a kind of empty imitation through which the colonized emerges in a 'flawed colonial mimesis', as *'almost the same, but not quite'*.[19] Despite the analogies between postcolonial parody and colonial mimicry, the latter, as defined by Bhabha, is much more concerned with the ambivalences produced *within* colonial discourse. Although Bhabha has censured Said's *Orientalism* for implying that power is always in the hands of the colonizer, at times in this essay Bhabha can be seen to be guilty of his own criticism. As Ania Loomba has observed, Bhabha's theory undermines the importance of native resistance in its assumption that any 'interrogation of colonialism is shaped primarily by its own discourse'.[20] While Bhabha does concede that colonized people are sometimes responsible for producing this 'double vision', as, for example, when a missionary from Bengal in 1817 reported that the natives happily accepted a copy of the Bible to use as waste paper, he does not develop the point fully. Mimicry leads to ambivalence not only in colonial documents but also in the narratives of postcolonial nations, where writers imitate colonial writing in order to 'produce its slippage, its excess, its difference'.[21] In this sense, the menace that Bhabha claims to be almost always located within colonial discourse is also generated outside it, and it is all the more powerful for this.

Although for his definition of mimicry Bhabha draws upon Jacques Lacan, who has described how the phenomenon 'reveals something in so far as it is distinct from what might be called an *itself* that is behind', the term was initially used in zoological circles.[22] Indeed, applying the concept of mimicry to the subversive strategies of the *novela de la selva* is a homecoming of sorts, given that it was first used to designate the behaviour of butterflies in the

Amazon rainforest. Returning the practice of mimicry to its jungle habitat also restores some of the more radical implications lost in Bhabha's definition of the term. In nature, it is important to distinguish between mimicry and camouflage. While camouflage allows insects to avoid detection by blending into the background, through mimicry insects actively appropriate the guise of another, either to avoid attack by prey, or, in the case of 'self-mimicry', to aid in their own predatory activities. The postcolonial writer as mimic can therefore be seen as combative rather than passive. Although his or her narratives speciously replicate the style or content of the colonial text, this repetition is a mere sham, a parody, and a furtive assault on the original.

In the case of the *novela de la selva*, the authors appropriate tropes of European travel writing on the tropics, exaggerating the arrogant jingoism of the urban traveller, the menace of the landscape, and the 'savagery' of the indigenous people, to create fictions which seem radically anachronistic given the context of their production. It is this tone of belatedness in the *novela de la selva* – the incongruence between the protagonists' neocolonial conduct and the political realities of the postcolonial era in which the novels were written and first read – which is the source of much of the novels' irony.[23] González Echevarría has drawn a parallel between Carpentier's anonymous narrator-protagonist and Don Quijote, a comparison also made of Rivera's Arturo Cova by Otto Olivera.[24] The Quixotic comportment of the protagonists of the *novela de la selva* in the jungle, where they pose as conquerors, epic heroes, or frustrated Romantic poets, not only undermines their credibility as narrators, but, like Cervantes's eponymous anti-hero, also denatures the authority of writing more generally.

Claire Colebrook has argued that irony is always only perceptible to a few: 'to read the irony you do not just have to know the context; you also have to be committed to specific beliefs and positions *within* that context'.[25] Parody also demands the reader's close attention to both the text and the context.[26] Parody in the *novela de la selva*, then, like the Amazonian butterfly's recourse to mimicry, executes the double function of both evading and facilitating confrontation. This 'sly civility' clearly has important implications not only for postcolonial reworkings of imperial narratives but also for textual authority in general, especially the complex relationship between the author, the narrator, and the reader.[27]

Narrative Irony in the *novela de la selva*

Wayne Booth has argued that 'it is always good for an irony to be grasped when intended, always good for readers and authors to achieve understanding', yet this pact of complicity between the reader and the author is ruptured repeatedly throughout the *novela de la selva*, primarily through the use of untrustworthy narrators.[28] In three of the four novels central to this study, namely *Green Mansions*, *La vorágine*, and *Los pasos perdidos*, the ironic protagonist is also the primary narrator. The magnitude of this detail cannot be overemphasized. If the narrator-protagonists are, as I will show, parodies of the archetypal adventurer-hero of European travel writing, then their narratives must always be read as ironic and, hence, as unreliable. This is a fact which much criticism of the novels has overlooked, leading to fundamental textual misreadings, such as the interpretation of how in *La vorágine* Arturo Cova's use of archaisms such as 'dogo' for 'perro' or 'fatum' for 'sino' lend the narrative an air of 'elegancia y dignidad', rather than being a reflection of his megalomaniac desire to recreate the grand narratives of the conquistadors.[29] Likewise, autobiographical criticism of both *La vorágine* and *Los pasos perdidos*, playfully encouraged by the authors, has diminished the standing of these novels as works of fiction, focusing rather on the parallels between the chronology of the authors' real-life trips to the jungle and the novelistic action.

The authors' disingenuous myth-making is fundamental to the wider attempt within the *novela de la selva* to ironize the authority of narrative as an unambiguous reflection of reality.[30] In his discussion of the counter-hegemonic strategies of postcolonial writers in Latin America, Peter Beardsell states:

> one type of critical appropriation occurs [...] when writers [...] seize upon Europe's treatment of Latin America as an ideal, a Utopia, a blank space to be filled, a place where mankind may be close to nature, an environment for adventure and, by subverting those myths, demonstrate the reality of their regions.[31]

While they indisputably appropriate and ironize European representations of the tropics, the authors of the *novela de la selva* do not do so in order to 'demonstrate [...] reality'. Rather, they weave metanarratives, undercutting their fictions in the very act of writing them, and always gesturing at their artificiality, their fictitiousness, and their place in a long line of representations of America. González Echevarría has highlighted the imitative nature of the Latin American novel:

> The novel's origin is not only multiple in space but also in time. Its history is not, however, a linear succession or evolution, but a series of new starts in different places. The only common denominator is the novel's mimetic quality, not of a given reality, but of a given discourse that has already 'mirrored' reality.[32]

Texts are composed in ever-widening circles, further and further removed from any originary 'essence' of what they are attempting to represent. In the *novela de la selva* this displacement is epitomized by the fragmentation of the narrative voice, which moves from discourses of tropical degeneracy to Romantic raptures about the sublime to intricate botanical descriptions. The writers of the *novela de la selva* engage with the multiple seams of text inscribed on the American continent since the conquest, aware that each of their compositions will accrete another layer to be assimilated by writers of the future. The metaphor of South America as a palimpsest is central to the Creole novelists' postcolonial vision of the continent. This process – what Wilson Harris might term 'fossilization' – implies that although the past can never be obliterated, it can be overwritten by the postcolonial present: re-membered rather than forgotten.

In the rest of this chapter I will discuss the narrative structure in each of the four novels central to this study: *Green Mansions*, *La vorágine*, *Canaima*, and *Los pasos perdidos*. This will serve not just as an introduction to each of the novels, but will suggest what possibilities narrative irony might open up for the postcolonial writer.

Green Mansions

William Henry Hudson's *Green Mansions* [1904] is a novel about a young man, Abel Guevez de Argensola, who participates in a failed conspiracy to overthrow the Venezuelan government, and who flees from Caracas to the rainforest south of the Orinoco River, where he seeks shelter among an Amerindian tribe. It is while living with the tribe that he meets and falls in love with a strange, nymph-like woman, Rima, who has been brought up in the forest by a man she believes to be her grandfather. The sentimentalized and idyllic early stages of their romance turn to tragedy when Rima is murdered by the tribe (who believe she is a witch) and Abel is left alone to struggle for survival amid an increasingly hostile tropical environment.

From the outset, *Green Mansions* establishes itself as a book about the telling of stories. The frame narrator, through which Abel's 'first person' narrative will be mediated, opens his tale with an account of the motives for the text that we have before us – a work which purports to tell the 'whole truth about Mr Abel', in contrast to the 'conjectural matter' being bandied around in the local press:

> It is a cause of very great regret to me that this task has taken so much longer a time than I had expected for its completion. It is now many months – over a year, in fact – since I wrote to Georgetown announcing my intention of publishing, *in a very few months*, the whole truth about Mr Abel. [...] It has not been so; and at this distance from Guiana I was not aware of how much conjectural matter was being printed week by week in the local press [...]. Let us hope that now, at last, the romance-weaving will come to an end.[33]

The narrator is keen to stress the verisimilitude of the text and his reliability as a narrator via his careful amendment of the generalization 'it is now many months' to 'over a year, in fact'. So this is a text about 'fact[s]', and 'truth', and the end of 'romance-weaving'. How strange, then, that such a document should be subtitled: 'A Romance of the Tropical Forest' – a title which not only directly contradicts the narrator's professed fidelity to facts but also aligns the text with a long line of fictional antecedents, such as Bernardin's *Paul and Virginia* and Chateaubriand's *Atala*. More strange still is the manner in which, despite the truth-bearing claims of the story, the frame narrator uses metaphors of writing to describe the protagonist's life as a 'closed and clasped volume' (p. 6) and a 'hidden chapter' (p. 3). Indeed, far from eschewing literary models for his story, the frame narrator consistently appeals to the conventions of romance, of travel writing and, as James V. Fletcher has shown, of

Romantic poetry.[34] His description of how Abel was alleged to have journeyed to Georgetown 'from some remote district in the interior' (p. 3), travelling 'alone on foot across half the continent to the coast' (p. 4), and emerging 'penniless, in rags [and] wasted almost to a skeleton by fever and misery of all kinds' (p. 4), reads like a stereotyped travel narrative, and is deeply redolent of the misadventures of the sixteenth-century Spanish traveller Cabeza de Vaca.[35] Similarly, the novel's imagery and quest-like structure have been established by Jay Macpherson as archetypically Romantic.[36] Despite the narrator's insistence on the truth of the story, then, it is clear that *Green Mansions* draws heavily upon literary antecedents and, as a consequence, reads not only as stereotyped but also as palpably anachronistic.

Further to these troubling contradictions is the fact that, while the frame narrator eulogizes Abel for his 'personal charm', 'kindly disposition', and 'love of little children, of all wild creatures, of nature, and of whatsoever was furthest removed from the common material interests and concerns of a purely commercial community' (p. 4), this portrait is incompatible with Abel's conduct throughout much of the novel. Just two paragraphs later, the frame narrator describes how Abel viciously attacks him for his 'use of stimulants' (p. 5) (perhaps another reason to doubt the narrator's good judgement), and throughout the novel, far from registering as charming and kind, Abel is described as rash, greedy, arrogant, racist, and irascible. Furthermore, we learn that he has actually murdered a man – a member of the tribe with which he lives in the forest, albeit in self-defence – and that this act fills him with less remorse than his subsequent killing of a snake. This is a character whose values are radically distorted and who is prone to violence and madness, the full extent of which we never learn, given his suppression of the details of the 'secret dark chapter [...] of moral insanity' (p. 179) he suffers during his sojourn in the tropical forest.

While many critics of the novel have drawn parallels between Abel and Hudson, such biographical interpretations are undermined by these paradoxes in the text.[37] Although critics have generally attributed the incongruities between the idealization of the native Amerindians in *Idle Days in Patagonia* or *The Naturalist in La Plata* and the scarcely concealed racism of *Green Mansions* to inconsistencies in Hudson's perception of primitivism, this does not distinguish adequately between fact and fiction.[38] Abel is not a spokesperson for Hudson, and what Fletcher has termed his 'crazy-quilt of ideas', in which Romantic pantheism is 'pieced together' with an outmoded perception of native savagery, is not a translucent projection of the author's beliefs, but a complex and ironic commentary on discourses of tropical nature in European travel writing.[39] Indeed, in a valuable early article on *Green Mansions*, Carlos A. Baker has established that far from being autobiographical, Hudson's novel is based on an eighteenth-century novel by Lady Morgan entitled *The Missionary*, which is set in the 'exotic' locale of Cashmere.[40] This study seems conclusively to reveal that not only are the topographical descriptions of Hudson's novel inspired by this text but also that the character of Rima

– subject to so much critical speculation – is a reworking of Lady Morgan's heroine Luxima.[41]

What Baker does not consider is the possibility that it is not Hudson but Abel or the frame narrator who may have drawn upon Lady Morgan's novel as a source for *Green Mansions*. Why, for instance, does it take the narrator 'over a year' (p. 3) to write what purports to be a mere transcription of a story told to him in one evening? And even if his recording of the story is faithful to the original, should we trust Abel's version of events? In the prologue the narrator describes how, when Abel talked about the past, he would 'deal you out facts in a dry mechanical way *as if reading them in a book*' (p. 5; my emphasis). Moreover, in the opening chapter of his story Abel relates how, at the beginning of his travels, he used to keep a diary:

> a record of personal adventures, impressions of the country and people, both semi-civilised and savage; and as my journal grew, I began to think that on my return at some future time to Caracas, it might prove useful and interesting to the public, and also procure me fame. (p. 9)

Are we to believe that the man who had once yearned for literary fame, thwarted by an unfortunate accident which reduces his manuscript to 'sodden pulp' (p. 10), would not be tempted to embellish his story in line with the popular genre of travel writing? There is much evidence of Abel's aptitude for improvisation, and especially his tendency to resort to clichés of European travel writing. When he is under suspicion by the tribe for his long absence in the jungle, for instance, he fabricates a tale about how he had been searching for gold, drawing upon antiquated myths of the Americas as a site of boundless riches.[42] Likewise, in his descriptions of the forest wildlife, Abel is seen to borrow from naturalists such as Henry Walter Bates and Alfred Russel Wallace.[43] As Ian Duncan has noted, when Abel describes how the call of a forest bird sounded like a 'blithe-hearted child with a highly melodious voice' (p. 26) he seems to draw directly upon Bates's description of the song of the *Cyphorinus cantans* (a type of wren) as resembling a 'musical boy [...] gathering fruits in the thicket, and [...] singing a few notes to cheer himself'.[44]

These intertextual echoes, whether generated by Abel or the novel's frame narrator, greatly attenuate the reader's confidence in the text's narrative authority. It is not insignificant to note that, in the opening chapter, Abel repeats how a friend laughs at his despair when he discovers that his 'true-life' travel journal has been destroyed by rain: 'It was all a true narrative, he exclaimed; if I wished to write a book for the stay-at-homes to read, I could easily invent a thousand lies far more entertaining than any real experiences' (pp. 10–11). It is clear, then, that in *Green Mansions* Abel and the frame narrator (and, by extension, Hudson) are less concerned with invention than with re-invention. While within the fiction this recycling of tropes is geared towards entertainment and commercial success, for Hudson, as for the authors of the *novelas de la selva* to follow, such repetitions serve not to reaffirm but to interrogate and to refashion the past. It is left for the critic or the reader – the 'stay-at-home' armchair traveller – to unravel these complex narrative strands.

La vorágine

La vorágine [1924] is the first-person narrative of a poet, Arturo Cova, who elopes with his girlfriend from Bogotá to the plains of Colombia and who, through a series of mishaps, ends up trapped in the jungle with his premature baby, its mother, and provisions for six days. The story we read purports to be Cova's journal, which he has entrusted a friend to take to the Colombian Embassy, and which subsequently has been edited by José Eustasio Rivera – not José Eustasio Rivera, author of *La vorágine*, but José Eustasio Rivera, fictional editor of the text, who shares the reader's limited knowledge of the fate of the protagonists.[45] The tortuous narrative of *La vorágine* and the novel's ambiguous conclusion have frequently been held up as evidence of the work's flawed composition, and of its status as a 'primitive' early novel. Far from being a defect, however, the complex narrative structure of *La vorágine* is one of its most important assets. The layers of narrators – from the fictional editor to the first-person narrative of Cova, and the internal narratives of Clemente Silva, Helí Mesa, and Ramiro Estévanez – certainly contribute to what R. H. Moreno-Durán has described as the novel's intricate '[v]oces, ecos, polifonías'.[46] This fusion of voices – the dislocation between the rural dialect of the *llaneros* and *caucheros*, indigenous expressions, and Cova's florid prose – produces a deeply fractured text, which at every turn diminishes the authority of the narrator as a bearer of truth and discloses his capriciousness, his propensity for fabrication, for wild fantasies, and for occlusion.

The first reviewers of *La vorágine* considered it 'visiblemente autobiográfica',[47] an unsurprising fate, given that in the first edition Rivera included a photograph of himself with the caption: 'Arturo Cova, en las barracas de Guaracú – Fotografía tomada por la madona Zoraida Ayram.'[48] Likewise, the socio-political aspects of the novel (principally its denunciation of the abuses of the Peruvian Amazon Company, a rubber company based in the disputed border region of the Putumayo at the turn of the century) have resulted in its interpretation as a factual *documento de denuncia*. Rivera never discouraged such readings. In fact, as Alonso has argued, the author seems to have encouraged the reception of his novel as an indictment of the rubber industry by placing a notice in three Bogotá newspapers to herald its publication:[49]

> *La vorágine*. Novela original de José Eustasio Rivera. Trata de la vida de Casanare, de las actividades peruanas en la Chorrera y en el Encanto y de la esclavitud cauchera en las selvas de Colombia, Venezuela y Brasil. Aparecerá el mes entrante.[50]

Upon its publication, Rivera was even more insistent upon the documentary quality of the novel and his philanthropic motives for writing it: 'Al componer mi libro no obedecí a otro móvil que el de buscar la redención de esos infelices que tienen la selva por cárcel.'[51] While Rivera insisted that he had witnessed the atrocities narrated in his novel during a trip he made to the jungle in 1922, remarks such as: 'Yo vi todas esas cosas. Los personajes que allí figuran son todos entes vivos y aun algunos de ellos llevan sus nombres propios,' have now been revealed as spurious.[52] Although, for example, the horrific description of a group of Amerindians being sprinkled with petrol and set alight in Part 2 of the novel is historically accurate, this notorious incident took place well before Rivera's travels to the jungle and was reported as early as 1907 by the Peruvian journalist Benjamín Saldaña Rocca in *La Felpa*.[53] The parallels between the description in *La vorágine* of the Amerindians 'abriéndose paso hacia las corrientes, donde se sumergieron agonizando' (p. 258), and the factual account of the incident in *La Felpa*, are telling. In the novel, the account of events by the rubber worker Clemente Silva, evidently embellished in Cova's journal, describes the burning indigenous people as 'coronadas de fuego lívido' (p. 258) and refers to 'el hedor de la grasa humana' (p. 258) – images which, despite their sensationalism, are broadly literary.

So why did Rivera suppress the artistry of his novel and encourage a misreading of the text as purely documentary? While one might cynically conclude that Rivera wanted to cash in on the proven commercial viability of accounts of the Putumayo scandal, such as W. E. Hardenburg's *The Putumayo: The Devil's Paradise* [1912], such an interpretation is discredited by the literary aspects of *La vorágine*, including its mythical reverberations, complex narrative structure, and painstaking novelistic gestation and revisions.[54] Instead, Rivera's myth-making about the construction of *La vorágine* should be seen as part of the wider ludic propensities of the novel and its attempt to undermine the unquestioned reliability of the transcendent narrator of European travel writing. Rivera's weaving of critical lore around his novel adds one more layer to the fictions that the reader must unstitch to gain access to the 'truth' of the text – a 'truth' which is sadly lacking in the ever-evasive jungle, and in a narrative which concludes with the terrified and nihilistic exclamation: '¡En nombre de Dios!' (p. 384).

Rivera's concern with the reception of *La vorágine* is matched intra-textually by Cova, who constantly alludes to the composition of the novel. The first two sections of *La vorágine*, and about half of the third and final section, are narrated by Cova in the past tense. Suddenly, shortly after Cova encounters an old friend in the jungle, the narrative switches to the present tense:

> Va para seis semanas que, por insinuación de Ramiro Estévanez, distraigo la ociosidad escribiendo las notas de mi odisea, en el libro de Caja que el Cayeno tenía sobre su escritorio como adorno inútil y polvoriento.
>
> [...] No ambiciono otro fin que el de emocionar a Ramiro Estévanez con el breviario de mis aventuras. (pp. 345–46)

This admission comes as quite a shock to the reader, for despite the melodramatic proclivities of Cova's narration, this is the first time that we have been confronted with a palpable untruth: as Richard Ford has insisted in his analysis of the narrative structure of *La vorágine*, 'obviamente Cova está pensando en otros lectores'.[55] Ford has dismissed Cova's philanthropic claims to have written the narrative for the diversion of his sick friend on the grounds that not only does Cova's story relate the massacre of the rubber workers at San Fernando de Atabapo, first told to him by Estévanez, who was an eyewitness to the event, but also that he continues to keep a diary even after he bids his friend goodbye. Indeed, the fact that Estévanez is almost blind makes Cova's narrative all the more redundant.

Cova's account of his expedition through the Colombian rainforest, far from being personal scribbles for the amusement of a friend, is stylistically consistent with the tradition of European travel writing on the tropics. The very layout of the novel, which includes a map, a glossary of indigenous words, and photographs of the protagonists, subscribes to a long-established pattern of travel writing.[56] The work includes the stock characters and loci of any tropical adventure tale: the intrepid (urban) explorer, trusty guides, easily beguiled natives; the infernal jungle, the river, the native village.

One of the most important sources of tropical imagery in *La vorágine* is Humboldt's writings on South America.[57] Although Elba R. David has fruitfully traced some of the parallels between *La vorágine* and Humboldt's *Personal Narrative*, he makes the common error of confounding the status of the narrator and the author when he asserts: 'No intentamos quitar nada de su [Rivera's] merecido prestigio al indicar que el recuerdo de la documentada obra de Humboldt pudo haber cruzado por su inspiración.'[58] In fact, the Humboldtian reverberations throughout the novel are testimony to Cova's wider ambition to fashion himself after the great continental explorer and are ironized implicitly by Rivera. As David demonstrates, both Humboldt and Cova write in great detail about the plant and animal life of tropical South America, such as electric eels, piranhas, mosquitoes, and the jungle vegetation. Nevertheless, there are some interesting textual parallels beyond the day-to-day particulars inevitable in any account of life in the tropics that Elba omits to mention. One example is Cova's reference to the phenomenon of horses on the plains instinctively locating sources of water (p. 194). A century earlier Humboldt had offered an analogous description of how 'as soon as you open the stable doors you see the horses [...] rush off into the savannah [...] until they finally announce by neighing that water has been found'.[59] Although this could be attributed to coincidence, it does seem significant that Cova should repeat such a story, especially as it would have been a well-worn anecdote for his supposed audience, Estévanez. Another important intersection between *La vorágine* and Humboldt's *Personal Narrative* is Cova's relaying of Correa's homespun wisdom about filtering the water found on the *llanos*: 'Tápelo con el pañuelo pa que le sirva de cedazo' (p. 166). Such advice is not only present in José Gumilla's eighteenth-century *El Orinoco ilustrado y defendido*, as Ordóñez has observed,[60] but in Humboldt's *Personal Narrative*, when an old man warns the explorer to 'cover the jug with a cloth and to drink the water through a filter so as not to smell the stink, and not to swallow the fine yellowish clay'.[61]

There are also many stylistic parallels between Humboldt and *La vorágine*, not least due to the ubiquity of Romantic themes in Rivera's novel. Cova's musings on the ephemeral life of man are suffused not only with Romantic but with specifically Humboldtian motifs, as when he describes how the forest trees are:

> siempre condenados a retoñar, a florecer, a gemir, a perpetuar, sin fecundarse [...] hasta borrar de la tierra el rastro del hombre y mecer un solo ramaje en urdimbre cerrada, cual en los milenios del Génesis, cuando Dios flotaba todavía sobre el espacio como una nebulosa de lágrimas. (p. 213)

This passage is reminiscent of the climactic conclusion to the chapter 'Cataracts of the Orinoco' in Humboldt's *Views of Nature* (although Rivera's version is, characteristically, much bleaker):

> Thus pass away the generations of men! [...] Yet when every emanation of the human mind has faded – when in the storms of time the monuments of man's creative art are scattered to the dust – an ever new life springs from the bosom of the earth. Unceasingly prolific nature unfolds her germs.[62]

Although designed to enhance the realism of the text, these parallels with Humboldt have quite the opposite effect. The inclusion of episodes from one of the canonical travel accounts of South America alerts the reader not only to the derivative nature of the novel but also to Cova's radical instability as narrator.

Cova's insistence that he is writing a true story – claims which are supported by the fictional editor's inclusion of a letter to a government official regarding the disappearance of Cova, a fragment from a letter, and an epigraphic telegram bearing the novel's most famous line: '¡Los devoró la selva!' (p. 385) – are undermined, then, by the flagrant literary echoes of his narrative, and its parallels with not only travel writing but also Romantic poetry, epic, and myth.[63] Green affirms that Rivera 'instila en Cova la conciencia de que está contando una historia', and indeed the text abounds in references to the processes of its composition.[64] Likewise, the fluctuations in medium from diary to epistolary form do not stress the novel's verisimilitude, but draw attention to its artificiality. After all, these formats are notoriously subjective and full of the '[p]eripecias extravagantes, detalles pueriles, páginas truculentas' (p. 345), which Cova admits to including in his narrative. Similarly, the predominance of first-person *testimonio* throughout the novel, especially in relation to the abuses of the rubber industry in the Putumayo, does not stress the reliability of eyewitnesses, but their proclivity for bias and misrepresentation. The reader of *La vorágine* has to grapple not only with the unreliability of narration in general but with that of Cova in particular, who reveals himself throughout the novel as prone to daydreaming and, more importantly, as mentally unstable.[65] His distorted perceptions, which make Alonso's reading of the text as 'fraught with irony' not just compelling but a critical exigency, attenuate the credibility of both his narrative and the accounts of the secondary narrators which are recorded by Cova.[66] Perhaps the final comment should be left to Cova himself, who in the antepenultimate paragraph of the novel says, in a moment of uncharacteristic candour: 'Son la historia nuestra, la desolada historia de los caucheros. ¡Cuánta página en blanco, cuánta cosa que no se dijo!' (pp. 383–84). *La vorágine* is a novel which is as much about the textual lacunae, the 'página en blanco', as about the words themselves.

Canaima

In Rómulo Gallegos's *Canaima* [1935], the protagonist, Marco Vargas, a well-educated Creole man, leaves the city to work in the Venezuelan rainforest. Once there he 'goes primitive', joining an Amerindian tribe and marrying a native woman. The novel ends with Marcos Vargas's son, also called Marcos Vargas, arriving in the city to be educated – a conclusion which has often been interpreted as symbolizing the reconciliation of culture and nature or, recast in the terms of that classic Latin American divide, civilization and barbarism. Nevertheless, the complexity of *Canaima* – a novel abounding in doublings, inversions, and ironies – seems to disallow any such straightforward reading. The final few lines of the novel, which describe the various tributaries of the Orinoco River crashing together before flowing into the sea, denote that far from being concluded, the arduous task of marrying nature and culture in Latin America is still to be undertaken:

> Bocas del Orinoco. Aguas del Padumu, del Ventuari... Allí mismo está esperándolas el mar. Apoyado sobre la barandilla del puente de proa va otra vez Marcos Vargas. Ureña lo lleva a dejarlo en un colegio de la capital donde ya están dos de sus hijos, y es el Orinoco quien lo va sacando hacia el porvenir... El río macho de los iracundos bramidos de Maipures y Atures...Ya le rinde sus cuentas al mar....[67]

It is significant that the final words of the novel are divided by ellipses, which both visually and etymologically imply a textual omission. This aporia reflects not only the uncertainty as to whether the young Marcos Vargas will be able to achieve the reconciliation of culture and nature but also the lack of sincerity in the novel's final lines. The description of the river as 'macho', an epithet much contested and ultimately derided in the novel, combined with the hyperbolic description of its 'iracundos bramidos', registers as mock-heroic, and seems to have been enunciated not by a transcendent authorial spokesperson but by an ironic narrator. Irony here, and throughout the novel, produces a fractured and resistant text, which relinquishes the expected 'happy ending' – the nuptials of civilization and barbarism – in favour of narrative ambiguity.

Unlike *Green Mansions*, *La vorágine*, and, as I will discuss shortly, *Los pasos perdidos*, which are all narrated by unreliable first-person narrators, throughout *Canaima* Gallegos uses free-indirect style. Colebrook has observed that free-indirect style, 'where discourses are presented as forces in their own right, as though language circulated with its own energy and power of transformation', is particularly open to 'postmodern irony'.[68] According to this schema, the subject becomes a channel rather than a source of language. *Canaima*, consistent with the *novela de la selva* tradition, merges various discourses (ethnology, anthropology, topography, and the expansionist rhetoric of the imperial romance) and mediates them through different characters. If *Canaima* is perceived as 'un libro enigmático' it is because the novel, lacking any unifying narrative voice, melds together an unlikely jumble of idioms and opinions, from the rural dialect of Encarnación Damesano to Childerico's florid classical metaphors.[69]

Parody is present from the novel's opening chapter, which fulfils the traditional function in travel literature of setting the scene. The narrator describes the birds, the mangrove swamps, and the native Amerindian villages in a narrative suffused with stereotypes of the tropics as Other. The land evoked is one of 'paisaje inquietante' (p. 10), 'donde imperan tiempos de violencia y de aventura' (p. 9), and where the natives are the 'degenerados descendientes del bravo caribe legendario' (p. 10). Violence, adventure, fear, and cannibalism (the word 'cannibal' derives from 'caribe') – the stock ingredients of European travel writing on the tropics – are all present, then, from the very first paragraphs of the novel. Pilar Almoina de Carrera has stated that 'entre la Crónica y la *novela de la selva* desarrollada casi cuatro siglos después existe un nexo', yet this bond is not one of unchallenged influence of the earlier texts on the later ones.[70] In *Canaima* the inclusion of episodes which would not be out of place in Columbus's journals (for example, the transcription of two Amerindians bartering: 'Yo dándote moriche canta bonito, tú dándome papelón. Yo dándote chinchorro, tú dándome sal' (p. 10)) registers as belated and derivative. Although Marcos is frequently interpreted as an authorial spokesperson, his view of the jungle as a site of unrivalled adventure, riches, and 'salvajes panoramas' (p. 17) is patently literary.[71] The figure of Don Quijote looms over Marcos, particularly in his desire for a life of adventure in the rainforest, inspired by the tales of the rubber workers: 'la selva sin fin, el vasto mundo del itinerario gigantesco vislumbrado a través de los cuentos de los caucheros, sembrado de hermosos peligros' (p. 61). Other literary references in the novel include the fashioning of Marcos's trip into the jungle as a descent into a mythical underworld and, as I shall discuss later, allusions to *Hamlet* and *King Lear*.[72]

If there is any remaining doubt as to the derivative nature of Marcos, it is dispelled by Janine Potelet, who has shown that many of the protagonist's observations about Amerindian culture can be traced back to a number of prominent South American anthropologists, including Elías Toro, who instituted the study of anthropology in the University of Caracas in 1905.[73] Of particular significance is Potelet's tracing of the theme of 'el mal de la selva' in *Canaima* back to Toro, who recorded how, while in the jungle, travellers often suffered from 'fascinación [...] voluntad inerte [...] y un secreto e inexplicable temor'.[74] Nevertheless, it is unlikely that this was Gallegos's main source for the theme of 'el mal de la selva'. The propensity for travellers to slip into depression or madness in the jungle is a staple not only of European travel writing on the tropics but also of South American fiction more generally. Indeed, it explicitly parallels the phenomenon of 'el embrujamiento de la selva' (p. 294) in *La vorágine*, a novel which, lest we forget, Gallegos was once accused of plagiarizing.[75] Allusions to *La vorágine* run throughout *Canaima*, not least in Gallegos's portrait of the iniquities of the rubber industry.[76] Images of the jungle as a prison, the anthropomorphizing of nature, and the novel's quest-like structure all conform to the paradigm of the earlier *novela de la selva*. Even the description of Guayana as 'una tierra de promisión' in Chapter 2 of *Canaima* (p. 14) recalls Rivera's celebrated collection of sonnets on the different landscapes of Colombia, *Tierra de promisión* [1921]. These intertextual currents are fundamental to the ironic narrative structure of *Canaima* and its introspective and metatextual proclivities. In this later *novela de la selva*, the Latin American writer no longer merely disassociates himself from European travel writing through parody, but actively affirms his adherence to a new, home-grown tradition of writing on the tropics by allusions to the *novela de la selva*.

Despite the ubiquity of literary references in *Canaima*, critics have frequently proposed autobiographical readings of the novel, a tendency encouraged by the discovery of a travel journal that Gallegos made on a trip to Guayana in 1931, which remained unexamined in the novelist's archive until 1984.[77] Although Gallegos went on this trip specifically to carry out research for a *novela de la selva*, carefully noting down topographical features and local expressions, the transfer from a personal diary to a novel entails a radical shift.[78] While it is interesting to note the parallels between many of the locals that Gallegos encountered on his trip and the characters in the novel, the myriad literary resonances of *Canaima* discussed above disbar an interpretation of the novel merely as a true-life travel account.[79] If autobiographical readings hold any value at all it is in their correlation of Gallegos with Gabriel Ureña, for if Ureña is an authorial alter ego, it is not insignificant that he is repeatedly described as looking at Marcos with 'miradas [...] secas de ironía'(p. 85).[80] Ureña's scepticism towards Marcos, a character whose warped vision of the jungle imperils the reliability of the entire novel via the use of free-indirect style, is an important cue for the reader: 'para el de los atónitos ojos irónicos él [Marcos] no era sino un espectáculo entretenido' (p. 85). Marcos, and the discourse of tropical adventure and escape he embodies, is thus heavily ironized by the author. Narrative irony, intertexuality, and inconclusivity ensure that ultimate 'meaning' is always evaded in *Canaima*.

Los pasos perdidos

Although Alejo Carpentier's *Los pasos perdidos* was published in 1953, decades after *La vorágine* and *Canaima* and almost half a century after *Green Mansions*, it not only shares the postcolonial concerns of the earlier novels but in many respects intensifies their parodic assault on the legacy of colonial travel writing on the tropics. The plot of *Los pasos perdidos* is paradigmatic within the *novela de la selva* genre. An anonymous first-person narrator, a Latin American musicologist living in the United States, relates in diary form his journey to the Venezuelan rainforest in search of indigenous musical instruments. Once in the jungle he falls in love with a local woman and renounces his old life (and wife) in favour of a more 'natural' and 'timeless' existence. At first the novel reads as a conventional travelogue, yet as the narrator travels deeper into the forest the stereotypes of travel literature give way to a vision of unrestrained botanical excess – a vertiginous 'mundo de la mentira, de la trampa y del falso semblante', where meaning is cleaved from language in a perpetual assault on ontological truth.[81] This is also, as I shall trace here, a fitting characterization for the novel's own auto-deconstructive textual praxis.

One of the central themes of *Los pasos perdidos* is the demystification of the figure of the artist, particularly of the Western author. While Carpentier presents Amerindian art (petroglyphs, clay pottery, primitive musical instruments) as mysterious and transcendent, the products of the Western imagination are deflated as mundane and utilitarian. The narrator's relinquishment of the threnody he is inspired to compose in the jungle due to a lack of paper (ironic, surely, given the fact that he is surrounded by trees, the raw material of paper) epitomizes the unglamorous nature of artistic production:

> Nunca pensé que la imaginación pudiera toparse alguna vez con un escollo tan estúpido como la falta de papel. Y cuando más exasperado me encuentro, Rosario me pregunta a quién estoy escribiendo cartas, puesto que aquí no hay correo. (pp. 226–27)

Rosario, presented by the narrator throughout the novel as a simple-minded woman of 'campesina lógica' (p. 228), is characteristically incisive in her belief that writing must always have a destination – that aesthetic production is not an end in itself but is directed at 'los demás' (p. 227). The narrator's detailed description of his approach to composing music, which does not preclude minutiae relating to writing materials (just as Cova in *La vorágine* tells us he is writing his narrative in an old account book), highlights the artificiality of art in general and of the novel we are reading in particular, which partakes of the same process of inscription, redrafting, and elision.

The demystification of authorship in *Los pasos perdidos* takes place as much outside the text as within it, principally via the mischievous and contradictory critical lore circulated by Carpentier regarding the novel's inception and composition. His assertion that *Los pasos perdidos* was spawned in a quasi-mystical 'iluminación' and 'en pocos segundos completamente hecha, estructurada, construida',[82] is incompatible with the author's admission to having rewritten the novel three times prior to its publication, and with his insistence in numerous interviews and in the novel's epilogue that many of the characters were based on real people.[83] As is the case with *La vorágine*, interpretations like that of *Los pasos perdidos* as Carpentier's 'autobiographical travel narrative' have flourished, and this is hardly surprising given that Carpentier

maintains that the novel was inspired by two trips he made to the Venezuelan rainforest in 1947 and 1948, just as a previous visit to Haiti had planted
the seed for *El reino de este mundo*.[84] Indeed, as Alexis Márquez Rodríguez
has observed, '[e]l protagonista innominado [...] tiene mucho, en efecto, del
autor', not only because of his mixed European and American parentage but
also his interest in music, architecture and American history.[85]

One of the key sources when assessing to what degree the novel might
be autobiographical is Carpentier's unfinished travel account of his trip to
Venezuela, *El libro de la Gran Sabana*, which González Echevarría considers
the 'primitive text of the novel'.[86] This travelogue, much of which was serial-
ized in *El Nacional* in the column 'Visión de America', coincides somewhat
in lexicon and content with the account of the narrator-protagonist. Both
narratives mention the sensation of receding in time as one moves forward
through the forest, both show an acute awareness of the tradition of European
writing on the New World, and both draw upon tropes of the American
tropics as 'virginal' and unexplored. Despite these convergences, as González
Echevarría has convincingly argued, *Los pasos perdidos* is only 'coherent if read
as fiction', and even more so, as an ironic commentary on travel writing on
the Americas.[87] Unlike those of his fictional narrator-protagonist, Carpentier's
awestruck descriptions of American topography throughout *El libro de la Gran
Sabana* do not attempt to diminish Otherness through linguistic domestica-
tion. Struggling to describe a vast formation of rocks, for example, Carpentier finally dismisses a comparative approach: 'Las rutinas imaginativas de mi
cultura occidental me hacen evocar, en el acto, el castillo de Macbeth o el
castillo de Klingsor. Pero no. Tales imágenes son inadmisibles, por lo limitadas,
en este riñón de la América virgen.'[88] In *Los pasos perdidos* these 'inadmissible'
images are the stock repertoire of the narrator's portrait of the tropics, which
as we shall see, is burdened by many of the stylistic and thematic conventions
of travel writing.

In *Los pasos perdidos* the narrator's description of how he had 'pasado largas
horas mirando a las riberas, sin apartar mucho la vista de la relación de Fray
Servando de Castillejos' (p. 113), exemplifies how in the novel travel writing
comes to embody a mediating presence between life and art. Rather than gaze
directly at the landscape, the narrator uses a 300-year-old text to translate the
experience.[89] Nancy Stepan has explained that in the nineteenth century, the
public thirst for tales of exploration produced a picture of the tropics which
was 'an imaginative construct as much as it was an empirical description of
the natural world'.[90] Far from being uncharted, the tropical rainforest visited
by the narrator in *Los pasos perdidos* is already mapped with meaning, and his
awareness of this recalls what Tzvetan Todorov has described as Columbus's
'finalist' approach to the New World, where 'the ultimate meaning is given
from the start'.[91]

There are many parallels between *Los pasos perdidos* and factual travel
accounts of tropical South America. González Echevarría regards Schomburgk's *Travels in British Guiana* as the 'secret source' of the novel, and Pratt

has described *Los pasos perdidos* as a 'dystopic rewriting of Humboldt'.[92] While the correspondence between *Travels in British Guiana* and Carpentier's novel is well documented, critics have failed to establish the significant textual analogies between *Los pasos perdidos* and Humboldt's *Personal Narrative*. Nevertheless, some episodes in the novel, such as the one cited below, seem to be drawn straight out of Humboldt:

> El Adelantado me muestra entonces, un paredón de roca, unos signos trazados a gran altura por artesanos desconocidos – artesanos que hubieran sido izados hasta el nivel de su tarea por un andamiaje imposible [...]. A la luz de la luna se dibujan figuras de escorpiones, serpientes, pájaros, entre otros signos sin sentido para mis ojos, que tal vez fueran figuraciones astrales. [...] un día, al regresar de un viaje, cuenta el Fundador, su hijo Marcos, entonces adolescente, le dejó atónito al narrarle la historia del Diluvio Universal. En su ausencia, los indios habían enseñado al mozo que esos petroglifos [...] fueron trazados en días de gigantesca creciente. (p. 198)

Humboldt related the same myth some 150 years before:

> A few leagues from Encaramada a rock called Tepu-mereme (Painted Rock) rises in the middle of the savannah. It is covered with animal drawings and symbolic signs [...] – stars, suns, jaguars, crocodiles [...]. These hieroglyphic figures are frequently carved so high up that only scaffolding could reach them. When we asked the Indians how they could have carved those images, they answered, smiling, as if only whites could ignore such an obvious answer: 'During *the great waters*, their ancestors reached those rocks in their canoes.'[93]

The parallels between the accounts of this phenomenon by Humboldt and by the narrator cannot be explained solely by the endurance of certain myths surrounding Amerindian culture. Indeed, we know that Carpentier was familiar with Humboldt's description of the petroglyphs, given that he writes about them in 'Visión de América'.[94] Rather, it signals the narrator's conscious or unconscious reworking of Humboldt's *Personal Narrative* – a notion compounded by the fact that in both works the discussion of the petroglyphs is directly juxtaposed with a meditation on Amerindian diluvial myths. In fact, many of the incidents central to *Los pasos perdidos*, such as the discovery of Rosario almost dead from altitude and dehydration, recall strikingly similar events in Humboldt's *Personal Narrative*.[95]

While the Humboldtian reverberations in the novel are widespread, the allusions to travel writing do not end there. The influence of European travel narrative is also apparent in the narrator's fidelity to the genre's stylistic conventions, such as the use of a diary format and frequent recourse to the present tense to create an atmosphere of dramatic immediacy or suspense. Indeed, at times, the narrator's engagement with travel writing strikes the reader as delusional, as when he pretends that he and his fellow travellers are 'Conquistadores [...] en busca del Reino de Manoa' (p. 161), whose party includes a series of colonial archetypes: the missionary, the governor, the astrologer, the musician, and the native female. González Echevarría's comparison of the anonymous narrator to Don Quijote is an astute one. Fed on a diet of colonial travel writing, the narrator surveys the modern American landscape through a lens mottled with tropes. Early on in his account he describes how he experienced 'una suerte de Descubrimiento' (p. 80) on the fifth day of his trip. The capitalization of the noun 'Descubrimiento' indicates that the narrator is alluding specifically to the 'Discovery' of America, yet the heroic overtones of this comment are undermined by the fact that at this moment the self-styled conquistador is travelling on a bus – a bus that is very unheroically 'gimiendo por los ejes' (p. 80). The characters of *Los pasos perdidos* are also far from heroic. The Adelantado's lofty title, steeped in allusions of sovereignty and 'grandes hechos' (p. 194), does not denote his monarchical disposition but is an enduring nickname, just as his 'city' falls far short of the narrator's expectation of a beacon of civilization in the jungle. The anachronistically quest-like structure of the narrator's journey through the forest, combined with his mock-heroic conduct, immediately alerts the reader to the ironic nature of the text.

Los pasos perdidos is a ceaselessly self-referential text which draws attention to its narrative deceits in the very act of writing them. It is significant that at the beginning of the fourth chapter the narrator admits that he is writing a novel, and on his return to the city he decides to sell 'una patraña que h[a] ido repasando durante el viaje', relating how he had been held prisoner by a tribe and had escaped 'atravesando, solo, centenares de kilómetros de selva' (p. 244). The stereotyped adventure tale created by the narrator, with the help of 'una novela famosa [...] en que se precisan los nombres de animales, de árboles, refiriéndose leyendas indígenas, sucedidos antiguos, y todo lo necesario para dar un giro de veracidad' (pp. 244–45), is not so unlike the text that we have before us, and the reader is left to ponder whether the story sold by the narrator to the press is the very one that we have been reading all along. Despite the narrator ridiculing Rosario's conviction that 'lo que los libros dicen es verdad' (p. 103), his own novelistic aesthetic is embedded in the concept of verisimilitude. The narrator's oxymoronic attempt to maintain 'veracidad' throughout his 'patraña' – a paradox which is compounded by his recourse to a work of fiction to enhance his novel's credibility – destabilizes the authority of both the fictive text (the travel journal of the narrator-protagonist) and the physical text (Alejo Carpentier's *Los pasos perdidos*). It is enticing to speculate about the 'novela famosa' that the narrator uses to glean material for his bogus travel account. This is not a factual travelogue – not Humboldt's *Personal Narrative*, or Schomburgk's *Travels in British Guiana* – but a classic *novela de la selva*.[96] Parody turns to self-parody, as the *novela de la selva* is lampooned for inscribing yet another layer of narrative on the already emblazoned jungle.[97]

The ironic postures of the genre come to maturity in this late novel in its concession that to parody a discourse one must necessarily partake of it. The reference to the narrator's plagiarized travel journal (a text within a text within a text) issues the coup de grâce to the notion of a pre-colonial tabula rasa to which the postcolonial writer can return. It is not a coincidence that even in the 'virgin' American jungle the narrator encounters a burgeoning city. The foundations of Latin American narrative must always be laid upon the vestiges of the past.

★　★　★

Narrative irony in the *novela de la selva* functions, then, on a number of different levels. Firstly, the novelists' use of parody serves to undermine European discourses of the tropics in travel literature and adventure fiction, particularly in relation to landscape aesthetics and ethnography. Yet no less significant is the *novela de la selva*'s interrogation of issues of literary identity, textual authority, and power through what Hutcheon has termed the 'transideological' force of irony.[98] The inherent ambiguity of irony – its potential to be comprehended or not – vitiates semantic stability and facilitates a reinvention of history via language 'by loosening the grip of a mythology that depends on fixed meanings and fixed truths'.[99] For the postcolonial writer, such confusion is a welcome antidote to the static literary tropes of the imperial period. Yet, for the reader of the *novela de la selva* these ungrasped ironies can, and do, disrupt the traditional paradigm of literary 'consumption'. Sommer has discussed at length the rhetorical function of 'unwilling' texts: 'The slap of refused intimacy from uncooperative books can slow readers down, detain them at the boundary between contact and conquest, before they press particularist writing to surrender cultural difference for the sake of universal meaning.'[100] It is not only the complex narrative structure of the *novela de la selva* which precludes definitive meaning, but also, as will be discussed in the following chapter, the jungle itself. Throughout these novels, the narrator (and, by extension, the reader) is forced to surrender to the unrepresentability of the tropical landscape, as the narrative trails off in ellipsis, horrified exclamation, or unglossed native words. Such textual lacunae draw attention not only to the shortcomings of the narrator as a reliable commentator but also to the limits of European landscape aesthetics – what Paul Carter has described as the 'dissonance between language and land'.[101] Like the 'horror' of Joseph Conrad's *Heart of Darkness*, the labyrinthine jungle of the *novela de la selva* becomes a metaphor for the untranslatable Otherness of postcolonial space, where words conceal rather than reveal, and act as shibboleths policing access to the hidden recesses of cultural experience.

Notes

1　Andrés Bello, *Obra literaria*, ed. Pedro Grases, 2nd edn (Caracas: Biblioteca Ayacucho, 1985), p. 20.
2　Bello, *Obra literaria*, p. 21.
3　Carlos Fuentes, *La nueva novela hispanoamericana* (México: Mortiz, 1969), p. 9.
4　Mario Vargas Llosa, 'Primitives and Creators', *Times Literary Supplement*, 14 November 1968.
5　Paul Connerton, *How Societies Remember* (Cambridge: Cambridge University Press, 1989), p. 6.

6 Djelal Kadir, *Questing Fictions: Latin America's Family Romance* (Minneapolis: University of Minnesota Press, 1986).

7 Said, *Culture and Imperialism*, pp. 34–35. See also, for instance, Helen Tiffin, 'Postcolonial Literatures and Counter Discourse', in Ashcroft et al (eds.), *Post-Colonial Studies Reader*, pp. 95–98. She argues that, for the postcolonial writer, 'the rereading and rewriting of the European historical and fictional record are vital and inescapable tasks. These subversive manoeuvres, rather than the construction or reconstruction of the essentially national or regional, are what is characteristic of post-colonial texts' (p. 95).

8 Lois Parkinson Zamora, *The Usable Past: The Imagination of History in Recent Fiction of the Americas* (Cambridge: Cambridge University Press, 1997), p. 5.

9 Rose, *Parody*, dedicates a chapter to the definition of the term parody, see pp. 5–55.

10 See Rose, *Parody*, pp. 281–82.

11 The prevalence of parody in postcolonial writing has been noted by a number of critics, including Robert Fraser, *Lifting the Sentence: A Poetics of Postcolonial Fiction* (Manchester: Manchester University Press, 2000), pp. 189–212.

12 Rose, *Parody*, p. 51.

13 See, for example, Fraser, *Lifting the Sentence*, pp. 200–02, where he discusses the function of parody as an exercise in practical criticism, giving as an example Jean Rhys's engagement with *Jane Eyre* in *Wide Sargasso Sea*.

14 Andrea Giunta, 'Strategies of Modernity in Latin America', in Gerardo Mosquera (ed.), *Beyond the Fantastic: Contemporary Art Criticism from Latin America* (London: Institute of International Visual Arts, 1995), pp. 53–67 (p. 64).

15 Neil Larsen, 'Foreword', in D. Emily Hicks, *Border Writing: The Multidimensional Text* (Minneapolis: University of Minnesota Press, 1991), pp. xi–xxi (p. xiii).

16 Coco Fusco, *English is Broken Here: Notes on Cultural Fusion in the Americas* (New York: New Press, 1995), p. 70.

17 Homi K. Bhabha, *The Location of Culture* (London: Routledge, 2002), p. 85.

18 Bhabha, *Location of Culture*, p. 86.

19 Bhabha, *Location of Culture*, p. 87; p. 86.

20 Ania Loomba, 'Overworlding the "Third World"', *Oxford Literary Review*, 13 (1991), pp. 164–91 (p. 180).

21 Bhabha, *Location of Culture*, p. 86.

22 Jacques Lacan, *The Four Fundamental Concepts of Psychoanalysis*, ed. Jacques-Alain Miller, trans. Alan Sheridan (London: Norton, 1998), p. 99. This quotation opens Bhabha's essay 'Of Mimicry and Man' in *Location of Culture*, p. 85.

23 There have been a number of discussions of irony in *Los pasos perdidos* and *La vorágine*, including those by Roberto González Echevarría, 'Ironía y estilo en *Los pasos perdidos*, de Alejo Carpentier', in Klaus Müller-Bergh (ed.), *Asedios a Carpentier: once ensayos críticos sobre el novelista cubano* (Santiago de Chile: Editorial Universitaria, 1972), pp. 134–45; and Alonso, *Regional Novel*, p. 148.

24 González Echevarría, 'Ironía y estilo', pp. 139–40. Otto Olivera, 'El romanticismo de *La vorágine*', in Montserrat Ordóñez (ed.), *La vorágine: textos críticos* (Bogotá: Alianza Editorial Colombiana, 1987), pp. 259–67 (p. 264).

25 Claire Colebrook, *Irony* (London: Routledge, 1994), p. 12.

26 Wayne C. Booth, *A Rhetoric of Irony* (Chicago: University of Chicago Press, 1974), has argued that 'in reading parody, we make use of external reference to other authors in order to understand how the parody attacks those same authors: the thing referred to, externally, to assist in comprehension is the same thing referred to, externally, as the object of ridicule' (p. 123).

27 'Sly civility' is Bhabha's term. See Bhabha, *Location of Culture*, pp. 93–101.

28 Booth, *Rhetoric of Irony*, p. 204.

29 Edmundo de Chasca, 'El lirismo de *La vorágine*', in Ordóñez (ed.), *Textos críticos*, pp. 239–57 (p. 254).

30 Such a position seems to foreshadow the postmodern understanding of irony, as defined, for instance, in Linda Hutcheon, *Irony's Edge: The Theory and Politics of Irony* (London: Routledge, 1994).

31 Beardsell, *Returning the Gaze*, p. 203.

32 González Echevarría, *Myth and Archive*, p. 8.

33 W. H. Hudson, *Green Mansions: A Romance of the Tropical Forest*, ed. Ian Duncan (Oxford: Oxford University Press, 1998), p. 3. All further references are to this edition and are given after quotations in the text.

34 James V. Fletcher, 'The Creator of Rima, W. H. Hudson: A Belated Romantic', *Sewanee Review*, 41 (1933), pp. 24–40. Fletcher has listed Wordsworth's Lucy and Shelley's Cythna as possible antecedents of Rima.

35 See, Alvar Núñez Cabeza de Vaca, *Naufragios* [1542], ed. Juan Francisco Maura (Madrid: Cátedra, 1989). Cabeza de Vaca is shipwrecked off the coast of Florida and is forced to undertake a long journey through America to reach safety.

36 Jay Macpherson, *The Spirit of Solitude: Conventions and Continuities in Late Romance* (New Haven: Yale University Press, 1982), pp. 182–218.

37 Roberts, *W. H. Hudson*, has contributed to this tendency by speculating about Rima being based on a childhood sweetheart of Hudson, see p. 99.

38 One instance of this idealization is in W. H. Hudson, *The Naturalist in La Plata* (London: Chapman and Hall, 1892), pp. 7–8, when Hudson describes a group of Amerindians looking for stray horses on the pampas as 'motionless and silent, like bronze men on strange horse-shaped pedestals of dark stone; so dark in their copper skins and long black hair, against the far-off ethereal sky, flushed with amber light'.

39 Fletcher, 'Creator of Rima', p. 24.

40 Carlos A. Baker, 'The Source-book for Hudson's *Green Mansions*', *PMLA*, 61 (1946), pp. 252–57.

41 Among the many parallels he draws between Rima and Luxima, Baker, 'Source-book for Hudson's *Green Mansions*', has pointed out that they both live in a forest and are described as being rainbow-coloured. When Luxima dies at the end of Lady Morgan's novel, her lover, like Abel, stores her ashes in a decorated urn.

42 In this tale (pp. 168–69) Abel seems to appeal specifically to Columbus's journals and to the myth of El Dorado.

43 Roberts, *W. H. Hudson*, p. 131, has related how Hudson had never visited the tropics and seems to have acquired knowledge of its flora and fauna from his readings of Bates, Bell, and Wallace.

44 Duncan (ed.), in Hudson, *Green Mansions*, n. 31, p. 205. This passage from Bates was included in Hudson's *Idle Days in Patagonia*.

45 Joan R. Green has discussed the gap between the author and editor in *La vorágine* in 'La estructura del narrador y el modo narrativo de *La vorágine*', in Ordóñez (ed.), *Textos críticos*, pp. 269–77 (p. 270), as has Raymond L. Williams, 'La figura del autor y del escritor en *La vorágine*', *Discurso Literario*, 4 (1987), pp. 535–51.

46 R. H. Moreno-Durán, 'Las voces de la polifonía telúrica', in Ordóñez (ed.), *Textos críticos*, pp. 437–52 (p. 437).

47 Eduardo Castillo, '*La vorágine*', in Ordóñez (ed.), *Textos críticos*, pp. 41–43 (first published in *Cromos* 13 December 1924). Jorge Añez, *De 'La vorágine' a 'Doña Bárbara'* (Bogotá: Imprenta del Departamento, 1944), p. 20, has argued, '*La vorágine* está basada e inspirada en hechos reales, en acontecimientos absolutamente históricos.'

48 José Eustasio Rivera, *La vorágine* (Bogotá: Editorial Cromos, 1924), p. 10.

49 Alonso, *Regional Novel*, p. 142.

50 Cited in Eduardo Neale-Silva, *Horizonte humano: vida de José Eustasio Rivera* (Madison: University of Wisconsin Press, 1960), p. 298.

51 Neale-Silva, *Horizonte humano*, p. 306.

52 Neale-Silva, *Horizonte humano*, p. 305.

53 Eduardo Neale-Silva, 'The Factual Bases of *La vorágine*', *PMLA*, 54 (1939), pp. 316–31. It is noteworthy that in the novel Clemente Silva describes how this very report 'empezó a circular subrepticiamente en gomales y barracones', José Eustasio Rivera, *La vorágine*, ed. Montserrat Ordóñez (Madrid: Cátedra, 1998), p. 268. All further references are to this edition and are given after quotations in the text.

54 Miguel Rasch Isla, 'Cómo escribió Rivera *La vorágine*', in Ordóñez (ed.), *Textos críticos*, pp. 83–88, has described the process of revisions within the text from its first publication until Rivera's death.

55 Richard Ford, 'El marco narrativo de *La vorágine*', in Ordóñez (ed.), *Textos críticos*, pp. 307–16 (p. 312).

56 These features changed from edition to edition, especially in the first few years after its publication. The first edition (Bogotá: Editorial Cromos, 1924) included photographs, but neither a map nor a glossary; instead, foreign and specialist vocabulary was italicized in the text. The glossary was introduced in the third edition (Bogotá: Editorial Minerva, 1926), and the maps replaced the photographs in the fifth edition (New York: Editorial Andes, 1928). Hernán Lozano has provided a useful account of the different versions of the novel in *La vorágine: ensayo bibliográfico* (Bogotá: Instituto Caro y Cuervo, 1973).

57 Neale-Silva, *Horizonte humano*, has reproduced an interview in which Rivera admits to having read 'los viajes de Humboldt, Crévaux, Michelena y Rojas, Chaffanjon, Hamilton Rice, para no citar sino forasteros' (p. 293), before commencing his own trip into the Amazon region.

58 Elba R. David, 'El pictorialismo tropical de *La vorágine* y *El viaje* de Alexander von Humboldt', *Hispania*, 47 (1964), pp. 36–40 (p. 38).

59 Alexander von Humboldt, *Personal Narrative of a Journey to the Equinoctial Regions of the New Continent*, trans. and ed. Jason Wilson (Harmondsworth: Penguin, 1995), p. 165.

60 Ordóñez (ed.), in Rivera, *La vorágine*, p. 166.

61 Humboldt, *Personal Narrative*, p. 164.

62 Alexander von Humboldt, *Views of Nature: The Sublime Phenomena of Creation*, trans. E. C. Otté and Henry G. Bohn (London: Bohn, 1850), p. 173.

63 For a discussion of Romantic imagery in *La vorágine* see Jean Franco, 'Image and Experience in *La vorágine*', *Bulletin of Hispanic Studies*, 41 (1964), pp. 101–10, and Olivera, 'El romanticismo de *La vorágine*'. For a discussion of epic see De Chasca, 'El lirismo de *La vorágine*'. In relation to myth see Seymour Menton, '*La vorágine*: Circling the Triangle', *Hispania*, 59 (1976), pp. 418–34; Leonidas Morales, '*La vorágine*: un viaje al país de los muertos', in Ordóñez (ed.), *Textos críticos*, pp. 149–67; and José Angel Valente, 'La naturaleza y el hombre en *La vorágine* de José Eustasio Rivera', *Cuadernos Hispanoamericanos*, 67 (1955), pp. 102–08.

64 Green, 'Estructura del narrador', p. 272.

65 See Luis B. Eyzaguirre, 'Arturo Cova, héroe patológico', in Ordóñez (ed.), *Textos críticos*, pp. 373–90. Sharon Magnarelli, *The Lost Rib: Female Characters in the Spanish-American Novel* (Lewisburg, PA: Bucknell University Press, 1985), has described Cova as 'seriously demented' (p. 40).

66 Alonso, *Regional Novel*, p. 148.

67 Rómulo Gallegos, *Canaima*, 12th edn (Madrid: Colección Austral, 1977), p. 245. All further references are to this edition and are given after quotations in the text. The

description of the river here echoes one in the first chapter of the novel: 'el río macho de los iracundos bramidos de Maipures y Atures' (p. 10).

68   Colebrook, *Irony*, pp. 161–62.

69   Charles Minguet, 'Introducción', in Rómulo Gallegos, *Canaima: edición crítica*, ed. Charles Minguet (Madrid: Archivos, CSIC, 1991), pp. xvii–xxii (p. xix).

70   Pilar Almoina de Carrera, '*Canaima*: Arquetipos ideológicos y culturales', in Minguet (ed.), *Canaima*, pp. 325–39 (p. 326).

71   Many critics have failed to distinguish adequately between Gallegos and Marcos Vargas. For instance, Almoina de Carrera, 'Arquetipos ideológicos y culturales', has described how 'para Gallegos [...] la presentación del indio no pasa de ser una visión externa y prejuiciada' (p. 337), which overlooks the fact that the resulting portrait is always mediated through an ironic narrator.

72   Françoise Pérus, 'Universalidad del regionalismo: *Canaima* de Rómulo Gallegos', in Minguet (ed.), *Canaima*, pp. 417–73 (pp. 447–48), has discussed the mythical and epic aspects of the novel, and has identified Cholo Parima as a keeper who must be slain by Marcos before he can pass into the underworld (forest).

73   Janine Potelet, '*Canaima*, novela del Indio Caribe', in Minguet (ed.), *Canaima*, pp. 377–416. Potelet has argued that two travel accounts in particular, *Por las selvas de Guayana* (Caracas, 1905) by Elías Toro, and *Río Negro* (Ciudad Bolívar, 1906) by B. Tavera-Acosta, 'aparecen como las fuentes inmediatas y obvias de *Canaima*', p. 378.

74   Cited in Potelet, 'Novela del Indio Caribe', p. 409.

75   Añez, *De 'La vorágine'*, pp. 20–22, accused Gallegos of having plagiarized *La vorágine* in *Doña Bárbara*.

76   Almoina de Carrera, 'Arquetipos ideológicos', says that 'en cuanto a los antecedentes literarios de *Canaima* [...] es imposible dejar de mencionar *La vorágine*', p. 327. Also see Olga Carreras González, 'Tres fechas, tres novelas y un tema: estudio comparativo de *La vorágine, Canaima y Los pasos perdidos*', *Explicación de Textos Literarios*, 2 (1974), pp. 169–78 (p. 172).

77   This document is reproduced in full in Minguet (ed.), *Canaima*, pp. 277–300.

78   See Gustavo Guerrero, 'De las notas a la novela: el memorándum de Gallegos y la génesis de *Canaima*', in Minguet (ed.), *Canaima*, pp. 359–75 (p. 371).

79   Efraín Subero, 'Génesis de *Canaima*', in Minguet (ed.), *Canaima*, pp. 309–16, has claimed that 'casi todos los personajes de *Canaima* son reales' (p. 313).

80   Numerous critics have identified parallels between Gallegos and Ureña, including Subero, 'Génesis de *Canaima*', p. 311, and Potelet, 'Novela del Indio Caribe', p. 393. There are several descriptions of Ureña as an ironic commentator in the novel. For example: 'Allí estaba, con sus grandes ojos [...] un poco irónicos' (p. 84).

81   Alejo Carpentier, *Los pasos perdidos* (Madrid: Alianza Editorial, 1998), p. 169. All further references are to this edition and are given after quotations in the text.

82   Ramón Chao, *Conversaciones con Alejo Carpentier* (Madrid: Alianza Editorial, 1998), p. 152.

83   See, for instance, Carlos Santander T., 'Lo maravilloso en la obra de Alejo Carpentier', in Helmy F. Giacoman (ed.), *Homenaje a Alejo Carpentier: variaciones interpretativas en torno a su obra* (New York: Las Americas, 1970), pp. 99–144, who quotes Carpentier as saying: 'me costó no poco esfuerzo escribir [*Los pasos perdidos*]. Tres veces la reescribí completamente' (p. 108).

84   Pratt, *Imperial Eyes*, p. 196.

85   Alexis Márquez Rodríguez, *La obra narrativa de Alejo Carpentier* (Caracas: Ediciones de la Biblioteca, Universidad Central de Venezuela, 1970), p. 55.

86   Roberto González Echevarría, *Alejo Carpentier: The Pilgrim at Home* (Ithaca, NY: Cornell University Press, 1977), p. 170.

87 González Echevarría, *Alejo Carpentier*, p. 169.

88 Alejo Carpentier, *Visión de América* (Barcelona: Seix Barral, 1999), p. 21.

89 This recalls Carpentier's own admission that he had travelled up the Orinoco River with copies of Gumilla and Humboldt, 'constantemente cotejando lo que se veía en la orilla del río y lo que habían pintado estos dos autores', cited in Chao, *Conversaciones*, p. 151 – evidence of yet more of Carpentier's playful blurring of the distinction between himself and the fictional protagonist of *Los pasos perdidos*.

90 Nancy Stepan, *Picturing Tropical Nature* (London: Reaktion Books, 2001), p. 11.

91 Tzvetan Todorov, *The Conquest of America: The Question of the Other*, trans. Richard Howard (New York: Harper & Row, 1984), p. 17.

92 González Echevarría, *Alejo Carpentier*, pp. 175–80 (p. 176); Pratt, *Imperial Eyes*, p. 196.

93 Humboldt, *Personal Narrative*, p. 188.

94 Carpentier, *Visión de América*, pp. 30–31. He also mentions the petroglyphs in 'El gran libro de la selva', pp. 83–85.

95 Humboldt, *Personal Narrative*, describes how his party found a young Amerindian girl on the savannah: 'She was exhausted with fatigue and thirst, with her eyes, nose and mouth full of sand [...]. We revived her by washing her face and making her drink some wine. She was scared when she found herself surrounded by so many people, but she slowly relaxed and talked to our guides' (p. 172). In *Los pasos perdidos* the narrator describes the discovery of Rosario in parallel terms: 'Una mujer estaba sentada en un contén de piedra, con un hato y un paraguas dejados en el suelo, envuelta en una ruana azul. Le hablaban y no respondía, como estupefacta, con la mirada empañada y los labios temblorosos, meciendo levemente la cabeza mal cubierta por un pañuelo rojo cuyo nudo, bajo la barba, estaba suelto. Uno de los que con nosotros viajaban se acercó a ella y le puso en la boca una tableta de maleza, apretando firmemente, para obligarla a tragar. Como entendiendo, la mujer empezó a mascar con lentitud, y volvieron sus ojos, poco a poco, a tener alguna expresión' (p. 82).

96 González Echevarría, 'Canaima y los libros de la selva', in Charles Minguet (ed.), *Canaima: textos críticos*, 2nd edn (Madrid: CSIC, 1996), pp. 503-14, has argued that the source that the narrator alludes to 'no puede ser otra que *Canaima*, especialmente si tomamos en cuenta que Carpentier residía en Caracas por esa época, y recordamos que Rosario, amante del protagonista de *Los pasos perdidos*, se casa con un joven llamado Marcos, clara alusión al Marcos Vargas de Gallegos' (p. 503).

97 González Echevarría, *Myth and Archive*, has noted that in *Los pasos perdidos* '[t]here is writing everywhere in the jungle' (p. 2).

98 Hutcheon, *Irony's Edge*, pp. 29–31.

99 Vera Kutzinski, *Against the American Grain: Myth and History in William Carlos Williams, Jay Wright, and Nicolás Guillén* (Baltimore: Johns Hopkins University Press, 1987), p. 26.

100 Sommer, *Proceed with Caution*, p. ix.

101 Paul Carter, *The Road to Botany Bay: An Essay in Spatial History* (London: Faber and Faber, 1987), p. 45.

CHAPTER TWO

Tropical Nature and Landscape Aesthetics

It is almost impossible to think of any natural space on earth which has not been written about: 'everywhere we look we encounter a pre-interpreted landscape, or a landscape made legible', as Jonathan Smith has argued.[1] Tropical landscapes, in particular, are cultural as well as natural constructs – spaces both real and imaginary which have inspired utopian fiction, visual art, and countless sensationalist travel accounts. Within a European literary tradition key places within the tropics such as 'Amazonia' have often been reduced to little more than discursive constructs, conceived variously as lands of promise and adventure or as green hells of disease and savagery.[2] David Arnold has compared Western attitudes and ideas about the tropics – what he terms 'tropicality' – to Said's definition of 'Orientalism'.[3] Just as representations of the Orient in European art and letters have centred on the region's dissimilarity to the Occident, so has the tropics been understood as embodying all that the 'temperate' zone is not. In *Tristes Tropiques* Claude Lévi-Strauss exemplifies the pervasiveness of stereotypes of the tropics as 'radically different':

> Brazil and South America did not mean much to me. However, I can still remember, with absolute clarity, the pictures conjured up [...]. I imagined exotic countries to be the exact opposite of ours, and the term 'antipodes' had a richer and more naïve significance for me than its merely literal meaning. [...] I expected each animal, tree or blade of grass to be radically different, and its tropical nature to be glaringly obvious at a glance.[4]

The prevalence of readily accessible tropes of tropical nature helps to explain why writers on the tropics so often coincide in word choice and image, from early modern accounts of tropical America to twentieth-century travel writing by André Gide, Lévi-Strauss, and Redmond O'Hanlon. Indeed, latter-day travel writers on the tropics often admit to being overburdened with the weight of these images and with the challenge of writing something unique and original – an anxiety of influence which is well disguised by their quick recourse to canonical texts of the travel writing genre.[5]

If Lévi-Strauss travelled with Jean de Léry (whom he described as 'the anthropologist's breviary'), and Gide with Joseph Conrad, the writers of the *novela de la selva* journeyed not only with imperial travel writing on the tropics but also with each other.[6] By the time that Carpentier's narrator comes to travel through the Venezuelan jungle he brings with him not only a number of early modern South American topographies but also, as González Echevarría has argued convincingly, a copy of *Canaima*.[7] Nevertheless, for writers of the postcolonial era, the inscription of tropical nature is not just a question of blindly repeating clichés, but a re-semanticizing exercise. The conventional categories of landscape aesthetics – 'nature', 'man', 'the sublime', and William Gilpin's 'the picturesque' – are disrupted in the *novela de la selva* as worn-out staples of European travel literature. Rather than recapitulate these dusty tropes, the genre engages with traditional representations of tropical nature only to ironize and subvert them. The sublime, in particular, is invoked only to reveal its incompatibility with a postcolonial view of the tropics as not amenable to rational description of any sort, and even what seems to be the uncomplicated distinction between man and nature is undermined.

The previous chapter showed how narrative irony is used by postcolonial writers to distance themselves from colonial narratives. This chapter will discuss a particular strand of this irony, directed against imperial stereotypes of the jungle as a space of the sublime, of horror, and of unknowability. Through parody, the *novela de la selva* transforms these colonial tropes into empowering concepts, presenting a vision of the jungle as an enormous heart of voracious vegetation and lurking evil, ready to engulf the unwary traveller. This chapter will also examine the dystopian representation of the rainforest throughout the *novela de la selva*, with reference to Conrad's *Heart of Darkness*. The latter anticipates the South American authors' efforts to forge a new aesthetics of nature – a descriptive vocabulary which, far from attempting to humanize the telluric, emphasizes the radical disjunction between man and tropical nature, and holds up the mysterious and often terrifying jungle flora as a direct challenge to European landscape aesthetics.

Tropes of the Tropics

Before discussing specific reworkings of European landscape aesthetics in the *novela de la selva* it will be useful briefly to revisit some of the most pervasive tropes in factual and fictional representations of the American tropics. From the early years of imperial exploration, tropical South America, and in particular its vast rainforests, challenged the conventional categories of European aesthetics. In Christopher Columbus's 'Diario del primer viaje' [1492] hyperbolic and rather breathless descriptions of the Americas as brimming with 'aves y paxaritos de tantas maneras y tan diversas de las nuestras que es maravilla. Y después ha árboles de mill maneras, y todos [dan] de su manera fruto, y todos güelen qu'es maravilla', set the tone for centuries of writing on the tropics.[8] His stress on the superabundance and wondrousness of tropical nature is repeated time and again in travel-writing. Indeed, in the early colonial period America's tropical flora and fauna were perceived as nothing short of magical.

Gonzalo Fernández de Oviedo's awestruck description of the taste of coconut milk in his *Historia general y natural de las Indias* [1526] – a tropical taxonomy modelled after Pliny's *Natural History* – epitomizes the view of the tropics as a repository of the marvellous:

> es la mas sustancial, la mas excelente y la mas preciosa cosa que se puede pensar ni beber, y en el momento paresce que así como es pasada del paladar ninguna cosa ni arte queda en el hombre que deje de sentir consolación y maravilloso-contentimiento.[9]

Oviedo's hyperbolic assessment of the delicious (and pleasingly laxative) coconut milk helps to found a tradition of writing on the American tropics which places the region not only on the boundaries of perceived topographical, climatic, and agricultural 'norms' but also on the borders of European thought: 'es [...] la más preciosa cosa que *se puede pensar*'. Stephen Greenblatt has argued that the discourse of the marvellous in early modern writing on the Americas functioned as a means to possess or discard 'the unfamiliar, the alien, the terrible, the desirable, and the hateful'.[10] Categories such as the marvellous, the grotesque and, in the eighteenth century, the sublime all helped to conceal a gap in the knowledge of the European observer of the tropical landscape.

In fact the tropics has more often than not left travellers confused or overwhelmed. While many early modern travellers attempted to describe tropical landscapes through reference to their similarity (or difference) to a European, particularly Spanish, norm, this comparative principal often failed. Columbus's repeated references to nightingales and the Andalusian climate seem like wishful thinking in a narrative that constantly threatens to break down before a completely unfamiliar environment. Oviedo also struggles to convey the tropical vegetation. At one point he describes strange, thorny trees, 'que al parecer ningun árbol ni planta se podria ver de mas salvajez ni tan feo, y segun la manera de ellos, yo no me sabria determiner ni decir si son árboles ó plantas'. Oviedo concludes this attempt by acknowledging that in the tropics language constantly fails him: 'la lengua falta'.[11] Nature in the torrid zone is 'cosa mas apropriada al pincel para darlo á entender, que no á la lengua'.[12]

Oviedo's reference to the ugliness of tropical nature was a common aesthetic response up until the advent of the European Enlightenment, prior to which wild spaces such as forests and mountains were considered unholy topographical aberrations. Advances in the natural sciences in the eighteenth century helped to forge a view of the cosmos as ordered and harmonious, thus ordained by God. By the late eighteenth century, inspired by the writings of Burke and Kant on the sublime, wild nature and its metonyms (the abyss, the whirlpool, and the cataract), had come into vogue as a source of peculiar aesthetic pleasure. Late eighteenth- and nineteenth-century European novels, such as Bernardin's *Paul and Virginia* and Chateaubriand's *Atala*, contributed to the monumentalization of the tropics as a source of the sublime.

The aestheticization of tropical South America in the European mind was also in a large part mediated through the writings of Humboldt, who described the tropics (particularly around the Orinoco River) as 'wild and gigantic nature' – a space of bewildering variety:

> Fantastic plants, electric eels, armadillos, monkeys, parrots: and many, many, real, half-savage Indians.
>
> What trees! Coconut palms, 50 to 60 feet high; *Poinciana pulcherrima* with a big bouquet of wonderful crimson flowers; pisang and whole host of trees with enormous leaves and sweet smelling flowers as big as your hand, all utterly new to us. As for the colours of the birds and fishes – even the crabs are sky-blue and yellow!
>
> Up till now we've been running around like a couple of mad things; for the first three days we couldn't settle to anything; we'd find one thing, only to abandon it for the next. Bonpland keeps telling me he'll go out of his mind if the wonders don't cease soon.[13]

Humboldt's account of his South American explorations from 1799 to 1804 inspired generations of nineteenth-century European naturalists to go to the continent and chart its flora and fauna. Natural histories by tropical travellers such as Charles Waterton, Henry Walter Bates, and Richard Spruce are united in their astonishment at 'the marvellous diversity and richness of trees, foliage, and flowers' of Amazonia.[14] Their descriptions of mass migrations of butterflies or enormous flocks of brightly coloured birds popularized views of the rainforest as a luxuriant other world. In this scientific tradition tropical plants and animals were often conveyed as superabundant or gigantic, and often, as in the following example, both:

> The rain brought out multitudes of toads and frogs; and in walking through the forest the following morning after the sun broke forth we came on a huge toad, nearly as big as a man's head.[15]

In this period, illustrations of tropical South America, especially of the Amazon, stressed the immensity of the jungle and its labyrinthine vegetation. In nineteenth-century iconography of the tropics, mysteriousness often slipped into menace, as in the pictures accompanying Carl Friedrich Philipp von Martius's *Flora brasiliensis*, 1840–46.[16] The aesthetic 'darkening' of the tropics corresponded to an increasing awareness of the links between the tropical landscape and ill-health. Tropes of abundance and fertility gave way to a picture of the tropics as ungoverned, chaotic, and dangerous – an aesthetic shift captured in Algot Lange's 1912 travel account, *In the Amazon Jungle*: 'The jungle no longer seemed beautiful or wonderful to me, but horrible – a place of terror and death.'[17] Tropes of the forest as a heart of darkness, a prison, or a green hell became the discursive norm for the tropics in the late nineteenth and early twentieth centuries, exemplified by the anti-Edenic landscape descriptions in *Heart of Darkness*:

> Trees, trees, millions of trees, massive, immense, running up high, and at their foot, hugging the bank against the stream, crept the little begrimed steamboat

like a sluggish beetle crawling on the floor of a lofty portico. It made you feel very small, very lost.[18]

The wondrous giganticism of the nineteenth-century scientific tradition was replaced in Conrad by a vision of nature in which man is not only diminutive but also superfluous. It is this vision of the tropics as unremittingly wild and gloomy which finds its fullest expression in the *novela de la selva*.

Jungles and the Vanishing Subject

'[A]hora voy a enseñarles otro Marcos Vargas que quizás ustedes desconozcan: el que habla con los palos del monte y lo ha sido él también algunas veces' (p. 218). The anecdote that follows, one of the many *cuentos de caucheros* that proliferate throughout *Canaima*, relates how one day a rubber worker witnessed Marcos Vargas walking over to a cluster of 'cuatro palos del monte que estaban separados de los demás y realmente como personas reunidas conversando' (p. 219). When the worker approached the trees in pursuit of Marcos he was puzzled to see that his friend had disappeared – '¡Ni rastro de hombre por todo aquello!' (p. 219) – and that, instead of the previously counted four trees, there were actually five, anthropomorphically poised as if in conversation. Any reader familiar with *La vorágine* will immediately be alerted to the expression, 'Ni rastro de hombre'. Its resemblance to the penultimate line of Rivera's novel – 'Ni rastro de ellos' (p. 385) – which precedes the chilling exclamation, '¡Los devoró la selva!', is less than accidental in a novel which so patently imitates the earlier text. Indeed, the leitmotif of the lost or disorientated traveller recurs throughout the *novela de la selva*, from Hudson's Abel, who finds himself 'hopelessly lost' (p. 57) in the woods during a storm, to Rivera's Clemente Silva, a pathfinder who is forced to pronounce the fateful words: 'Andamos perdidos' (p. 307).

The grounds for all of these novelists using the motif of the vanishing subject could reasonably be explained by the preponderance of travel literature relating to people going missing in the tropics.[19] Nevertheless, I do not consider incidents of man merging with or being obliterated by nature in the *novela de la selva* as strategies of realism, but as symbols for the dissolution of the boundaries of selfhood in the jungle. The relationship between man and nature has been at the centre of Western philosophy since Descartes. While Cartesian thought promoted a schismatic view of man and the world, philosophers such as Hegel problematized this division. Kate Soper has summarized Hegel's rather complex description of this shift:

> Nature may appear as an utterly separate, other and indifferent realm of being, but it does so only to a consciousness that is not yet aware of its own conceptual role in positing Nature *as other* to itself. As consciousness proceeds to an awareness of its own alienation in presenting Nature as 'alien' to it, it transcends this alienation.[20]

This displacement was intensified in the twentieth century, when philosophers and human geographers united in their opposition to a panoramic view of the world. In *Art as Experience* John Dewey typifies this tradition in his affirmation that:

> the uniquely distinguishing feature of esthetic experience is exactly the fact that no such distinction of self and objects exists in it, since it is esthetic in the degree in which organism and environment cooperate to institute an experience in which the two are so fully integrated that each disappears.[21]

The disappearance of the subject is once again yoked to aesthetic experience, or, rather, to the impossibility of aesthetic experience. The subject's phenomenal perception of the natural world is predicated on the effacement of Otherness, where nature is experienced as an extension of the self and vice versa: 'The relationship of man and world is so profound, that it is an error to separate them. [...] The world is our home, our habitat, the materialization of our subjectivity.'[22]

While such theories might help to elucidate Marcos's transitory transmogrification into a tree in *Canaima* as, perhaps, a metaphor for the intimate union between the human and the telluric, they do not account for man's aesthetic experience of inhospitable regions such as the jungle, or distinguish between the perception of the visitor and the resident. The dichotomy between the outsider and what E. Relph has termed the 'existential insider' is highlighted throughout the *novela de la selva*.[23] In *Los pasos perdidos*, for example, the narrator's assumption that birdsong could not have any 'sentido musical-estético para quien lo oye constantemente en la selva' (p. 203) implies that the urban outsider has greater aesthetic awareness than those native to the forest. While Yi-Fu Tuan agrees that the 'visitor's evaluation of environment is essentially aesthetic', he shows that his or her spatial awareness is far less complex than that of the resident:

> only the visitor (and particularly the tourist) has a viewpoint; his perception is often a matter of using his eyes to compose pictures. The native, by contrast, has a complex attitude derived from his immersion in the totality of his environment. The visitor's viewpoint, being simple, is easily stated. [...] The complex attitude of the native, on the other hand, can be expressed by him only with difficulty and indirectly through behavior, local tradition, lore, and myth.[24]

This suggests that representations of the jungle in travel writing and imperial topographies are always deficient, oversimplified not only through the outsider's 'easily stated' observations, but his or her recourse to aesthetic categories which are incommensurate to the scale of tropical nature.

So what are the implications of all of this for the *novela de la selva*? How do the writers in this tradition undermine the notion of the human being as distinct from the natural world – and thus capable of reflecting upon it – without resorting to idealized narratives of millennial harmony between the human and the telluric?

The turn away from panoramic views of nature in European aesthetics is welcomed by the *novela de la selva* as an opportunity to destabilize many of the categories which underpin external representations of tropical nature. Whether utopian or dystopian, empirical or fanciful, travel writing on the tropics has normally rested upon at least two fundamental assumptions. The first is that the narrator of a travelogue is a stable subject, capable of carefully observing his or her surroundings and reporting them in a manner appropriate for the intended audience. The second is that there is a stable environment to be observed and reported – data such as 'landscape' and 'natives' benignly poised for the panoptic eye of the writer. The *novela de la selva* undermines not only the notion of 'landscape' as a self-evident fact but also the existence of an autonomous subject capable of observing it.

Current use of the term 'landscape' is a legacy from the realm of aesthetics, specifically from painting. It was introduced into English in the sixteenth century from the Dutch term *landskip*, referring to a painting of inland natural scenery, and its use is tied up with the notion of observation and always presumes the presence of a human being to order or appreciate the natural surroundings.[25] As Eric Hirsch has stressed, 'The painterly origin of the landscape concept is significant. What came to be seen as landscape was recognized as such because it reminded the viewer of a painted landscape, often of European origin.'[26] The idea of landscape therefore provided people with a way of assimilating nature, especially non-European nature, and of imposing order on the land.[27] Even a cursory glance at the terms habitually employed by travel writers reinforces the idea of human pre-eminence over the telluric. Just as the term 'landscape' implies a viewer with a raised vantage point, the etymology of nouns such as 'environment' and 'surroundings' always locates the observing subject at the centre of the scene. David Spurr has discussed the correlation between surveillance of landscape and imperialism, with the 'commanding view' as 'an originating gesture of colonization itself, making possible the exploration and mapping of territory which serves as the preliminary to a colonial order'.[28] Pratt also has identified the 'monarch-of-all-I-survey' scene as an emblem of Romantic and Victorian travel literature, leading to the visual archetype of the intrepid traveller, perched on top of a promontory or mountain, equipped with writing materials or an easel.[29]

There is no environment more capable of thwarting the traveller's desire for unobstructed views than the jungle. In his short essay, 'Seker Ahmet and the Forest', John Berger has discussed the phenomenology of a densely wooded space: 'this experience [...] depends upon your seeing yourself in double vision. You make your way through the forest and, simultaneously you see yourself, as from the outside, swallowed by the forest.'[30] So it is not only the fate of Cova, but any forest-wanderer, to be 'devoured' by the jungle – an ingestion which, as Berger makes clear, is not the result of grizzly bears or piranhas but a diminution of the subject's ability to distinguish between him or herself and the natural milieu. Tuan has also identified the chief characteristic of the jungle as human habitat to be 'its all-enveloping nature. It is not differentiated as to sky and earth; there is no horizon; it lacks landmarks;

it has no outstanding hill that can be recognized [...]; there are no distant views.'³¹

Cova's apostrophe to the jungle, which opens Part 2 of *La vorágine*, epitomizes the all-encompassing nature of the jungle, and the concomitant sense of self-alienation that this engenders:

> ¡Oh selva, esposa del silencio, madre de la soledad y de la neblina! ¿Qué hado maligno me dejó prisionero en tu cárcel verde? Los pabellones de tus ramajes, como inmensa bóveda, siempre están sobre mi cabeza, entre mi aspiración y el cielo claro, que sólo entreveo cuando tus copas estremecidas mueven su oleaje, a la hora de tus crepúsculos angustiosos. [...] ¡Cuántas veces suspiró mi alma adivinando al través de tus laberintos el reflejo del astro que empurpuraba las lejanías, hacia el lado de mi país, donde hay llanuras inolvidables y cumbres de corona blanca, desde cuyos picachos me vi a la altura de las cordilleras! [...] ¡Tú me robaste el ensueño del horizonte y sólo tienes para mis ojos la monotonía de tu cenit [...]! (p. 189)

Cova's yearning for a horizon (and his comparison of the jungle to a 'cárcel' and 'laberinto') not only betokens the claustrophobia of the dense undergrowth – his desire to see – but also his desire to be seen. In this passage Cova is less concerned with describing the reality of the jungle than his ever-dwindling sense of selfhood. His persistent self-referentiality ('mi cabeza', 'mi aspiración', 'mi alma', 'mis ojos') seems a proto-Adamic bid to reassert the boundaries of selfhood against the ever-encroaching branches and creepers, bearing down 'sobre [su] cabeza' in an abnegation of Otherness. Gaston Bachelard has described how, for the visitor, the forest can seem like a 'limitless world': 'Soon, if we do not know where we are going, we no longer know where we are.'³² For Cova, the forest's 'limitless' nature is not related merely to its vast scale, but to its incursion on the body. Cova's allusion to Humboldt's triadic vision in *Views of Nature* of the American landscape as forests, savannahs, and snow-capped mountains signals a last attempt to reassert the boundaries of selfhood, and the aesthetic tradition of viewing 'landscape' at a physical, and thus noumenal, remove. Unsurprisingly, this bid fails. The gaze, fundamental to European representations of tropical nature, is stymied not only by the impenetrably thick jungle foliage but also by Cova's ever-diminishing ability to distinguish between the landscape and himself.

Nowhere in the *novela de la selva* is this disorientation more explicit than in *Los pasos perdidos*, when the protagonist is travelling by boat amid thick undergrowth:

> se perdía la noción de la verticalidad, dentro de una suerte de desorientación, de mareo de los ojos. No se sabía ya lo que era del árbol y lo que era del reflejo. No se sabía ya si la claridad venía de abajo o de arriba, si el techo era de agua, o el agua suelo; si las troneras abiertas en la hojarasca no eran pozos luminosos conseguidos en lo anegado. [...] Con el trastorno de las apariencias, en esa sucesión de pequeños espejismos al alcance de la mano, crecía en mí una sensación de desconcierto, de extravío total, que resultaba indeciblemente angustiosa. (p. 164)

This is a topsy-turvy world, where reality and illusion are interchangeable, where light seems to emanate from below and water pours from above, and where the eyes suffer, synaesthetically, from 'mareo'. The narrator responds to this environmental disorder with revulsion and fear, admitting to 'una sensación de desconcierto, de extravío total, que resultaba indeciblemente angustiosa'. Yet, if the human and telluric are so intimately connected, why is this experience of oneness with nature so frightening? Why *unspeakably* awful? It seems that what is unspeakable in this passage is not the disorientating surroundings, but the narrator's concealed desire for cognitive supremacy over nature – a supremacy which, as the *novela de la selva* is keen to stress, belongs only to the pages of European literature on the tropics. In both *La vorágine* and *Los pasos perdidos*, novels which on the surface seem to perpetuate the ascendancy of the all-knowing subject who wishes to 'comprenderlo todo, anotarlo todo, explicar en lo posible' (*Los pasos perdidos*, p. 212), the protagonists are plunged into existential angst by the all-enveloping jungle.

Berger's belief that the experience of forest is predicated on 'double vision' helps to explain the vertigo of Carpentier's narrator while he is sailing through the jungle.[33] Far from allowing himself to be effaced by nature, 'going with the flow' both literally and figuratively, he insists on aestheticizing the scene according to the traditional precepts of landscape art – precepts which explicitly do not make provision for the inversion of earth and sky, or for the observing subject to be anywhere but in the centre. Indeed, the narrator of *Los pasos perdidos* has had (successful) recourse to European landscape aesthetics earlier in the novel. Shortly before he enters the rainforest, he offers a panoramic view of the plains, steeped in the imperial trope of the all-seeing traveller:

> contemplo esta llanura inmensa, cuyos límites se disuelven en un leve oscureci-
> miento circular del cielo. Desde mi punto de vista de guijarro, de grama, abarco,
> en su casi totalidad, una circunferencia que es parte cabal, entera, del planeta
> en que vivo. [...] De lejanía en lejanía se yergue un árbol copudo y solitario,
> siempre acompañado de un cacto, que es como un largo candelabro de piedra
> verde, sobre el cual descansan los gavilanes, impasibles, pesados, como pájaros
> de heráldica. [...] Llevo más de una hora aquí, sin moverme, sabiendo cuán inútil
> es andar donde siempre se estará al centro de lo contemplado. (pp. 112–13)

The division of the scene into the watcher and 'lo contemplado', a typical binary in colonial discourse, confers on the narrator the power of seeing – the imperial gaze which objectifies the world around him while he remains omnipotently in the centre. '[N]o tengo ya que alzar los ojos para hallar una nube' (p. 112) he asserts: from his raised vantage point, the narrator has a panoptic sweep of the landscape, glimpsing 'una nube', 'un árbol copudo', '[e]l río', 'un venado'. He has in his sights the earth and the sky, the animal and the vegetable kingdoms. There is a strong sense of the pictorial in this passage. The narrator is keen to stress the '*Silencio*' (p. 112: italics in original) of the scene, significantly the chapter's opening word: 'Nada hace ruido, nada toca con nada, nada rueda ni vibra' (p. 112). Here, the proliferation of 'nada' stresses not only the narrator's solitariness but also the stasis of the surrounding landscape.[34] The narrator's description of the deer as being 'tan inmóvil [...] que su figura tiene algo de monumento y algo, también, de emblema totémico' (p. 113) is telling. Not only is this image frozen like a painting but it is also actually evoked in aesthetic terms. A living animal is reduced to a monument, a totem, an emblem, objectified and distorted, like the landscape itself, in the narrator's stare.

The jungle of *Los pasos perdidos* constantly defies the travel writer's cognitive trickery before nature, and the attendant production of a one-dimensional and static picture of telluric Otherness. What the narrator perceives as his 'desorientación' in the tropical jungle can therefore also be seen as 're-orientation' – an overdue corrective to the tropes of European landscape aesthetics, which will lead to a more subtle and impartial view of nature and man's place in it.

The *novela de la selva* clearly has far-reaching implications for representations of tropical nature. Far from being a backdrop to the action, the jungle in these novels is an ever-present force, which not only thwarts the gaze of the subject but also diminishes his or her ability to describe nature in anything like an objective narrative. In *Green Mansions* Abel exemplifies the impossibility of writing about the jungle from within: 'Perhaps I was not capable of thinking quite coherently on what had just happened until I was once more fairly outside of the forest shadows – out in that clear open daylight, where things seem what they are' (p. 36). This distinction between the dim forest and clear, open space is not only phenomenological – not merely the ocular enhancement from blindness to sight – but noumenal. Thinking about nature seems to necessitate a step away from it. Yet if the urban traveller in the *novela de la selva* is incapable of describing the jungle from within (owing to the inseparability of the self and the environment) and incapable of describing it from without (owing to lack of knowledge) then how can he ever hope to represent it? The rest of this chapter will examine the *novela de la selva*'s various responses to this question.

The Sublime

One of the principal ways that writers of travel literature from the mid-eighteenth century onward attempted to convey the immensity of tropical nature was via recourse to the sublime. Although initially employed by pseudo-Longinus as a figure of literary rhetoric, the sublime was incorporated into the realm of landscape aesthetics in the eighteenth century by Edmund Burke and Immanuel Kant to designate objects too large or powerful to grasp cognitively. Burke was the first to locate the sublime in woodland: 'it [the sublime] comes upon us in the gloomy forest, and in the howling wilderness, in the form of the lion, the tiger, the panther, or rhinoceros'.[35] We might add to this list, as did Kant, 'massive mountains climbing skyward, deep gorges with raging streams in them, wastelands lying in deep shadow and inviting melancholy meditation',[36] indeed anything which makes 'some sort of approach towards infinity' (Burke, p. 58).

For Burke and Kant the sublime 'is a pleasure that arises only indirectly: it is produced by the feeling of a momentary inhibition of the vital forces followed immediately by an outpouring of them that is all the stronger' (Kant, p. 98). The sublime, therefore, is a sensation which is produced in the mind of the person, rather than in nature itself. Kant, in particular, is explicit about this: 'the sublime must not be sought in things of nature, but must be sought solely in our ideas' (p. 105). It is little wonder, then, that the sublime became a trope among Romantic and Victorian travellers in the tropics, for inbuilt in Kant's definition of the sublime is the idea that human reason always triumphs over nature: that mankind is rationally empowered not only with the ability to comprehend landscape of any scale and might but also with the means to gain pleasure from such encounters – an oxymoronic delight occasioned 'by *amazement* bordering on terror, by horror and a sacred thrill' (Kant, p. 129). The sublime clearly had important implications for European imperialism, as it equipped travellers not only with an adjectival catch-all to counter immense forests, cataracts, and mountain ranges but also with the power to transform a vertiginous instantiation of Otherness into a source of self-edification. In the late eighteenth and early nineteenth centuries, the aesthetic of the sublime ceased to be literary camouflage for the indescribable and became the sine qua non of travel itself.

Given the sublime's implications for colonialism, it would be surprising if the *novela de la selva* adopted it unreservedly as a means of representing the American landscape. While many descriptions of the jungle in these novels seem to draw on tropes of the sublime, they do so in a way which destabilizes the Romantic tradition, and which reveals it as both egocentric and idealizing. The Romantic archetype of the intrepid traveller in an elevated reverie of signification amidst an immense and powerful nature is substituted in the *novela de la selva* for a vision of telluric chaos, terror, and speechlessness. Both Kant and Burke stress that the sublime is contingent upon the onlooker being in a safe place.[37] Throughout the *novela de la selva* the protagonists find themselves time and again without sanctuary. Abel in *Green Mansions* is bitten by a poisonous snake, Cova is lost in the jungle, and Carpentier's protagonist is reduced to tears by a raging storm.

Burke's *Enquiry* identifies one of the principal terms associated with the sublime as 'Astonishment' (p. 53), the etymology of which derives from the Old French *estoner*, from Vulgar Latin *extonāre* – 'to strike with thunder'. It is perhaps not coincidental, then, that the thunderstorm should be a recurrent motif of the sublime throughout Romantic travel writing on tropical South America, a leitmotif which, as we shall see, is embraced by the *novela de la selva* as an instance ripe for postcolonial mimicry. In *Views of Nature* Humboldt provides a textbook instance of the sublime storm:

> For an hour and a half we remained exposed to a fearful thunder-storm. Night was approaching, and we in vain sought shelter in the fissures of the rocks. Meanwhile our anxiety increased every moment, lest, drenched as we were and

deafened by the thundering roar of the falling waters, we should be compelled to spend the long tropical night in the midst of the Raudal.[38]

Humboldt builds up the nervous tension of the scene by stressing the precarious position of his party. Sodden with rain, unable to hear clearly, and about to be plunged into darkness, their circumstances are a typical prelude to the sublime, conforming to Burke's prescription of 'obscurity' (p. 54) and 'excessive loudness' (p. 75) as requisite to the experience. Despite the propinquity of danger, the terror of wild nature is allayed by the arrival of a group of Amerindians with a canoe who accompany the travellers to a safe viewing point:

> On gaining the summit, a wide prospect of the surrounding country astonishes the beholder. From the foaming bed of the river rise hills richly crowned with woods, while beyond its western bank the eye rests on the boundless Savannah of the Meta. On the horizon loom like threatening clouds the mountains of Uniama.[39]

This paradigmatic instance of the sublime hardly requires a commentary. The scene is aestheticized by Humboldt as if it were a painted landscape, with a foreground of nearby hills and a background of far-away mountains, with a horizon and the boundless savannah beyond. The displacement from the terror of the storm to an awed appreciation of the beauty of tropical nature (a beauty born out of man's capacity to order his surroundings) vindicates the supremacy of the human mind over the telluric. The fact that Humboldt describes the scene with recourse to painting analogies confirms this ascendancy. As Pratt has argued, the notion of a prospect suggests that 'the landscape was intended to be viewed' from the very point where the observer is standing, and that the scene is thus 'deictically ordered with reference to his vantage point'.[40]

Humboldt's ritualized Romantic response to the tropical storm is replayed throughout eighteenth- and nineteenth-century accounts of the tropics. In the case of the *novela de la selva*, though, far from testifying to the triumph of human reason over nature – what Kant terms the 'supersensible vocation' (p. 115) – jungle storms reveal the vulnerability of man and his lightly concealed terror before the immensity of tropical nature. In *Green Mansions* Abel finds himself doubly doomed when he is caught in a thunderstorm immediately after being bitten by a poisonous snake:

> That sudden twilight and a long roll of approaching thunder, reverberating from the hills, increased my anguish and desperation. Death at that moment looked unutterably terrible.
> [...] At intervals a flash of lightening would throw a vivid blue glare down into the interior of the wood and only serve to show that I had lost myself in a place where even at noon in cloudless weather progress would be most difficult; and now the light would only last a moment, to be followed by thick gloom; and I could only tear blindly on, bruising and lacerating my flesh at every step, falling again and again only to struggle up and on again, now high above the surface climbing over prostrate trees and branches, now plunged to my middle in a pool or torrent of water. (pp. 56–57)

It is significant that Abel's main preoccupation in this passage is his being 'hopelessly lost' (p. 57). The Romantic definition of the sublime hinges upon a transitory feeling of disorientation, followed by increased self-awareness. Abel's experiences in the wood certainly verge on aesthetic transcendence. The scene is set for a paradigmatic moment of the sublime, yet this is too long in coming and instead, the protagonist is made to fight his way through the woods for 'perhaps two or three hours' (p. 58) (almost three pages of the novel) before arriving at the edge of a precipice. In this irrevocably dystopian scene the promontory description – a stock ingredient of Romantic and Victorian travel literature – is given a new twist. Although Abel's response to finding himself on the summit of a cliff is paradigmatically Romantic (he rejoices at the sight of the 'open savannah country beyond') this momentary loftiness is cut short by his 'swift flight through the air before losing consciousness' (p. 58). There are no epiphanies for this would-be Romantic hero: far from elevating man's reason, wild nature plunges Abel into a literal and metaphorical abyss. Hudson does not just imply that the sublime is absent here – that reason is left wanting – but that reason is overwhelmed, and that Abel slips into oblivion because he can no longer fathom reality.

Throughout the *novela de la selva* tropical nature consistently elicits unconsciousness rather than an experience of the sublime. Despite his predilection for aestheticizing the tropical landscape, the narrator of *Los pasos perdidos*, like Abel, falls into a stupor when he is caught in a raging jungle storm:

> De pronto, hay turbamulta en el cielo: baja un viento frío que levanta tremendas olas, los árboles sueltan torbellinos de hojas muertas, se pinta una manga de aire, y, sobre la selva bramante, estalla la tormenta. Todo se enciende en verde. [...] esa luz de cataclismo, de lluvia de aerolitos, me produce un repentino espanto, al mostrarme la cercanía de los obstáculos, la furia de las corrientes, la pluralidad de los peligros. No hay salvación posible para quien caiga en el tumulto que golpea, levanta, zarandea, nuestra barca. Perdida toda razón, incapaz de sobreponerme al miedo, me abrazo de Rosario, buscando el calor de su cuerpo, no ya con gesto de amante, sino de niño [...]. Agotado por la tensión nerviosa, me duermo sobre el pecho de Rosario. (pp. 172–74)

While references to a cataclysm and a whirlwind invoke the sublime, as in *Green Mansions* there is no attendant gratification here. Reason most explicitly does not overcome the chaos of the telluric but is 'perdida': man does not lord over, but is lorded over by, nature. The image of a person asleep in the jungle has important implications for a possible reformulation of the aesthetics of nature in the *novela de la selva*. Asleep or unconscious, human beings cease to distinguish themselves from their surroundings and become fully integrated into nature. Indeed, falling asleep is perhaps the ultimate negation of human reason in its capitulation to the oneiric. This is not as idealistic as it might sound. Carpentier's protagonist has not dozed off in a forest glade because of a primal feeling of well-being, but has been overcome by relentless sensory bombardment. Unlike Romantic descriptions of the sublime, which, although alluding to the importance of hearing or smell, most often portray the landscape pictorially as a static picture 'out there', Carpentier's narrator experiences the storm three-dimensionally. Arnold Berleant has said that 'more forcefully than in any other situation, environmental perception engages the entire, functionally interactive human sensorium'.[41] In *Los pasos perdidos*, the narrator experiences the storm in multiple ways: the water churns beneath him, the waves crash over him, lightning flashes overhead, and the forest trees are buffeted around him. While he succeeds in conveying this assault on the senses, he does so in a narrative which, far from schematizing or aestheticizing the storm, merely lists the myriad sounds and sights, eschewing his habitual recourse to European landscape aesthetics as interpretative tools for tropical nature, and submitting to a more animal sensation of the phenomenology of a storm.

Marcos Vargas's experience of the eponymous 'Tormenta' of Chapter 14 of *Canaima* can also be interpreted as largely physical. In a highly stylized sequence, predicated on the lyrical repetition of key phrases, the narrator describes how Marcos strips off his clothes and submits himself to the sensorial assault of a tropical storm. The scene is loaded with symbolism – a glut of meaning which seems to diminish rather than to fortify any didactic purpose. Marcos is Lear-like in his defiance of the might of nature; Hamletesque in his twice-repeated 'Se es o no se es' (p. 189; p. 190), and archetypally Romantic as he stands undaunted while the wind and rain whip his face, and trees fall around him. Indeed, his composure during the storm recalls that of Cova in *La vorágine*, who is also unruffled by a collapsing 'palmera heroica' (p. 170). Cova's oxymoronic perception of the sight as 'bello y aterrador' (p. 170) is a direct allusion to the sublime, and aligns him, as Jean Franco has argued, with a long line of Romantic heroes, particularly Shelley's Alastor, the eponymous hero of a narrative poem which relates how a poet is almost sucked into a vortex while sailing along a river.[42] So Marcos's comportment in the storm is really just Gallegos's version of Rivera's version of Shelley (or even Humboldt), which itself is predicated on the sublime of Burke and Kant. The sublime is thus revealed as a rhetorical figure, and one which has become so tropological as to render it insipid. There is nothing convincing about Marcos's conduct in the storm; from his tearing off his shirt, 'haciendo saltar los botones' (p. 188), to his angry shouting at the forest trees, this twentieth-century imitation of the Burkean and Kantian sublime entails an inevitable semantic dislocation and produces a character who seems not only overwrought but ridiculous.

Far from being a useful tool for describing the enormity of tropical nature, the sublime is revealed as both clichéd and ideologically suspect. It is no coincidence that all of the *novelas de la selva* discussed here incorporate a tropical storm into their narratives, for the storm is not only a staple of the travel writing genre but also a classic moment for the protagonist to demonstrate metaphorically his elevation (or lack thereof) over nature. These narratives take the stock ingredients of the sublime – the woodland setting, the thunderstorm, and the habitual telluric trimmings such as 'the cataract' and 'the precipice' – and subject them to parody. Burke's and Kant's characterization of responses to the sublime certainly did not accommodate fainting or undressing, but then these versions were disseminated in an age when it was acceptable to lay claim to exotic 'landscape' for human elevation, and where the human in question was inevitably an educated European man. While the subjects of the *novela de la selva* conform largely to the traditional pattern (they are all educated, urban, white males), the landscape most certainly does not, resisting time and again appellations of the sublime in favour of a vision of tropical nature as unreservedly terrifying and inassimilable.

Towards a Postcolonial Aesthetics: the Ugly and the Unknowable

So far in this chapter I have discussed how European landscape aesthetics are questioned and even lampooned in the *novela de la selva*. This final section will examine the alternative environmental aesthetics proposed by the authors of the *novela de la selva*, which, far from marking a complete break with European perceptions of the tropics actually intensifies their view of the region as frightening and strange. Throughout the *novela de la selva* the appropriation of colonial stereotypes succeeds in destabilizing tropes of the tropics. Although stereotypes have traditionally been used within imperial discourse to fix difference, they also reveal the anxieties of empire and are often exploited by postcolonial writers. This strategy is consistent with what Neil L. Whitehead has perceived as the emergence of an ironic counter-narrative in recent travel-writing from Latin America, which, as a response to the over-processing of the tropics in science and popular culture 'provokes a nostalgic, even atavistic, search for some last hidden tokens of its former wild savagery and exoticism'.[43] By representing the jungle as unknowable, for example, the authors of the *novela de la selva* are not simply repeating a colonial trope, but attempting to locate the American tropics outside European landscape aesthetics. In post-independent Spanish America there was not only an ecological imperative to preserve the jungle from European expansionism but also a cultural exigency to shield it from the domesticating inclinations of European writing on the tropics. In works ranging from Domingo F. Sarmiento's *Facundo* to Gallegos's *Doña Bárbara*, wildness is portrayed not only as an inherent attribute of South American nature but often as more potent and alluring than the alternatives of culture and civilization.

Heart of Darkness is clearly a foundational text for any postcolonial inscription of tropical nature and adumbrates the treatment of the jungle in the *novela de la selva*. Many charges of racism have been levelled against *Heart of Darkness*, most famously by Chinua Achebe during a lecture delivered at the University of Massachusetts in February 1975, in which he argued that Conrad's novella had painted a picture of Africa as 'the antithesis of Europe and therefore of civilization, a place where man's vaunted intelligence and refinement are finally mocked by triumphant bestiality'.[44] However, it is also possible to regard Conrad's descriptions of African nature as following the pattern of colonial mimicry outlined by Bhabha and, therefore, as embodying an ironic, critical view of European perceptions of the tropics. This is clear in the following passage, for example:

> At last I got under the trees. My purpose was to stroll into the shade for a moment, but no sooner within than it seemed to me I had stepped into the gloomy circle of some Inferno.
> [...] Black shapes crouched, lay, sat between the trees, leaning against the trunks, clinging to the earth, half coming out, half effaced within the dim light, in all the attitudes of pain, abandonment, and despair. Another mine on the cliff went off followed by a slight shudder of the soil under my feet. The work was going on. (p. 20)

This sequence is central to an understanding of what might be termed Conrad's 'anti-colonial' vision of the African landscape. Marlow's portrait of the forest as a Dantean 'Inferno' could not be further from the upbeat jingoism of conventional Victorian travel writing on Africa. The discovery rhetoric, which Pratt considers fundamental to nineteenth-century imperial discourse, is conspicuously absent in Marlow's description of the forest.[45] Far from being perched on a promontory, or in a position of elevated meaning-making, Conrad's protagonist is trapped in a murky grove surrounded by scarcely intelligible shapes and sounds. Bhabha has argued that, in common with other early modernist 'colonial' literature such as *A Passage to India*, *Heart of Darkness* addresses the difficulty of representing the Other. Hazy descriptions, such as 'the horror', are, for Bhabha, indicative of an 'uncertain colonial silence that mocks the social performance of language with their non-sense; that baffles the communicative verities of culture with their refusal to translate'.[46] The tropical rainforest in *Heart of Darkness* is not a tabula rasa awaiting imperial inscription, but is full of indigenous people, of ominous drumbeats, and the infamous 'Sticks, little sticks [...] flying about, thick' (p. 45). Later in the novel, while steaming up the river, Marlow notes in surprise a face staring at him through the leaves: 'suddenly, as though a veil had been removed from my eyes, I made out deep in the tangled gloom, naked breasts, arms, legs, glaring eyes – the bush was swarming with human limbs in movement' (p. 46). Throughout these passages there is a sense that the jungle is animate and that the human limbs, strangely contorted and reified as branches or trunks (as in the painting *La selva* by the Cuban artist Wilfredo Lam), are extensions of the forest, 'leaning', 'clinging', and 'half coming out' of the ground.

Of course, we must not overlook the quick resumption of the imperial work ethic in the above passage. The exploding mine and the attendant return to work mark the narrative conclusion of the incident. Marlow quickly turns away from the shade, abandoning the dark thoughts that this vision had precipitated, only to be greeted by the comforting sight of the snow-white accountant who, 'in the great demoralisation of the land [...] kept up his appearance' (p. 21). Nevertheless, this glimpse of the 'Other' side of colonialism – the concealed indigenous population and the perennial stare of the wilderness – suggests that the colonial regime in the Belgian Congo was less stable and diffuse than it might have wished to be, forever teetering, like

Kurtz, on the edge of an abyss of incomprehension and horror.

Many *novelas de la selva*, and in particular *La vorágine* and *Los pasos perdidos*, are remarkably similar to *Heart of Darkness*, both thematically and stylistically. Although Sylvia Molloy has alluded to the 'notables semejanzas' between *La vorágine* and *Heart of Darkness*, no one has established that Rivera had actually read Conrad's novella.[47] Likewise, Klaus Müller-Bergh's search for the literary antecedents of *Los pasos perdidos* lists *Heart of Darkness* as just one of ten possible sources.[48] Despite what Frances Wyers has termed the 'certain curious coincidences', then, between *Heart of Darkness* and the *novela de la selva*, I am less concerned with establishing any direct textual parallels than with the novelists' shared exploitation of the imperial trope of telluric horror.[49] While it is likely that Rivera and Carpentier had read, or at least were familiar with, *Heart of Darkness*, the convergence between the novels can be attributed less to conscious imitation than to the collective impulses of postcolonial writing which aspires, as Said has argued, to 'revised visions of the past tending towards a new future'.[50] *Heart of Darkness* and the Spanish-American *novelas de la selva* that followed all engage in this process of revision, glimpsing in the hackneyed tropes of occidental travel writing and adventure stories – particularly those of the tropical jungle as a space of unrestrained degeneration and savagery – the seeds of a powerful postcolonial counter-narrative.[51]

The rainforest of *La vorágine* surpasses the horrors of Conrad's *Heart of Darkness*, for it is full not only of dying workers but also of armies of fire ants, lethal swamps, and whirlpools. Although Cova's journal purports to be a conventional travel document on the Americas, including information about endemic flora and fauna, clothes, food, and the native population, we must bear in mind that it is not composed in the safe confines of an urban dwelling following a harrowing journey in the tropics, but is written in the midst of the jungle shortly before his death. The lack of a point of safe return in Rivera's text injects new meaning into the imperial trope of telluric horror. The landscape is no longer just another hurdle on the traveller's path to self-fulfilment – a dusty and harmless rhetorical figure – but a terrifying and possibly insurmountable threat. Take the following passage, for example:

> Por primera vez, en todo su horror, se ensanchó ante mí la selva inhumana. Árboles deformes sufren el cautiverio de las enredaderas advenedizas, que a grandes trechos los ayuntan con las palmeras y se descuelgan en curva elástica, semejantes a redes mal extendidas, que a fuerza de almacenar en años enteros hojarascas, chamizas, frutas, se desfondan como un saco de podredumbre, vaciando en la yerba reptiles ciegos, salamandras mohosas, arañas peludas.
>
> Por doquiera el bejuco de matapalo – rastrero pulpo de las florestas – pega sus tentáculos a los troncos, acogotándolos y retorciéndolos, para injertárselos y trasfundírselos en metempsicosis dolorosas. Vomitan los bachaqueros sus trillones de hormigas devastadoras, que recortan el manto de la montaña y por anchas veredas regresan al túnel, como abanderadas del exterminio, con sus gallardetes de hojas y de flores. El comején enferma los árboles cual galopante sífilis, que solapa su lepra supliciatoria [sic] mientras va carcomiéndoles los tejidos y pulverizándoles la corteza. (pp. 295–96)

The sense of a brooding, animistic nature is overwhelming in this passage – what Michael Taussig has described in his analysis of the rubber plantations of the Putumayo region of Colombia as the forest's 'miasmic subspecies of terror, the pressing in of somethingness in the nothingness'.[52] In the first paragraph the sense of claustrophobia invoked by references to the 'enredaderas' and 'redes', and the adjective 'elástica', is enhanced by the equally enmeshing long sentence, punctuated by multiple subordinate clauses, and this is consistent with the novel's extended metaphor of the jungle as a 'cárcel verde' (p. 189). Far from the vital and luxuriant nature of Humboldt's South American corpus, these trees are 'deformes', a word which suggests the violation of some extant botanical norm, just as the reptiles are aberrant in their blindness. The only testimonies to life in this forest are the dead leaves, branches, and fruits of the forest trees. The many references to disease, from leprosy to syphilis, are particularly pessimistic and inimical to the conventional European view of wild nature as a place for promoting masculine brawn, or, as in Romantic fiction, intellectual vigour. The dark side of tropical superfluity and fecundity, including rampant biota and unrestrained disease, is a post-Romantic staple for the writers of the *novela de la selva*.

Despite the apparent pessimism of the above passage, throughout *La vorágine* – and the *novela de la selva* more widely – descriptions of the telluric horror of the jungle are marked not only by revulsion but also by gratification on the part of the observer, as when Cova regards the death of two Amerindians who are sucked into a vortex to be imbued with 'una ráfaga de belleza' (p. 233). Although such sentiments directly invoke the Burkean and Kantian belief in the excitation of pain and danger as a source of the sublime, as was established earlier, the chaotic tropical landscape does not sit easily with this literary convention. Cova himself debunks the literary proclivity to idealize tropical nature, attributing such visions to poets who 'sólo conocen las soledades domesticadas' (p. 296) – a criticism steeped in irony given his own formerly Edenic image of the jungle. The antithesis he postulates between literary representations of nature and the terrifying and inassimilable reality of the jungle stresses the need for writers to develop a new vocabulary for tropical nature – an aesthetics that eschews categories such as the sublime in favour of a more impartial vision of nature, which does not seek in the landscape human elevation (the jungle is, after all, 'antihumana', p. 295), but mere sensory experience. In the passage cited above, images such as the ivy's 'tentacles' gripping hold of trunks, or ants being 'vomited' out of the earth, are among the most imaginative and memorable of the entire novel and seem to belong less to any conventional literary tradition than to what might be termed an aesthetics of the horrid, or of the ugly. This departure by the writers of the *novela de la selva* – their oxymoronic celebration of the unaesthetic properties of tropical nature – is a key element of their postcolonial vision of the Americas as a space outside the categories of European landscape aesthetics.

Los pasos perdidos refines this aesthetics of the ugly. The narrator describes his first vision of the horror of the primeval rainforest in terms strongly reminiscent of *La vorágine*:

> Con los remos, con las manos, había que apartar obstáculos y barreras para llevar adelante esa navegación increíble, en medio de la maleza anegada. Un madero puntiagudo cayó sobre mi hombro con la violencia de un garrotazo, sacándome sangre del cuello. De las ramazones llovía sobre nosotros un intolerable hollín vegetal, impalpable a veces, como un plancton errante en el espacio. [...] Con esto, era un perenne descenso de hebras que encendían la piel, de frutos muertos, de simientes velludas que hacían llorar, de horruras, de polvos cuya fetidez enroñaba las caras. (p. 163)

Such descriptions proliferate through the second half of *Los pasos perdidos* and forge a dystopian vocabulary for the American tropics, which jars with the idealization of nature in the writings of Romantic travellers. This passage repels the senses of the reader, especially those of smell and touch. Everything is bristling, chafing, stinging, rotting, and dying. Yet, as in *La vorágine*, the reader is impressed by the intricacy of the imagery and the narrator's paradoxical satisfaction in the horror of nature. Just a few pages later he glimpses 'una cosa horrenda':

> un caimán muerto, de carnes putrefactas, debajo de cuyo cuero se metían, por enjambres, las moscas verdes. Era tal el zumbido que dentro de la carroña resonaba, que, por momentos, alcanzaba una afinación de queja dulzona, como si alguien – una mujer llorosa, tal vez – gimiera por las fauces del saurio. (p. 165)

This description captures perfectly the dialectic between the jungle's power to entrance and repel. While the narrator is repulsed by the sight of the maggot-eaten alligator, he feels compelled to stare at it and intricately describe it in his journal. The simile he adopts, which compares the buzzing flies to a woman crying, does not succeed in offsetting the dreadfulness of the sight. In fact, it seems overly literary and out of place (there are parallels between this description and Baudelaire's 'Une charogne' in *Les Fleurs du mal*). Nevertheless, it is interesting to note the adjective 'dulzona', which, although conveying a sense of nauseating abundance, still seems incompatible with the narrator's description of putrefying flesh. The allusion to sweetness not only acts as a foil to the heady smell of decay but also seems to conflate traditional judgements of perception by aligning sweetness with 'una cosa horrenda' – by glimpsing beauty in the hideous. Although on the threshold of accepting a new aesthetics of nature, the narrator flees the scene, just as he later turns his back on the teratological 'fetos vivientes' (p. 186) – dwarfs which he encounters in an Amerindian settlement – in a disavowal not only of the horrors of the jungle but also of his own incapacity to verbalize them.

Attributing the recurrent motif of the hideous throughout the *novela de la selva* to a guiding aesthetic of 'the ugly' may seem as restrictive as categories such as the sublime or the picturesque. Indeed, the notion of ugliness is alluded to throughout Burke's *Enquiry* and Kant's *Critique of Judgement*, and has been the subject of a book by Karl Rosenkranz: *Ästhetik des Hässlichen*. So how do the writers of the *novela de la selva* enlist the concept in defence of their postcolonial, post-subliminal, self-imaginings?[53] Firstly, it is important to remember that the presentation of the jungle as a locus of grotesque Otherness is not confined to the *novela de la selva*, but is a trope of travel writing on tropical South America from the earliest years of conquest. Within the *novela de la selva* descriptions of the tropics as ugly can be seen as an example of colonial mimicry where, as Lawrence Buell has explained, writers 'try to turn the European perception of the (post)colonial periphery into a cultural asset'.[54] Moreover, the ugly has traditionally evaded aesthetic classification. While Kant, for example, alludes to the existence of wild scenery which is not embraced by the sublime, such as 'shapeless mountain masses piled on one another in wild disarray, with their pyramids of ice, or the gloomy raging sea', ugliness is pushed to the borders of aesthetic thought as something which is not quite definable.[55] Ugliness is thus correlated with that which exceeds, rather than elevates, the imagination. It is only defined as ugly – that is, chaotic, grotesque, or horrific – because it is beyond the representational powers of the onlooker.

It will be clear by now that descriptions of landscape are fundamental to colonial constructions of the tropics. Yet what happens when there is a complete lack of correspondence between the imperial lexicon and non-European topography? From the earliest accounts of the New World, travellers to the Americas have despaired at the disparity between the landscape and their capacity to describe it, especially, as Christopher Mulvey has shown, when confronted with colossal sights such as the Niagara Falls.[56] Carpentier has described how the eighteenth-century German traveller Richard Schomburgk was overawed as he stood at the base of Mount Roraima, where he recognized the limits not only of language but also of man's imaginative capacity before nature: 'el romantico descubridor afirma que "no hay palabras para pintar la grandeza de este cerro, con sus ruidosas y espumantes cascadas de prodigiosa altura"'.[57] Descriptions of the tropics as unrepresentable can be ambivalent, for while they subscribe to the colonial strategy of 'Othering', they also undermine the tendency in travel writing linguistically to domesticate nature. The *novela de la selva* exploits this inherent ambivalence in European discourses of tropicality, drawing paradoxically upon imperial tropes of unknowability in order to affirm the distinctiveness of tropical nature and its position outside European conceptual frameworks. This desire for cultural hermeticism might help to explain the *novela de la selva*'s somewhat paradoxical project: to celebrate tropical nature, but to do so in a narrative which persistently shirks definite meaning, and which, through the profusion of indigenous words, maintains a façade of incorrigible Otherness which cannot be penetrated by a universal readership.

In his influential 1948 article on *La vorágine*, William E. Bull censured Rivera for being 'algo confuso respecto a su trabajo de novelista' by creating characters who are 'particularmente incapaces de describir la naturaleza de una manera objetiva'.[58] Bull has obviously overlooked the introspective and parodic elements of Rivera's novel which, far from attempting to describe nature in 'una manera objetiva', affirms that such a representation can never exist. As Said has argued, 'there is no such thing as a delivered presence, but a *re-presence*, or a representation'.[59] Images of nature can only ever be distortions, mediated through a range of socio-cultural stereotypes. Like so many travellers to the tropics, Cova rails against the difficulty of finding a lexicon which is able to convey the immensity of nature:

> ¡Nada de ruiseñores enamorados, nada de jardín versallesco, nada de panoramas sentimentales! Aquí, los responsos de sapos hidrópicos, las malezas de cerros misántropos, los rebalses de caños podridos. Aquí, la parásita afrodisíaca que llena el suelo de abejas muertas; la diversidad de flores inmundas que se contraen con sexuales palpitaciones y su olor pegajoso emborracha como una droga; la liana maligna cuya pelusa enceguece los animales; la pringamoza que inflama la piel, la pepa del curujú que parece irisado globo y sólo contiene ceniza cáustica, la uva purgante, el corozo amargo. (p. 296)

The lack of a conjunction in Cova's inventory of the jungle plants, 'la uva purgante, el corozo amargo', suggests a dizzying array of flora and undermines his complete linguistic mastery of the scene, conforming to George Santayana's interpretation of landscape as 'an infinity of different scraps and glimpses given in succession'.[60] Cova's description of the 'pepa del curujú que parece irisado globo y sólo contiene ceniza cáustica', is particularly interesting. This analogy is not a 'taming metaphor'; it does not correspond to what Anthony Pagden has termed the 'principle of attachment', but rather conforms to a pattern of what might be called, after Bhabha, *telluric mimicry*, a recalcitrant doubling which, in its curiously 'off' imitation, produces menace.[61] The use of the verb 'parecer' suggests a certain agency on the part of nature, a purposeful replication, which tricks the onlooker into admiring the plant's gaudy exterior before revealing its rotting centre. The sense of the tropic's impenetrability is further accentuated in this passage by the use of native orthography, and it is not insignificant that the indigenous word 'curujú' is omitted from the glossary appended to the end of the novel.

The theme of nature as unknowable is equally redolent in *Canaima*. Marcos Vargas's initial glimpse of the rainforest results in a feeling of disappointment: 'Al principio fue la decepción. Aquello carecía de grandeza; no era, por lo menos, como se lo había imaginado' (p. 150). Stepan's observation that the 'theme of disappointment, when representations do not live up to reality, or better put, when reality does not live up to its representations, is common in many tropical journeys', helps to elucidate Marcos's initial disenchantment.[62] His imagined forests, fed on the myths of the jungle workers he meets as a young man, have no place in the reality of the Venezuelan rainforest. Almost immediately, Marcos's feeling of disillusionment gives way to an awed comprehension of the abundance of trees, stretching before him ad infinitum:

empezó a sentir que la grandeza estaba en la infinidad, en la repetición obsesio-
nante de un motivo único al parecer. ¡Árboles, árboles, árboles! Una sola bóveda
verde sobre miríadas de columnas afelpadas de musgos, tiñosas de líquenes,
cubiertas de parásitas y trepadoras, trenzadas y estranguladas por bejucos tan
gruesos como troncos de árboles. ¡Barreras de árboles, murallas de árboles,
macizos de árboles! [...] Verdes abismos callados... Bejucos, marañas... ¡Árboles!
¡Árboles!

[...] Por la selva virgen, que es como un templo de millones de columnas,
limpio de matojos el suelo hasta donde la fronda apretada no deja llegar los rayos
solares, solemne y sumida en penumbra misteriosa, con profundas perspec-
tivas alucinantes. Las jornadas de andar cabizbajo y callado ante la abrumadora belleza extraña del panorama, siempre igual y siempre imponente: verde
sombrío y silencio. (pp. 150–51)

The repetition of the word 'árboles' signals not only the dizzying proliferation of greenery but also Marcos's inability to verbalize it. Marcos grasps
for images to convey the immensity of the rainforest, resorting to the almost
synonymous and inadequate nouns 'barreras', 'murallas', 'macizos'. At the
end of the first paragraph his description trails off into halting, ungrammatical
sentences, which omit verbs and end in ellipses, thus signalling the extra-
linguistic nature of the tropics. In the second paragraph there is an attempt
to restore human dominion in the forest, as Marcos resorts to tropes of virgin
jungle and a taming metaphor which compares the trees to 'un templo de
millones de columnas'. The appeal to architecture, especially ecclesiastical
buildings, is a constant of travel writing on the tropics and has been reinvoked
throughout the *novela de la selva*.[63] In *La vorágine* Cova describes the jungle
as a 'catedral de la pesadumbre' (p. 189), and in *Los pasos perdidos* the narrator
compares a marvellous rock formation – 'la Capital de las Formas' – to 'una
increíble catedral gótica, de una milla de alto, con sus dos torres, su nave, su
ábside y sus arbotantes' (p. 175). Such analogies not only impose a man-made
order on a natural phenomenon but also invert the idea of origin in their
suggestion that art does not imitate nature, but vice versa. Fanny Calderón de
la Barca, a Victorian traveller in Mexico, uses an almost identical technique in
her comparison of a cavern to 'a subterranean Egyptian temple':

The architecture was decidedly Egyptian.[...] pillars covered with gigantic
acanthus leaves, pyramids of ninety feet high losing their lofty heads in the
darkness of the vault, and looking like works of the pre-Adamites: yet no being
but He who inhabits eternity could have created them.[64]

In the *novela de la selva*, these metaphors are left wanting. In *Canaima* the
comparison of the jungle to a 'templo de millones de columnas' fails given
the fact that such a prodigy of architecture is as difficult to imagine (and as
unlikely to exist) as the cathedral 'de una milla de alto' imagined by Carpentier's narrator. In *Green Mansions*, Abel also rejects such metaphors:

Lying on my back and gazing up, I felt reluctant to rise and renew my ramble.
For what a roof was that above my head! Roof I call it, just as the poets in their
poverty sometimes describe the infinite ethereal sky by that word; [...] Nature,

we know, first taught the architect to produce by long colonnades the illusion of distance. (pp. 23–24)

Marcos discontinues the appeal to metaphor, and instead characterizes the landscape hazily as 'abrumadora' and 'extraña', as beautiful, but strangely so – a 'beauty lying in the Lap of Horrour'.[65] In *Canaima*, then, Marcos's representation of the jungle remains determinedly ambiguous. His stress on the 'verde sombrío' and 'silencio' is predicated on absence – on what is not there – without actually filling in the gaps. The much-repeated apostrophe to the '¡Árboles, árboles, árboles!' becomes a fitting metonym for the immense unknowability of the South American rainforest.

The narrator of *Los pasos perdidos* is no more successful at conveying the reality of tropical nature. His cognitive struggle to describe the excesses of the jungle via analogy is countered insistently by the forest's magnitude and unrecognizable natural features. Even perched on top of a mountain, gazing at his surroundings in a stereotyped posture of imperial mastery, the narrator fails to take verbal possession of the landscape:

allá abajo, se enrevesa, se enmaraña, se anuda, en un vasto movimiento de posesión, de acoplamiento, de incestos, a la vez monstruoso y orgiástico, que es suprema confusión de las formas. 'Éstas son las plantas que han huido del hombre [...]' me dice el fraile. 'Las plantas rebeldes, negadas a servirle de alimento, que atravesaron ríos, escalaron cordilleras, saltaron por sobre los desiertos, durante milenios y milenios, para ocultarse aquí en los últimos valles de la Prehistoria.' (pp. 207–08)

The 'confusión de las formas' lamented by the narrator in this passage becomes a linguistic labyrinth, where the landscape 'se enmaraña, se anuda', shirking ultimate meaning in a semantic knot. The anthropomorphized plants, almost mock-heroic in their flight from civilization to the farthermost outposts of the jungle, are no longer passive tools of foreign expansion (through the provision of rubber or wood) but empowered with the will to self-possession. The narrator may well try to assert his authority by demonizing the jungle vegetation using the same dusty tropes of sexual excess that he employs in his descriptions of the indigenous inhabitants ('acoplamiento', 'incesto', 'orgiástico'), but this lightly conceals his terror at the heady potency of the plants and their indifference to his human presence. One could well switch the referent of the noun 'confusión' in the opening sentence from the vegetation to the narrator. It is the observer's cognitive impuissance before nature, and not the landscape itself, which is the cause of this linguistic impasse.

The interplay between knowability and the unknown is a constant of the *novela de la selva*. It is the juxtaposition between Conrad's depiction of imperial control and the elusive 'heart of darkness', the contrast between Cova's bucolic daydreams of a forest retreat and the dystopian reality he discovers there, and the constant menace of the jungle in *Los pasos perdidos* as a site of amorphous Otherness against the urban traveller's attempts at linguistic mastery. The narrator of *Los pasos perdidos* epitomizes this dichotomy in his description of the jungle as '[e]l mundo de la mentira, de la trampa y del falso semblante; allí todo era disfraz, estratagema, juego de apariencias, metamorfosis' (p. 169). The ludic propensities of the rainforest, its menacing capacity for 'inacabable mimetismo' (p. 169) and metamorphosis, counter the travel writer's desire for textual mastery. Such linguistic impotence approaches Jean-François Lyotard's outline of the 'postmodern sublime', defined by Johannes Bertens as 'an art of negation, a perpetual negation [...] based on a never-ending critique of representation that should contribute to the preservation of hetero-geneity, of optimal dissensus'.[66] As such, Carpentier uses the colonial trope of unknowability counter-discursively in order to stress the limits of European representations of the tropics. Pedro Henríquez Ureña has characterized the literary history of Latin America since independence as 'la historia del flujo y reflujo de aspiraciones y teorías en busca de nuestra expresión perfecta'.[67] The *novela de la selva* was not so concerned with finding *the* perfect expression, as with forging a plural Latin American literary identity, which not only spurned linguistic monologism in favour of heterogeneity but also acknowledged the fissure between tropical nature and man's capacity to describe it within the framework of European landscape aesthetics.

★　★　★

While Abel, Cova, Marcos, and Carpentier's narrator attempt to maintain a precarious grasp on their experiences in the rainforest by appealing to the dusty tropes of landscape aesthetics, their failure to describe adequately their surroundings is illustrative of the limits of European models of the tropics: of the linguistic hinterlands beyond the grasp of the colonial idiom, or the unrep-resentability of a monstrous nature which plunges the seer into confusion and terror. The sublime, in particular, is revealed as an arbitrary figure of colonial travel writing on the tropics – a metonym for the unknown, which glosses over a hiatus in human knowledge with a stock repertoire of lofty epithets. In the postcolonial idiom the sublime is replaced with an aesthetics of the ugly and of the unrepresentable, which redefines the unfathomable as something positive and liberating – less as a failure in human knowledge than a victory on the side of nature.

It is unsurprising that the postcolonial vision of the authors of the *novela de la selva* should be predicated on a negation of the positivism of European travel writing which, for centuries, had attempted to classify, codify, and domesticate the South American tropics. Instead, they stressed the inassimilable Otherness of the tropical rainforest – that dark and dystopian heart of equatorial vegeta-tion which defies linguistic and cerebral knowledge, inviting the reader into their illusory jungles, only to tangle us in labyrinthine creepers, or to taunt us, like Pan, with nebulous horrors.

Notes

1 Jonathan Smith, 'The Slightly Different Thing that is Said: Writing the Aesthetic Experience', in Trevor J. Barnes and James S. Duncan (eds.), *Writing Worlds: Discourse, Text and Metaphor in the Representation of Landscape* (London: Routledge, 1992), pp. 73–85 (p. 82).

2 For a discussion of literary constructions of Amazonia see Ana Pizarro, 'Imaginario y discurso: la amazonía', *Revista de Crítica Literaria Latinoamericana*, 61 (2005), pp. 59–74; Pedro Maligo, *Land of Metaphorical Desires: The Representation of Amazonia in Brazilian Literature* (New York: Lang, 1998); Rodríguez, 'Naturaleza/nación'; Candace Slater, *Entangled Edens: Visions of the Amazon* (Berkeley: University of California Press, 2002).

3 David Arnold, *The Problem of Nature: Environment, Culture and European Expansion* (Oxford: Blackwell, 1996).

4 Claude Lévi-Strauss, *Tristes Tropiques* [1955], trans. John and Doreen Weightman (New York: Penguin, 1992), p. 47.

5 Denis Porter, *Haunted Journeys: Desire and Transgression in European Travel Writing* (Princeton: Princeton University Press, 1991), discusses the concern for originality in travel writing (p. 12).

6 Lévi-Strauss, *Tristes Tropiques*, p. 81. André Gide constantly alludes to *Heart of Darkness* in his *Travels in the Congo*, trans. Dorothy Bussy (New York: Knopf, 1930). He also dedicates the book 'To the Memory of Joseph Conrad', and admits to be rereading Conrad's novella 'for the fourth time' (p. 292) while writing his journal.

7 González Echevarría, '*Canaima*', p. 503.

8 Cristóbal Colón, *Textos y documentos completos: relaciones de viajes, cartas y memoriales*, ed. Consuelo Varela (Madrid: Alianza Editorial, 1984), p. 41.

9 Gonzalo Fernández de Oviedo y Valdés, 'Sumario de la natural historia de las Indias', in Don Enrique de Vedia (ed.), *Historiadores primitivas de Indias* (Madrid: Ediciones Atlas, 1946), III, pp. 473–515 (p. 500).

10 Stephen Greenblatt, *Marvelous Possessions: The Wonder of the New World* (Oxford: Clarendon Press, 1991), p. 23.

11 Fernández de Oviedo, 'Sumario de la natural historia', p. 506.

12 Fernández de Oviedo, 'Sumario de la natural historia', p. 492.

13 Humboldt wrote this in a letter to his brother after arriving in America in July 1799, cited in Hugh Honour, *The New Golden Land: European Images of America from the Discoveries to the Present Time* (New York: Pantheon Books, 1975), p. 170.

14 Henry Walter Bates, *The Naturalist on the River Amazons* (London: Dent, 1969), p. 180.

15 Richard Spruce, *Notes of a Botanist on the Amazon and Andes*, ed. Alfred Russel Wallace, 2 vols (London: Macmillan, 1908), I, p. 49. Slater, *Entangled Edens*, has identified 'giganticism' as an important theme in writing on Amazonia.

16 Honour, *New Golden Land*, discusses *Flora brasiliensis*, p. 175.

17 Algot Lange, *In the Amazon Jungle: Adventures in the Remote Parts of the Upper Amazon River, including a Sojourn among Cannibal Indians*, ed. J. Odell Hauser (London: Putnam's Sons, 1912), p. 289.

18 Joseph Conrad, *Heart of Darkness: An Authoritative Text; Backgrounds and Sources; Criticism*, ed. Robert Kimbrough, 3rd edn (New York: Norton, 1988), p. 37. All further references are to this edition and are given after quotations in the text.

19 This is a theme of American travel literature from the earliest years of the colonial period. Many fictional and factual travellers have disappeared, including Cabeza de Vaca, Robinson Crusoe, and Colonel Percy Fawcett.

20 Kate Soper, *What is Nature? Culture, Politics and the Non-Human* (Oxford: Blackwell, 1995), p. 95. For a more detailed account of this philosophical shift see Soper, pp. 45–49,

or Max Oelschlaeger, *The Idea of Wilderness: From Prehistory to the Age of Ecology* (New Haven: Yale University Press, 1991), pp. 97–132.

21 John Dewey, *Art as Experience* (London: Allen & Unwin, 1934), p. 249.

22 J. H. Van den Berg, *The Phenomenological Approach to Psychiatry: An Introduction to Recent Phenomenological Psychopathology* (Springfield, IL: Thomas, 1955), p. 32.

23 E. Relph, *Place and Placelessness* (London: Pion, 1976), p. 55. 'Existential insideness' is defined as a 'form of insideness [...] in which a place is experienced without deliberate and selfconscious reflection yet is full with significances'.

24 Yi-Fu Tuan, *Topophilia: A Study of Environmental Perception, Attitudes, and Values* (Englewood Cliffs: Prentice Hall, 1974), p. 63.

25 For further discussion of the genealogy of the term 'landscape' see Steven C. Bourassa, *The Aesthetics of Landscape* (London: Belhaven Press, 1991), p. 3, and Eric Hirsch, 'Landscape: Between Place and Space', in Eric Hirsch and Michael O'Hanlon (eds.), *The Anthropology of Landscape: Perspectives on Place and Space* (Oxford: Oxford University Press, 1995), pp. 1–30 (p. 2).

26 Hirsch, 'Between Place and Space', p. 2.

27 Dick Harrison, *Unnamed Country: The Struggle for a Canadian Prairie Fiction* (Edmonton: University of Alberta Press, 1977), has discussed how writers and artists have struggled to come to terms with the vastness of the Canadian plains by trying to 'impose familiar patterns' on them (p. 24).

28 David Spurr, *The Rhetoric of Empire: Colonial Discourse in Journalism, Travel Writing, and Imperial Administration* (Durham, NC: Duke University Press, 1993), p. 16.

29 Pratt, *Imperial Eyes*, pp. 201–08.

30 John Berger, *About Looking* (London: Writers and Readers, 1980), p. 81.

31 Tuan, *Topophilia*, p. 79.

32 Gaston Bachelard, *The Poetics of Space* [1958], trans. Maria Jolas (Boston, MA: Beacon Press, 1994), p. 185.

33 Berger, *About Looking*, p. 81.

34 The importance of silence in this passage could also be related to what Spurr, *Rhetoric of Empire*, has termed the 'rhetorical strategy of negation by which Western writing conceives of the Other as absence, emptiness, nothingness, or death' (p. 92).

35 Edmund Burke, *A Philosophical Enquiry into the Origin of our Ideas of the Sublime and Beautiful* [1757], ed. Adam Phillips (Oxford: Oxford University Press, 1990), pp. 60–61. All further references are to this edition and are given after quotations in the text.

36 Immanuel Kant, *Critique of Judgement* [1790], trans. Werner S. Pluhar (Indianapolis: Hackett, 1987), p. 129. All further references are to this edition and are given after quotations in the text.

37 For example, Kant has said 'the sight of them [the trimmings of the sublime] becomes all the more attractive the more fearful it is, provided that we are in a safe place' (p. 120).

38 Humboldt, *Views of Nature*, pp. 169–70.

39 Humboldt, *Views of Nature* , p. 170.

40 Pratt, *Imperial Eyes*, p. 205.

41 Arnold Berleant, *The Aesthetics of Environment* (Philadelphia: Temple University Press, 1992), p. 17. Holmes Rolston III, in 'Aesthetic Experience in Forests', *The Journal of Aesthetics and Art Criticism*, 56 (1998), pp. 157–66, has described how '[t]he forest attacks all our senses – sight, hearing, smell, feeling, even taste' (p. 158).

42 Franco, 'Image and Experience', pp. 101–02.

43 Neil L. Whitehead, 'South America/Amazonia: The Forest of Marvels', in Peter Hulme and Tim Youngs (eds.), *The Cambridge Companion to Travel Writing* (Cambridge: Cambridge University Press, 2002), pp. 122–38 (p. 135).

44 This lecture, entitled 'An Image of Africa: Racism in Conrad's *Heart of Darkness*', is

reproduced in Chinua Achebe, '*Hopes and Impediments*': *Selected Essays, 1965–1987* (London: Heinemann, 1988), pp. 1–13 (p. 2).

45   Pratt, *Imperial Eyes*, pp. 201–08.

46   Bhabha, *Location of Culture*, p. 124.

47   Sylvia Molloy, 'Contagio narrativo y gesticulación retórica en *La vorágine*', in Ordóñez (ed.), *Textos críticos*, pp. 489–513 (p. 492). See also Jennifer L. French, *Nature, Neo-Colonialism, and the Spanish American Regional Writers* (Hanover, NH: Dartmouth College Press, 2005), pp. 133–143, who discusses *Heart of Darkness* and *La vorágine* in the context of the engagement of Latin American regional writers with British colonial writing.

48   Klaus Müller-Bergh, *Alejo Carpentier: estudio biográfico-crítico* (New York: Las Americas, 1972), pp. 74–75. Luis Harss, *Los nuestros* (Buenos Aires: Editorial Sudamericana, 1966) has said: 'Hay una indudable reminiscencia de Conrad en Carpentier, no sólo en la exuberancia de su estilo sino además en las tortuosas lucubraciones de su gótico-simbología' (p. 70). Frances Wyers, 'Carpentier's *Los pasos perdidos*: Heart of Lightness, Heart of Darkness', *Revista Hispánica Moderna*, 45 (1992), pp. 84–95 (p. 84), has claimed that *Heart of Darkness* 'looms behind this work', although she does not establish whether or not Carpentier was conscious of these parallels.

49   Wyers, 'Carpentier's *Los pasos perdidos*', p. 84.

50   Said, *Culture and Imperialism*, p. 34.

51   Wilson Harris, 'The Frontier on which *Heart of Darkness* Stands', in Conrad, *Heart of Darkness*, ed. Kimbrough, pp. 262–68.

52   Michael Taussig, *Shamanism, Colonialism, and the Wild Man: A Study in Terror and Healing* (Chicago: The University of Chicago Press, 1991), p. 78.

53   The French Caribbean poet J. S. Alexis from Haiti has discussed the concept of the ugly with regard to Haitian art in a 1965 paper, 'Of the Marvelous Realism of the Haitians': 'beauty of form is not in any of its fields an accepted premise, a primary purpose, but Haitian art achieves it from all angles of approach, even that of said ugliness', cited in Selwyn R. Cudjoe, *Resistance in Caribbean Literature* (Athens: Ohio University Press, 1980), p. 254.

54   Lawrence Buell, *The Environmental Imagination: Thoreau, Nature Writing and the Formation of American Culture* (Cambridge, MA: Belknap Press of Harvard University Press, 1995), p. 53.

55   Kant, *Critique of Judgement*, p. 113.

56   Christopher Mulvey, *Anglo-American Landscapes: A Study of Nineteenth-century Anglo-American Travel Literature* (Cambridge: Cambridge University Press, 1983), pp. 187–208.

57   Carpentier, *Visión de América*, p. 45.

58   William E. Bull, 'Naturaleza y antropomorfismo en *La vorágine*', in Ordóñez (ed.), *Textos críticos*, pp. 319–34 (p. 330).

59   Edward Said, *Orientalism: Western Conceptions of the Orient*, with a new afterword (London: Penguin, 1995), p. 21.

60   George Santayana, *The Sense of Beauty: Being the Outlines of Aesthetic Theory*, ed. William G. Holzberger and Herman J. Saatkamp, Jr., *The Works of George Santayana* (Cambridge, MA: MIT Press, 1988), II, p. 86.

61   Anthony Pagden, *European Encounters with the New World: From Renaissance to Romanticism* (New Haven: Yale University Press, 1993), p. 26.

62   Stepan, *Picturing Tropical Nature*, p. 62.

63   Even outside travel writing, forests have not infrequently been compared to churches. For example, Rolston III, 'Aesthetic Experience', has described the forest as 'a kind of church. Trees pierce the sky, like cathedral spires. Light filters down, as through stained glass' (p. 166).

64 Frances Calderón de la Barca, *Life in Mexico* (London: Dent, 1970), p. 314.
65 From William Gilpin's *Northern Tour to the Lakes, etc.*, [1786], cited in Christopher Hussey, *The Picturesque: Studies in a Point of View*, with a new preface (Hamden, CT: Archon Books, 1967), p. 84.
66 Johannes Willem Bertens, *The Idea of the Postmodern: A History* (London: Routledge, 1995), p. 133.
67 Pedro Henríquez Ureña, *Ensayos en busca de nuestra expresión* (Buenos Aires: Raigal, 1952), p. 54.

CHAPTER THREE

Salvaging the Savage

Until the first decades of the twentieth century European iconography of Native Americans tended to the extremes of idealization and demonization.[1] On the one hand, early modern commentators such as Juan Ginés de Sepúlveda considered the 'Indians' not only degenerate and sinful but also subhuman – a widespread belief which led to a prolonged debate in Valladolid in 1550 to determine whether Amerindians were humans or animals.[2] On the other hand, many writers and artists located the native peoples of America in a primordial 'golden age' – a trend that was not discouraged by Columbus's belief that he had discovered the garden of Eden at the end of the Orinoco River, nor his founding vision of the American people as 'desnudos como su madre los parió, y [...] muy bien hechos, de muy fermosos cuerpos y muy buenas caras'.[3] Early modern pictorial representations of American Indians, while frequently giving vent to anxieties about sexual impropriety or unrestrained cannibalism, were often guided by European concepts of beauty and morality, and depicted the Native Americans in the manner of classical statuary, with Herculean busts and flowing locks of hair. Jean de Léry's *Histoire d'un voyage fait en la terre du Brésil* [1578] was punctuated with flattering portraits of Amerindians, focusing on their muscular physiques and broadly European facial features. Likewise, a series of woodcuts by Hans Burgkmair from 1516–19 depicted Tupinamba Indians dressed in distinctly un-American garb and armed with swords.[4] Early modern representations of native American life in both the visual arts and letters tended to assimilation: as Todorov has affirmed in his account of the Spanish conquest of America, what was denied was 'the existence of a human substance truly other, something capable of being not merely an imperfect state of oneself'.[5]

In the centuries following the 'Discovery' of America, European attitudes towards Native Americans remained ambivalent. In the seventeenth and eighteenth centuries Amerindians were generally considered to be degenerate, while in the nineteenth century the Noble Savage replaced the Wild Man as the dominant literary trope. In Spanish America following independence, Creole writers appealed to the pre-Columbian past as a means of breaking their associations with Spain.[6] From the middle of the nineteenth century the

Amerindian was central to postcolonial literature in Spanish America, particularly in movements such as *Indianismo* and *Indigenismo*. Nevertheless, representations of Amerindians continued to be far from authentic. For the Argentine writers Domingo F. Sarmiento and Esteban Echeverría, for example, Amerindians were associated with savagery and barbarism, and even pro-indigenous novels tended to appeal to literary tropes, producing an 'unbelievable Indian who might be called a combination Tonto and René'.[7] Whether positive or negative, representations of Amerindian culture in European and Latin American fiction tended to lack objective empiricism: as Robert F. Berkhofer has argued, 'Native Americans were and are real, but the *Indian* was a White invention and still remains largely a White image, if not stereotype.'[8]

The urban narrators of the *novela de la selva* share these ambivalent views of native culture, often swinging between esteem and disdain for the indigenous tribes they encounter in the jungle. While such contradictions lead to internal inconsistencies in the narrators' representation of Amerindian culture, these are not necessarily at odds with many of the illogical racialist discourses which were forwarded by contemporaries of Hudson, Rivera, and Gallegos, if perhaps not of Carpentier. According to Mario Vargas Llosa, as late as the 1920s Peruvian *modernistas* such as Enrique López Albújar were espousing a vision of the Amerindian which was 'más fantaseosa que fundada en la experiencia, a menudo caricatural, a veces risible por lo estereotipada'.[9] Nevertheless, in contrast to their ironic narrators, the authors of the *novela de la selva* were all profoundly interested in Amerindian culture. Hudson, Rivera, Gallegos, and Carpentier had all met Amerindians and some had actually lived among rainforest tribes for a short period.[10] The narrators' recourse to stereotypes about native American culture throughout the *novela de la selva* should not, therefore, simply be taken as evidence of the authors' racism. Indeed, there is a clear variance between the authors' respectful views of Amerindian culture and the jingoistic behaviour of protagonists such as Cova, who at one stage threatens an indigenous tribe with a pack of dogs. Rather, the repetition of colonial stereotypes of the 'Indian' throughout the *novela de la selva* can be seen as an example of colonial mimicry, parallel to the genre's ironic appeal to European landscape aesthetics. The narrators' repetition of clichéd ethnographical observations makes explicit the mechanisms of imperial discourse underpinning many accounts of the Native American in both European and Latin American writing.

As I will explore in this chapter, the authors of the *novela de la selva* are interested not only in overturning imperial topoi of the 'Indian' but also in establishing new descriptive paradigms for native American culture. They try to achieve this by including Amerindian myths and words in their novels and by shifting the narrative perspective from the urban travellers to the Amerindians themselves. Nevertheless, the representation of Amerindian culture in the *novela de la selva* is not attempting to be – and should not be idealized as – an instance of self-description on the part of indigenous people. Although the proliferation of *costumbrista* literature in post-independence Latin America might be seen as an 'autochthonous' genre, the urban Creole elite's portrayal of jungle tribes is quite the opposite and is often no more successful than European descriptions of Amerindians. José Carlos Mariátegui has argued that the novels of *indigenismo* could not provide 'una versión rigurosamente verista del indio', given that they were written by whites or mestizos.[11] While this view might be challenged by, for example, the novels of José María Arguedas, it is merely compounded by the authors of the *novela de la selva*. These writers do not reject just colonial representations of Native Americans, but the vexed notion of 'representation' itself, which is shown to be hopelessly aporetic. Writing about postmodern aesthetics in the late 1980s, Linda Hutcheon argued that 'representation cannot be avoided, but it can be studied to show how it legitimates certain kinds of knowledge and, therefore, certain kinds of power'.[12] The authors of the *novela de la selva* were already engaged in this kind of study some eighty years before.

Facing the Extreme: The 'Indian' as Barbarian or Noble Savage

The inclusion of Amerindian tribes in the *novela de la selva* would seem to be a novelistic exigency, given that the central action of these works takes place in the midst of the South American rainforest. It is surprising, therefore, that Amerindians should play – on the surface at least – a relatively minor role in most of the novels. In line with their traditional function in colonial travel writing, the Amerindians in *La vorágine* and *Los pasos perdidos*, for instance, are a source of more or less picturesque detail – an intrinsic facet of the exotic jungle milieu on a par with the tropical vegetation and animal life. Although in these two novels the narrators provide quasi-ethnological portraits of the Amerindians they encounter, the indigenous people rarely speak, much less become characters. In *Green Mansions* several of the Amerindians with whom Abel resides in the jungle are named and their characters are developed, yet they never fully transcend imperial stereotypes. By the end of the novel they are presented as irredeemably inhuman, especially for their treatment of Rima, whom they burn to death, and thus receive what within the story is presented as 'poetic justice' – the complete annihilation of the tribe at the hands of rival Amerindians. In *Canaima* Amerindian culture is presented somewhat more sympathetically. The plaintive conclusion to the novel, which intimates the desperate future 'de la raza indígena, degenerada por enfermedades, sin cuidado ni precaución y por falta de cruzamientos y por alimentación insufi-ciente algo total y definitivamente perdido para la vida del país' (p. 242), strikes a chord with the modern reader, as Jorge Marcone has observed, in its prefiguring of the eradication of wild natural spaces and the native communi-ties which populate them.[13] Nevertheless, although the protagonist of *Canaima* joins a native tribe and marries an Amerindian woman, the novelistic action does not manage to transcend racial stereotypes and, significantly, concludes with Marcos Vargas's mestizo son being sent away from the forest to the city to be educated.

Throughout much of the *novela de la selva* Amerindians are compared to the stock colonial figure of the barbarian – a characterization which is greatly at odds with the novels' postcolonial credentials. Throughout their Amazonian travel accounts the narrators quite literally demonize the native inhabitants with appellations such as 'devils in human shape' (*Green Mansions*, p. 166). In *Los pasos perdidos* Fray Pedro describes the murder of fellow religious crusaders in the Americas – the 'padres despedazados por los indios del Marañón', 'un beato Diego bárbaramente torturado por el último Inca' and the 'cuarenta frailes degollados' (pp. 171–72) – and these stories are given greater credibility in the novel by the fact that Fray Pedro himself is ultimately discovered 'atrozmente mutilado, en una canoa echada al río' (p. 263). Such traveller's tales quickly escalate into groundless colonial fantasies, as in *Green Mansions*, when Abel recollects his return journey through the forest:

> I see myself incessantly dogged by hostile savages. They flit like ghosts through the dark forest; they surround me and cut off all retreat, until I burst through them, escaping out of their very hands, to fly over some wide, naked savannah, hearing their shrill, pursuing yells behind me, and feeling the sting of their poisoned arrows in my flesh. (p. 199)

The 'hostile savages' supposedly tailing Abel remain nebulous and insubstantial in this dreamlike account, flitting 'like ghosts' through the gloomy tropical forest. Indeed, it seems likely from Abel's description of his miraculous 'escape' that they never existed at all. In *Canaima* the third-person narrator suffers from a parallel apprehension of invisible but belligerent Otherness when he hears distant shouts in the forest:

> Ya se oyen gritos de un lenguaje naciente. Son los guaraúnos del bajo Orinoco, degenerados descendientes del bravo caribe legendario [...].
>
> Pero a veces los gritos son alaridos lejanos, sin que se acierte a descubrir de dónde salen y quizás no sean proposiciones amistosas, sino airadas protestas del indio indómito, celoso de la soledad de sus bajumbales. (p. 10)

In this instance, too, the narrator's interpretation of the faint, distant cries of the 'degenerate' Amerindians as being hostile seems merely speculative, and this is emphasized by his use of the subjunctive 'sean'. Such fantasies draw upon well-established colonial stereotypes which, as Frantz Fanon has argued, make the jump from racial Other to 'ugliness, sin, darkness, immorality'.[14] The proclivity among travellers to imagine native populations as savage and violent is indicative of their own anxieties, particularly their fear of transgressing in the unregulated spaces beyond the fringes of 'civilization'.

Fanon has argued that the insistent vilification of the black man in white society, particularly for his sexual voraciousness, is symptomatic of the latter's desire to bolster selfhood through the exclusion of the racial Other.[15] This kind of racial stereotyping is also very much at work in the *novela de la selva* regarding the Native Americans. If we return to Abel's description of him fleeing the hostile Amerindians, cited above, sexual undertones can be discerned, as, for example, in the reference to poisoned arrows piercing Abel's skin. Throughout *Green Mansions* Abel sexualizes the Amerindians he meets in the jungle. In chapter 1, he describes how he is embraced by one of the tribe when he fires his pistol (itself an action replete with phallic imagery):

> Runi at my side, in an access of fierce delight and admiration, turned and embraced me. It was the first and last embrace I ever suffered from a naked male savage, and although this did not seem a time for fastidious feelings, to be hugged to his sweltering body was an unpleasant experience. [...] I staggered to my hammock; but being unable to get into it, Runi, overflowing with kindness, came to my assistance, whereupon we fell and rolled together on the floor. (p. 19)

This episode abounds in homoerotic elements, from the reference to Runi's 'sweltering body' to the image of the two men rolling drunkenly on the floor. Here the borders of selfhood are in danger of collapsing, not only because of Abel's implied sexual transgressions but also because of the actual physical intermingling of the bodies (note that Runi is '*overflowing* with kindness'; my emphasis). In *La vorágine*, the boundaries of Cova's selfhood are also challenged when 'unas indias' (p. 211) follow him to his hammock and attempt to seduce him. The indigenous girls are perceived by Cova as sexual predators – rather like succuba demons, fabled to copulate with men while they sleep – and Cova, in turn, self-styled throughout his travel account as a Don Juan figure, suddenly adopts the rhetoric of a pious missionary travelling in savage lands: 'rechacé la provocación amorosa, con profundo deseo de liberarme de la lascivia y pedirle a la castidad su refugio tranquilo' (p. 211).

The sexual practices of the tribes encountered by the urban travellers in the jungle are almost always presented as immoderate and are sharply opposed to their own libidinal drives. For the narrators of the *novela de la selva*, references to the Amerindians' lack of sexual inhibition – from their imitation of 'amor animal' (*Canaima*, p. 182) during a dance to a description of the hammocks in which they 'yacen y fornican y procrean' (*Los pasos perdidos*, p. 186) – are almost always employed to debase the indigenous people, and rarely transcend Fanon's tongue-in-cheek characterization of the white man's fear of the African:

> What do you expect, with all the freedom they have in their jungles! They copulate at all times and in all places. They are really genital. They have so many children that they cannot even count them. Be careful, or they will flood us with little mulattoes.[16]

Images of the Amerindians as lustful partake of the broader colonial urge not only to objectify but also to 'abjectify' the Other. References to sexual depravity and to dirt – to 'the stink of the native quarter, of breeding swarms, of foulness, of spawn, of gesticulations' – fill the pages of the *novela de la selva*.[17] Citing Julia Kristeva's discussion of the abject in *Powers of Horror*, Spurr argues that the principal motive for the degradation of the Other is the fear of personal transgression:

> The abject is neither the subject nor the object. ... It represents the crisis of the subject ... insofar as it would not yet be, or would no longer be separated from the object. Its limits would no longer be established. It would be constantly menaced by its possible collapse into the object.[18]

The construction of Otherness can once again be seen as an attempt to preserve the frontier between the subject and the object – a frontier which, as I will demonstrate in Chapter 5, often breaks down when urban travellers enter the jungle. The narrators' insistence on the alterity of Amerindian culture in the *novela de la selva* can be regarded, then, as indicative of the fragility of selfhood and a projection of their fear of 'going native' in the jungle. Abel in *Green Mansions* makes exemplary recourse to the abject when he is offered a wife by the tribe with which he is living – a girl whom he perceives to be 'rather lean and dirty; [...] [a] copper-coloured little drab of the wilderness' (p. 47). So, too, does Marcos, a character distinguished in the *novela de la selva* for his sympathy towards Amerindian culture. When, for example, the Amerindian villagers imbibe a hallucinatory drug during a dance, Marcos describes the manner in which they fall on top of one another in 'una masa *inmunda* y jadeante' (p. 183), with 'el *inmundo* líquido negro y viscoso de la secreción nasal' running down their faces (p. 182: my emphases). Moreover, he refuses to share 'la convivencia maloliente bajo el techo de la churuata' or to adopt the 'desagradable costumbre de comer con la mano, de una sola fuente donde todos metían las suyas nada limpias' (p. 234). The narrator of *Los pasos perdidos* also appeals to the abject when he describes two captive dwarfs in 'un hueco fangoso, suerte de zahúrda hedionda, llena de huesos roídos' (p. 185).

Kristeva has described 'food loathing' as 'perhaps the most elementary and most archaic form of abjection'.[19] The reference to the chewed bones in the dwarfs' prison in *Los pasos perdidos* can therefore be related to one of the central images of the abject in the *novela de la selva*, which is the consumption of 'unclean' food, from both a literal and a ritualistic perspective. In Western thought from the Greeks onwards there has been a direct correlation between culinary practices and cultural degradation. As John Block Friedman has argued, 'characterisation by diet suggests the difference or remoteness of the other from the observer rather than the common bond of humanity'.[20] References to the Amerindians' diet throughout the *novela de la selva* revisit the colonial tendency to degrade native populations through images of the abject, as when, for instance, Cova describes the Amerindians biting the heads of 'gruesos gusanos' (p. 210) to drink their juice, or scraping corn off the ground and lifting it 'a la boca, con tierra y todo' (p. 330). Likewise, in *Los pasos perdidos*, the narrator stresses the Amerindians' lack of cleanliness in his description of their dietary norms. Invoking a hierarchical scale to distinguish between 'los tragadores de gusanos, los lamedores de tierra' (p. 186) and the bone-chewing dwarfs, the narrator describes how the Amerindians 'devoran larvas de avispa, triscan hormigas y liendres, escarban la tierra y tragan los gusanos y las lombrices que les caen bajo las uñas, antes de amasar la tierra con los dedos y comerse la tierra misma' (p. 185). The proliferation of verbs in the third person plural explicitly juxtaposes the Amerindians' eating habits with those of the narrator. The movement of the passage marks not only the Amerindians' descent through the levels of a food chain but also their physical prostration as they crawl increasingly closer to the ground – a lowering which is no doubt supposed to symbolize their cultural degradation. The verbs 'devorar' and 'amasar' not only reflect the Amerindians' famished search for sustenance but are endowed with overtones of greed and gluttony, heightened by the reflexive pronoun in the verb 'comerse'.

This passage has antecedents in both factual and fictional travel writing, as well as in earlier *novelas de la selva*. It mirrors a number of sixteenth-century commentaries, which describe how the New World inhabitants 'eat fleas, spiders and worms raw, whenever they find them',[21] and it recalls the description of the Yahoos in Swift's *Gulliver's Travels*, who 'dig up roots, eat several kinds of herbs, and search about for carrion [...] which they greedily devour'.[22] Descriptions of the Amerindians' consumption of raw insects is related not only to the notion of 'improper food' (Aristotle argued that insects belong to a 'lower' species of animals which are spontaneously generated) but also, arguably, to cannibalism. As Anthony Pagden has shown, in early modern accounts of the Amerindians, commentators believed that the frequency with which the indigenous population ate 'unclean' food was an indication of their readiness to engage in cannibalism: 'That men, who were so unselective in their food consumption as to fail to perceive this crucial division in the natural world, were equally prepared to eat their own kind was hardly surprising.'[23]

Although there are few direct references to cannibalism in the *novela de la selva*, there are a number of allusions to it. In *Los pasos perdidos* the dwarfs' diet of chewed bones aligns them closely to dogs, and this is significant given that early modern commentators such as Jean de Léry often compared Amerindians to dogs, *canis*, from which it was a short step – both culturally and orthographically – to cannibals.[24] Likewise, in *La vorágine* there is an implicit reference to man-eating:

'Y con los cristianos también son atrevíos [los indios]: ¡al dijunto Jaspe le salieron del matorral, casi debajo del cabayo, y lo cogieron de estampía y lo envainaron! Y no valió gritarles. ¡Aposta, andábamos desarmaos, y eyos eran como veinte y echaban flecha pa toas partes!' [...]

'Era que el Jaspe los perseguía con los vaqueros y con el perraje. Onde mataba uno, prendía candela y hacía como que se lo taba comiendo asao, pa que lo vieran los fugitivos o los vigías que atalayaban sobre los moriches.'

'Mama, jue que los indios le mataron a él la jamilia [...]. Ya ven lo que pasó en el Hatico: macetearon a tóos los racionales y toavía humean los tizones.' (p. 130)

Peter Hulme has argued that '[h]uman beings who eat other human beings have always been placed on the very borders of humanity.'[25] By repeating this tale of cannibalism, Cova's journal once again substantiates colonial myths of monstrous and belligerent Otherness, and attempts to extenuate in advance the murder of a group of Amerindians at the end of the novel's first section. Nevertheless, the density of this 'tit for tat' argument undermines any such simplistic interpretation. It appears that Jaspe not only provoked the Amerindians but did so through a mock-up of a cannibal feast, where he killed one of their party and pretended (it seems) to roast him. Thus, the boundaries between the white man and the *indio* – between so-called 'civilized' and 'barbarous' conduct – break down. Stereotypes of the Amerindians as cannibals seem obsolete in a Latin American novel of the 1920s. Their rhetorical force is inhibited by this sense of belatedness and by the fact that, as I will discuss further in Chapter 5, it is not only the Amerindians who are shown to transgress dietary taboos in these novels but also the white travellers, who eat raw meat, forage for insects and – it is hinted – also engage in cannibalism.

The defilement of Amerindians through tropes of monstrosity or abjection is not the only manner through which European and Latin American writers have sought to objectify America's native population. A more subtle though equally pernicious form of imperial domination is the celebration of indigenous people under what Gareth Griffiths has described as the 'mythologized and fetishized sign of the "authentic"'.[26] The narrator of *Los pasos perdidos* is particularly prone to such stereotypes, given his proto-Romantic view of jungle life as a path to emotional and intellectual rebirth. His first glimpse of an Amerindian village leads him to record:

> En torno mío cada cual estaba entregado a las ocupaciones que le fueran propias, en un apacible concierto de tareas que eran las de una vida sometida a los ritmos primordiales. [...] La soberana precisión con que éste flechaba peces en el remanso, la prestancia de coreógrafo con que el otro embocaba la cerbatana, la concertada técnica de aquel grupo que iba recubriendo de fibras el maderamen de una casa común, me revelaban la presencia de un ser humano llegado a maestro en la totalidad de oficios propiciados por el teatro de su existencia. (pp. 176–77)

In this passage the narrator endorses the mythologized notion of the communal nature of tribal life by presenting the entire population working together harmoniously. This is a milieu where 'no había oficios inútiles' (p. 177): the life of the Amerindian, unlike that of the observer, is purposeful and fulfilling. Nevertheless, despite his admiration for the Amerindians he encounters in this episode, the narrator is not able objectively to describe life in their village. His use of metaphors relating to music and theatre, as well as his description of one of the Amerindian men raising a blowgun 'choreographically', reveal his characteristic bent to idealize native life and assimilate it into the fold of the familiar.

The narrator's aestheticization of Amerindian life as a kind of stylized performance for the urban spectator upholds the binary of the 'watcher' and the 'watched' in anthropological discourse. It is also an example of the imperial strategy which Roger Célestin has termed 're-representing': 'the removal from a former, "authentic" context (but foreign to me) to a context foreign to it (but familiar to me)'.[27] This tendency is widespread not only in imperial travel literature but also in the *novela de la selva*. When, for example, Cova describes a group of Amerindian men as 'fornidos y jóvenes, de achocolatado cutis y hercúleas espaldas' (p. 193), he appeals to a classical analogy which would be unfamiliar to the indigenous population. Indeed, it is important to note that the narrators of the *novela de la selva* not only imbue the Amerindians with aesthetic qualities but also occasionally depict them as if they were objects of art. In *Green Mansions* Abel draws upon a statuary metaphor to describe a group of taciturn Amerindians as 'a set of hollow bronze statues' (p. 21) and, in a similar vein, the narrator of *Los pasos perdidos* describes the muscular chests of the indigenous rowers as '*esculpidos* por los remos' (p. 177: my emphasis). The reification of the native body throughout the *novela de la selva* and, especially, the implication that it is 'hollow' and lifeless – hence lacking in human feeling – is consistent with much earlier imperial ethnography.

The denial of aesthetic qualities in Amerindian life is also a staple of these novels. In *Canaima* a native dance is described as being 'sin arte alguno, bestia pura' (p. 182), and in *Green Mansions* Abel credits his whistling as being 'a style of music superior to that of the aboriginals' (p. 21). Likewise, in *Los pasos perdidos* the narrator assumes that birdsong has no 'sentido musical-estético para los que lo oyen constantemente' (p. 20), and although he is moved when he discovers a sacred jug decorated with a maternal motif, he appears to esteem it less for its artistic than for its ethnographic value. While such comments connote the aesthetic inferiority of the indigenous cultures of the Amazon, and hence could be seen to participate in imperial discourse more generally, the inverse – the admiration for indigenous art – can be seen to be equally problematic. Marianna Torgovnick has explained that this 'eleva-tion' of the primitive art object 'in a sense reproduces, in the aesthetic realm, the dynamics of colonization, since Western standards control the flow of the "administration" and can bestow or withhold the label "art"'.[28] This ambiva-lence is epitomized in *Los pasos perdidos* when the narrator expresses the belief that he has just witnessed the 'Nacimiento de la Música' (p. 188) in the chant of a witch doctor:

> Hay como portamentos guturales, prolongados en aullidos; sílabas que, de pronto, se repiten mucho, llegando a crear un ritmo; hay trinos de súbito cortados por cuatro notas que son el embrión de una melodía. Pero luego es el vibrar de la lengua entre los labios, el ronquido hacia adentro, el jadeo contratiempo sobre la maraca. Es algo situado mucho más allá del lenguaje, y que, sin embargo, está muy lejos aún del canto. [...] En boca del Hechicero, del órfico ensalmador, estertora y cae, convulsivamente, el Treno – pues esto y no otra cosa es un *treno*. (pp. 187–88)

Although the narrator is initially reluctant to call the shamanic chanting a 'song' ('está muy lejos aún del canto'), preferring instead to stress its primi-tive and even animalistic qualities, he eventually resorts to the technique of re-representation by intellectualizing the phenomenon, and attaching a name to it ('pues esto y no otra cosa es un *treno*') – an action which both elevates the chanting to the category of 'art' and, at the same time, circumscribes it within a European aesthetic category.

What ostensibly appear to be idealized portraits of Amerindian culture in the *novela de la selva* are often loaded with tacit racial and cultural stereotypes. In *Los pasos perdidos*, for example, the narrator's speciously flattering description of the Amerindians' harmony with their natural environment gives way to a crude vision of evolutionism:

> las mujeres tenían vientres *hechos* para la maternidad. [...] Por lo demás, *el desarrollo* de los cuerpos estaba cumplido en *función de utilidad*. Los dedos, *instrumentos* para asir, eran fuertes y ásperos; las piernas, *instrumentos* para andar, eran de sólidos tobillos. Cada cual llevaba su esqueleto dentro, envuelto en carnes *eficientes*. (p. 177: my emphasis)

The reification of the Amerindians' limbs as 'instrumentos' not only reduces them to the realm of inanimate objects but also insinuates that their bodies have only functional value in the jungle. According to the narrator, among this tribe the human body adapts to suit the natural environment and not vice versa, thus thwarting the widespread classical and early modern belief that God had bestowed nature unto man in order that he might transform it.[29] The narrator's description of how the Amerindians' legs are crafted especially 'para andar' is particularly absurd given that this is the leg's congenital function. The epithets used to describe the Amerindians' bodies ('fuertes', 'ásperos', 'sólidos', 'eficientes') implicitly recall Aristotle's theory of how it was possible to distinguish between the free man and the so-called 'natural slave' on the basis of the latter's more stalwart physique – a manner hotly debated in the sixteenth century in relation to the Amerindians, and which could not be unknown to a narrator who dedicates much of the second half of the novel to a discussion of the *polis*. The Aristotelian undercurrents of many of the narrator's seemingly innocuous observations unearth his complicity with the conquistadors he alludes to throughout his journal and lead to an associative free play between Amerindians and barbarians, the jungle and savagery.

References to cultural simplicity in the *novela de la selva* are also ambivalent, given the often fine line between the simple and the simple-minded. In *Los pasos perdidos* the narrator's description of how Rosario takes each day as it comes, 'sin poseer nada, sin arrastrar el ayer, sin pensar en el mañana' (p. 184) is, on the surface at least, approbatory, but it may be worth noting that, as late as the eighteenth century, travellers had cited the indigenous Americans' supposed lack of foresight as proof of their lack of humanity.[30] Just as in Rousseau's anecdote about the Caribbean Indian who sells his bed in the morning only to have to buy it back by nightfall, there is an element of disparagement in the narrator's perception of his lover's carefree nature, culminating in his description of her as 'desmemoriada' (p. 184).[31] Likewise, Abel's reference to the Amerindians as 'children of nature' (p. 28) in *Green Mansions* is highly ambivalent. While this description has a Rousseauesque air to it, as Johannes Fabian has insisted, '[a]side from the evolutionist figure of the savage there has been no conception more obviously implicated in political and cultural oppression than that of the childlike native.'[32]

It is important to note that in the *novela de la selva* the narrators' idealization of the 'primitive' is often quite unrelated to their esteem, or lack thereof, for Amerindian culture. In *Green Mansions* and *Los pasos perdidos* the characters lauded most for their 'primitivism' – Rima and Rosario – are not Amerindians but idealized, literary figures who, like the narrators, are not native to the forest. Described by the narrator of Carpentier's novel as 'india por el pelo y los pómulos, mediterránea por la frente y la nariz, negra por la sólida redondez de los hombros' (p. 84), Rosario is depicted as a living summation of the races that met on the American continent. Rima's racial make-up is even further removed from the indigenous American: her skin is described as ever-changing, from 'dim white' to 'pale-grey', and from 'dim, rosy purple to dim blue' (p. 53). Abel surmises that she must belong to 'a distinct race which had existed in this little-known corner of the continent' (p. 53). She is certainly much closer to European colouring than that of the Amerindians, if not positively fairylike. Duncan has suggested that Rima defines the role of the Amerindian women in the novel through binary oppositions: 'Historically the real wild folk of the woods, they appear here in the retrogressive guise of treacherous and bloodthirsty "savages", Rima's moral and symbolic negatives as well as her deadly foes.'[33] Abel idealizes Rima as the last of a dying race, without realizing that the Amerindians he is so quick to malign are in sight of a similar fate. Likewise, although Marcos marries a native woman in *Canaima*, this match falls far short of the love he had felt for his urban sweetheart, Aracelis. When his Amerindian wife repeats words that his former lover had said to him years before: '¡Y yo queriéndote tanto, tanto, tanto!', he is described as feeling compassion for her, 'mezclada con tristeza de sí mismo': 'la atrajo en silencio hacia su pecho, con ganas de llorar, como si con ella se hubiese quedado sólo por algo definitivamente perdido o que nunca llegó' (p. 243). This transracial love story is not like those idealized matches which proliferated in European literature in the eighteenth and nineteenth centuries, but is a more realistic exposition of the difficulties of cross-cultural relationships and the chasm that exists between Native American and Latin American cultures.

Clearly, then, many of the narrators' descriptions of native life in the *novela de la selva* are predicated on literary views of the 'Indian' rather than on the actual indigenous cultures they encountered in the tropical jungle. Their persistent reiteration of tropes relating to native barbarism or the 'noble savage' is calculated not only to stress the wickedness or naivety of the native population but also to insert them into a long-established discourse of Otherness. Dehumanization is one of the linchpins of colonial discourse and it is a technique frequently drawn upon by the narrators of the *novela de la selva*, who insistently attempt to diminish the humanity of the indigenous people featured in their travel accounts. Nevertheless, the narrators' hope for a return to imperial certainties in the jungle, with the Amerindian fulfilling the traditional role of servant, pathfinder, and exotic Other, is resolutely refused by the indigenous jungle tribes. This is not just a matter of simple rebellion, as we have in early twentieth-century British travel novels, such as Sir Arthur Conan Doyle's *The Lost World* or Evelyn Waugh's *A Handful of Dust*, where the urban traveller is abandoned by his indigenous servants and is forced to fend for himself in the forest. What threatens the narrators' desire for control of the Other in the *novela de la selva* is the breakdown of representational fixity, where imperial tropes succeed only in drawing attention to the limits of European knowledge, and where indigenous ways of naming and seeing threaten to displace those of the urban travellers.

Alternative Ethnographies

Inverse ethnography
Until the last decades of the nineteenth century, ethnography was not carried out by professional anthropologists, but was a sideline of explorers, naturalists, and missionaries, who described not only the topography of foreign countries but also the lives of the natives, their customs, religions, governments, and languages.[34] The institutionalization of anthropology as a discrete science led not only to an increase of Europeans who wished to go to exotic climes to study the native inhabitants but also to a recognition within the postcolonial states of Latin America that the study of indigenous American customs need no longer be in the hands of outsiders.[35] It is within this climate of pioneering research and retrospection that the *novela de la selva* was born.

In the past few decades there have emerged a number of works assessing the complicity of ethnology with imperial domination. For example, Talal Asad has argued that anthropology is made feasible by the power relationships between the 'dominating (European) and dominated (non-European) cultures'.[36] This contributes, as James Clifford has observed, to a refashioning of the view of the anthropologist less as a sympathetic observer than as a caricatured 'ambitious social scientist making off with tribal lore and giving nothing in return'.[37] The authors of the *novela de la selva* arguably initiated this caricature much earlier, for the figure of the anthropologist is present in each of the novels. In *Green Mansions*, for example, Abel, who is fleeing from the Venezuelan authorities, has it falsely recorded in his passport that he is visiting the Venezuelan interior in order to 'collect information concerning the native tribes' and subsequently takes to keeping a journal of observations he makes regarding the 'country and people, both semi-civilised and savage' (p. 9). While there are no explicit references to anthropology as a discipline in *La vorágine* and *Canaima*, the narrative often includes ethnographical material, as when Cova describes how cassava is prepared, or when Marcos observes a native dance. In *Los pasos perdidos* the narrator's search for indigenous musical instruments in the jungle functions as a pretext for a classic anthropological approach:

Al concluir los trueques que me pusieron en posesión de aquel arsenal de cosas creadas por el más noble instinto del hombre, me pareció que entraba en un nuevo ciclo de mi existencia. La misión estaba cumplida. En quince días justo había alcanzado mi objeto de modo realmente laudable, y, orgulloso de ello, palpaba deleitosamente los trofeos del deber cumplido. El rescate de la jarra sonora – pieza magnífica –, era el primer acto excepcional, memorable, que se hubiera inscrito hasta ahora en mi existencia. (p. 178)

It is important to note that, despite the narrator styling this find as the fulfilment of a mission, these instruments are not discovered by him but by his fellow traveller, El Adelantado. Indeed, as Bill Ashcroft has explained, the idea of 'discovery' is 'profoundly Euro-centric' since what travellers purported to have discovered was often already known, and in this instance, created, by the native population.[38] The narrator's use of words such as 'trofeo' or 'arsenal' to describe the musical instruments, compounds the already implicit suggestion that his 'rescate' of these artefacts is, in fact, cultural pillage.

Nevertheless, while being entangled in the production of imperial discourse, ethnography, as Clifford insists, is always 'complex, often ambivalent, potentially counter-hegemonic'.[39] The *novela de la selva* exploits the ambivalent qualities of ethnography in order to undermine the authority of traditional anthropological paradigms – object/subject, observer/observed, rational/irrational – and hence the power hierarchies they sustain. In these novels, anthropological discourse is discounted as a valid way of writing about the Other, and the categories of Self and Other themselves are disrupted. Throughout the *novela de la selva*, the perspective of subject and object frequently shifts and the urban outsider often finds himself not initiating, but at the brunt of, anthropological observation. This is consistent with Beardsell's belief that from the first years after the conquest the Native Americans 'returned the Europeans' gaze' by theorizing the outsider in much the same way as they themselves had been theorized.[40] This shift in perspective – what I will term 'inverse ethnography' – which overturns the naturalized role of the native population as the object of surveillance, takes place throughout the *novela de la selva* and is exemplified in *Canaima* when Marcos is approached by an Amerindian during an indigenous dance:

uno, acercándose a Marcos Vargas, a quien ya rodeaban varias guarichas, examinándolo con su impertinente curiosidad característica:
 'Ma cuareja mancatida' díjole. Pero comprendiendo que no lo entendía recurrió al castellano: 'Yo teniendo hija hembra. Yo ofreciéndote guaricha bonita si tú no siendo maluco con indio y dejándolo tranquilo bailando india Rosa.' (p. 180)

The approach of the Amerindian father intent on bartering away his daughter, and that of the young indigenous girls who have already surrounded Marcos, disrupts what is an archetypal anthropological pose: the urban outsider overlooking a native ritual in a position of elevation and immunity. In this episode the colonial tradition of surveillance of the Other is overturned: now it is the Amerindian who observes and addresses Marcos. Moreover, while in travel writing or anthropological discourse it is usually the urban outsider who is bilingual, here the Amerindian slips effortlessly from his native tongue into Spanish, proving much more articulate and persuasive than Marcos. Stephen Greenblatt has discussed the deep-rooted tendency in Western culture to correlate lack of speech with inhumanity, from the medieval Wild Man to Columbus's belief that the Native Americans had no language.[41] In line with this, the narrators of the *novela de la selva* usually stress the Amerindians' linguistic incompetence and describe them as speaking halting Spanish, impaired by 'gerundios y monosílabos' (*La vorágine*, p. 201), or talking in their own 'bárbaras lenguas' (*Canaima*, p. 59) – the etymological connection between 'bárbaro' and the Greek *barbaros*, 'babbler', surely not lost on Gallegos. During this episode in *Canaima* the Amerindian father demonstrates not only his proficiency in his own language and in Spanish but also his superiority over the urban traveller, who is at first unable to understand him. Indeed, his instigation of a deal between himself and Marcos regarding his daughter – 'Yo ofreciéndote guaricha bonita si tú no siendo maluco con indio' – exemplifies not only his sophisticated grasp of language but also his ability to negotiate and bargain, thus overturning the imperial stereotype of the Native American having no grasp of commercial value.[42]

Inverse ethnography is also present in *Green Mansions*. When Abel makes a homespun guitar and puts on a performance to 'entertain' the Amerindians, we suddenly glimpse him from their perspective:

> I also skipped about the floor, strum-strumming at the same time, instructing them in the most lively dances of the whites […]. It is true that these exhibitions were always witnessed by the adults with a profound gravity, which would have disheartened a stranger to their ways. They were a set of hollow bronze statues that looked at me, but I knew that the living animals inside of them were tickled at my singing, strumming, and pirouetting. (pp. 21–22)

Here, the urban traveller has become an exhibit for the Amerindians, rather than vice versa, and they are far from being impressed by him. Although Abel shrugs off their lack of enthusiasm, attempting to restore his dominance over them through the crude metaphor which describes them as expressionless statues, the description of his guitar-playing and dancing has the effect of defamiliarizing his actions, and enabling the reader, like the Amerindian observers, to see them as a strange ritual, witnessed for the first time. In *Los pasos perdidos* the narrator also becomes a curiosity for the locals, as is exemplified by Rosario's contempt for his clothes:

> Ayer, al ver una camisa de alta factura, que yo había comprado en una de las tiendas más famosas del mundo, Rosario se echó a reír, afirmando que tales prendas eran más propias de hembras. Junto a ella me desasosiega continuamente el temor al ridículo, ridículo ante el cual no vale pensar que los otros 'no saben', puesto que son ellos, aquí, los que saben. (pp. 115–16)

The narrator here explicitly acknowledges the inversion of the Self/Other binary in the jungle and the concomitant diminution of his status. This recalls a similar moment of slippage in Humboldt's *Personal Narrative*, when he relates how the Chaima tribe 'are ashamed – so they say – to wear clothes, and if they are forced to do so too soon they rush off into the jungle in order to remain naked. [...] The older women hid behind trees and burst into loud fits of laughter when they saw us pass by fully dressed.'[43] The reversal of the Western norm in both of these accounts – the correlation of wearing European clothes with embarrassment – succeeds in denaturalizing urban culture and deflates the persona of the traveller from a cultural arbiter to a figure of fun.

In all of these episodes, the referent of 'exoticism' shifts from the Amerindian characters to the urban travellers themselves. Indeed, in *Los pasos perdidos* the narrator actually admits that he is conscious of '[su] propio exotismo' (p. 110), particularly in front of his future lover, Rosario. From the early colonial period, the flora, fauna and indigenous peoples of the New World had been brought to major European cities and put on display for the public.[44] In the *novela de la selva* it is the urban and Europeanized outsider who becomes a spectacle for the Amerindian – an inversion which displaces the established boundaries of the 'familiar' and the 'exotic'.

Célestin has discussed the counter-discursive potential of the term 'exotic', especially in instances where non-Western writers make strange the everyday features of Western life.[45] This change in perspective in the *novela de la selva* consistently disrupts the urban traveller's will to cultural domination in the forest, where he is not only outwitted by the Amerindians but is also dependent upon them for his survival. In *Green Mansions* Abel is nursed back to health by an Amerindian tribe when he contracts a fever, and through most of the novel he relies upon Amerindians for food and shelter. In *Los pasos perdidos* the narrator reluctantly acknowledges that he and his fellow travellers are 'intrusos, forasteros ignorantes', so far removed from nature that 'si el fuego [...] se apagara de pronto, seríamos incapaces de encenderlo nuevamente por la sola diligencia de nuestras manos' (p. 182).[46] Likewise, Cova and his companions get lost in the jungle only after their Amerindian oarsmen die in an accident – a disorientation which leads to Cova's death.

This dependence is not just a case of the urban traveller and the Amerindian each being 'dueños de su cultura' (p. 176), as the narrator of *Los pasos perdidos* likes to believe. The single request that the Amerindians make to Marcos in *Canaima* – that he show them how to 'hacer hielo' (p. 238) – is denied, leaving them baffled as to 'cómo podía ignorar un racional lo que otros sabían, cuando entre ellos – los indios – era tesoro común la ciencia de las cosas necesarias para la vida' (p. 238). What the narrators cite as the Amerindians' designation of the white man as 'un racional' is thus revealed as a misnomer throughout these novels. The urban travellers not only lack technical and scientific knowledge in the jungle but also frequently give themselves over to irrational behaviour, as when Abel runs through the forest in a 'panic' (p. 31) – an appropriate ailment to have in the tropical rainforest, since it acquires its name from Pan, the malevolent god of the woods.

Myth-making

The turn to inverse ethnography among the Amerindian characters in the *novela de la selva* is just one of many ways in which the genre sought to disrupt the dynamics of imperial discourse. Another important strategy in the authors' arsenal of postcolonial tricks was the inclusion of indigenous stories and myths in their narratives. Although the articulation of native stories in the *novela de la selva* was consistent with an increasing interest in the 'indigenous' among Latin American intellectuals in the first half of the twentieth century, coming to a head in the 1930s and 40s in the *novela indigenista*, important differences can be discerned between the representation of native American culture in these two genres. While the focus of the *novela indigenista* tended to be on Andean culture, as in José María Arguedas's *Yawar Fiesta* or Ciro Alegría's *El mundo es ancho y ajeno*, the *novela de la selva* was interested in exploring the indigenous cultures of the tropical region broadly termed 'Amazonia'. As Sá explains, the mythical content of novels such as *Canaima* and *Los pasos perdidos* can be traced back to Pacaraima Carib literature and, more specifically, to the myth of Macunáima – the name of the hero of Mário de Andrade's 1928 novel. As such, the inclusion of indigenous myths in the *novela de la selva* can be seen not only as a celebration of autochthonous American culture but of a specifically tropical one at that.

One of the principal difficulties when discussing the repetition of Amerindian myths in the *novela de la selva* is that these stories are removed from anything like an original context, not only through their transformation from oral to written media but also through their articulation by outsiders. Nevertheless, even though Amerindian myths in the *novela de la selva* pass through an author and, in the majority of cases, an ironic first-person narrator, these indigenous stories retain much of their force and 'authenticity'. As Lévi-Strauss has shown, myths are exceptional in their ability to survive translation:

> Whatever our ignorance of the language and culture of the people where it originated, a myth is still felt as a myth by any reader anywhere in the world. Its substance does not lie in its style, its original music, or its syntax, but in the *story* which it tells.[47]

Throughout the *novela de la selva*, Amerindian myths are shown not only as capable of surviving but also of prospering within the novelistic form. In these novels native stories embody a powerful counter-discourse, decentring the urban traveller's view of the rainforest and offsetting his desire to mystify his adventures in the jungle with an alternative, indigenous mythopoesis. They also disrupt the strict verisimilitude of the travelogues of which they are a part, especially through their inclusion of magical or animal protagonists and their disregard for historical realism.

References to indigenous myths span the *novela de la selva* and even provide the title for Gallegos's novel, *Canaima*: 'El maligno, la sombría divinidad de los guaicas y maquiritares, el dios frenético, principio del mal y causa de todos los males, que le disputa el mundo a Cajuña el bueno. Lo demoníaco sin forma determinada y capaz de adoptar cualquiera apariencia, viejo Ahrimán redivivo en América' (p. 153). This malevolent forest god appears under a different name in *Green Mansions* – Curupitá (p. 31) – and resembles the Indiecita Mapiripana in *La vorágine*. Indigenous cosmogonies are also fundamental to *Los pasos perdidos*, which includes epigraphs from two Mayan books, the *Popol Vuh* and *Chilam Balam de Chumayel*.[48] In Carpentier's novel the narrator's speculations about Amerindian myths take on a more scholarly guise, seeming to derive principally from Lévi-Strauss, especially his observations on the 'portentosa unidad de los mitos' (p. 213).[49] As well as containing myths, the novels include a profusion of indigenous rituals, such as totemism, marriage rites and feasting. These rituals recuperate the primacy of an Amerindian world view and, particularly, the sanctity of the forest and the jungle animals, which tend to appear in the narrators' travelogues as annoyances or predators.

One of the most important functions of indigenous stories in the *novela de la selva* is their ability to contradict the dominant narratives of the travellers. In *Green Mansions*, for instance, it is significant that Rima is the source of much indigenous lore. When Abel first visits the forest in which he encounters Rima, the tribe with which he is residing tells him that it is 'a dangerous place', and he soon ascertains that their 'fear of the wood was superstitious' (p. 25). Indeed, Rima bears more than a passing resemblance to the much-feared forest demon, Curupitá, who, according to 'Indian beliefs' is a 'misshapen, man-devouring monster who is said to beguile his victims into the dark forest by mimicking the human voice – the voice sometimes of a woman in distress – or by singing some strange and beautiful melody' (p. 33). While Abel dismisses the tribe's beliefs as a product of the 'savage mind', Rima does appear to be invested with supernatural qualities, such as her ever-changing skin tone, and her ability to 'disappear' in the forest, or to tame wild creatures. This indeterminacy, coupled with her mysterious origins, lends weight to the Amerindians' view of her as a supernatural creature – an ambiguity which is never truly clarified in the story.

In *Canaima*, too, indigenous myths are forwarded as a means of comprehending Marcos's irrationality in the forest, where he takes to talking to trees or, like the Italian count also exiled in the jungle, bellowing like a wild animal.[50] The Amerindians insist that such behaviour is a manifestation of 'Canaima en cabeza de racional' (p. 185) – an interpretation that is not contradicted by a more rational explanation in the novel. Thus, indigenous knowledge supplants Western science, which might construe Marcos's malady to be the result of malaria or some psychological disorder.

Indigenous myth is also seen to eclipse scientific rationalism in *La vorágine*, when Cova suffers from a fever. It is significant that this episode is directly juxtaposed with Heli Mesa's story of the Indiecita Mapiripana, 'la sacerdotista de los silencios' (p. 225), who is reputed to haunt the forest. The tale relates how the Indiecita took revenge '[e]n otros tiempos' (p. 226) on a lascivious missionary who used to seduce prepubescent Indian girls, and who one night raped the Indiecita. The offspring of this encounter – an owl and a vampire bat – haunt the missionary nightly until he dies of fever in a cave. The tale ends chillingly with the words: 'quedó revolando entre la caverna una mariposa de alas azules, inmensa y luminosa como un arcángel, que es la visión final de los que mueren de fiebres en estas zonas' (p. 227). Although this story is improbable, Cova lends it credibility by relating how it was prompted by his discovery of an inexplicable 'huella humana' (p. 224) on a riverbank – the calling card of the Indiecita – and it can be no coincidence that he contracts a fever immediately after this discovery. Cova's sickness is thus invested with supernatural overtones in the novel and could be interpreted on a mythical level as punishment for his ill-treatment of the Amerindians. The return to myth in the *novela de la selva*, and especially its supplanting of Western science, recalls Theodor Adorno and Max Horkheimer's definition of the 'dialectic of enlightenment', where enlightened Europe 'returns to mythology, which it never really knew how to elude'.[51]

Indigenous myth also provides internal commentary on the novelistic action in *Los pasos perdidos*. In Carpentier's novel the inclusion of a passage from the *Popol Vuh*, the Quiché book of creation, which predicts 'con trágica adivinación, el mito del robot' (p. 206), appears to complement the narrator's description of the alienated labour he endures in the metropolis at the opening of the novel. Yet the repetition of this story also occasions dramatic irony. The narrator relates the myth of the 'amenaza de la máquina', and man's downfall at the hands of it, not long before he climbs into a helicopter which takes him back to the city and his life as a mechanized 'Hombre-Avispa' (p. 13). The *Popol Vuh* plays an important role in *Los pasos perdidos*, and it is interesting that its inclusion in Carpentier's novel came at a time when the myth was undergoing something of a renaissance, having provided the unifying principle for Miguel Angel Asturias's 1949 *Hombres de maíz*.[52] *Los pasos perdidos* shares the neo-indigenous impulses of Asturias's novel, and the sacred Mayan story seems to have been included for its ironic and metatextual undertones. It can be no coincidence in a novel so concerned with textual production and authority that the narrator should refer to a myth which was translated into Spanish in the seventeenth century from an indigenous manuscript, now missing, and which has undergone numerous translations ever since. The *Popul Vuh* is also, like the narrator's travelogue, a deeply reflexive text, as can be seen from the ending of Chapter 7, the episode in which Zipacna kills the Four Hundred Boys:

> Such was the death of those Four Hundred Boys. And it used to be said that they entered a constellation, named Hundrath after them, though perhaps this is just a play on words.[53]

In this episode the *Popul Vuh* warns us not to believe everything we read. References to this book in *Los pasos perdidos* therefore provide an internal commentary on the connections between myth (etymologically from Greek *muthos,* or fable) and fiction more generally – and particularly on the self-mythologizing novel being produced by the narrator.

Amerindian myths in the *novela de la selva* do not just embody an ironic counterpoint to the narrators' interpretations of the novelistic action. On several occasions they supersede Western modes of thinking and writing as the 'norm', such as when the urban travellers resort to mythology in order to communicate with the Amerindians. This happens in *Green Mansions* when Abel explains his long absence from the tribe by fabricating a story which accords with conventional Amerindian mythical and oral structures, abandoning his usual florid prose in favour of a simpler (and much more appealing) storytelling technique:

> In my own country, a hundred days from here, I was the son of a great chief, who had much gold, and when he died it was all mine, and I was rich. But I had an enemy, one worse than Managa, for he was rich and had many people. And in a war his people overcame mine, and he took my gold, and all I possessed, making me poor. (p. 168)

Likewise, in spite of the verbose tendencies of his travelogue, in the jungle Carpentier's narrator aspires to compose 'una suerte de cantata', 'un poema muy simple, hecho de vocablos de uso corriente, sustantivos como *hombre, mujer, casa, agua, nube, árbol,* y otros que por su elocuencia primordial no necesitaran del adjetivo' (p. 217) – in short, a sort of pared-down creation myth, after the *Popul Vuh.* In *La vorágine* Pipa – a white man who has 'gone native' in the forest – exemplifies Amerindian views of natural animism when he takes a hallucinogenic potion and sees 'procesiones de caimanes y de tortugas, pantanos llenos de gente, flores que daban gritos' (p. 213). On another occasion Cova participates, albeit mistakenly, in a totemic ritual.[54] When he arrives at an Amerindian village, Cova starts plucking a duck that he had been carrying in his knapsack, thus offending the Amerindians' belief that one's soul resides 'en distintos animales' (p. 207), and causing the village chief to think that he is dying. When Cova is informed of his misdemeanour by an interpreter he releases another duck, and describes how 'al verlo, el indio quedóse en éxtasis ante el milagro y siguió los zig-zags del vuelo sobre la plenitud del inmediato río' (p. 207). As such, the mythical and the quotidian are integrated in *La vorágine.* The forest ceases to be merely a topographical space, but is invested with supernatural qualities, giving an added twist to the novel's final line: '¡Los devoró la selva!' (p. 385).

If, in Amerindian culture, myth is a tool for comprehending the illogical and often contradictory nature of everyday life, then the protagonists of the *novela de la selva* can also be seen to appeal to their own myths, as when Cova blames his ill-fortune on fate, or the narrator of *Los pasos perdidos* interprets the females around him as if they were the dramatis personae of a Greek epic. Myth plays a particularly prominent role in Carpentier's novel, yet despite the narrator's frequent references to myths, he consistently misinterprets them.[55] When Rosario is reading the *Historia de Genoveva de Brabante,* for example, the narrator attempts to dispel her anxiety about the misfortunes of the heroine with the throwaway comment, 'Son cuentos de otros tiempos' (p. 103). Although Rosario's response seems naïve, 'Lo que los libros dicen es verdad' (p. 13), she shows a more developed understanding of myth than the narrator. Myths, always 'cuentos de otros tiempos' (hence the fairytale platitude, 'Once upon a time'), do, as Lévi-Strauss maintains, embody certain timeless truths about society: 'a myth always refers to events alleged to have taken place long ago. But what gives the myth an operational value is that the specific pattern described is timeless; it explains the present and the past as well as the future.'[56]

The indigenous myths included in *Los pasos perdidos* and in the *novela de la selva* as a whole often contradict the narrator's interpretation of his experiences in the forest, thus providing an alternative hermeneutic key to the novelistic action. Within a broader literary-historical context, the interest in Amerindian myth in the *novela de la selva*, and particularly the recourse to indigenous source material such as the *Popol Vuh* or *Chilam Balam*, correspond to a growing interest in indigenous American culture among Spanish-American authors. The repetition of indigenous stories and myths and the use of mythical structures in the *novela de la selva*, far from marking the straightforward continuity between these jungle novels and European ethnography, as some critics have suggested, marks an aesthetic shift towards indigenous American narrative patterns. The decentring of European narrative conventions in the *novela de la selva* is also achieved by the inclusion of indigenous words in these novels – the subject of the final section of this chapter.

Language as Cultural Difference

If, as Ngugi wa Thiong'o has claimed, 'language as culture is the collective memory bank of a people's experience in history', then the obliteration of native speech in colonial culture precedes cultural amnesia, and occasions the great colonial fallacy of the tabula rasa.[57] Many postcolonial writers have recorded the feelings of alienation precipitated by their education in a 'foreign' language and culture – the cerebral syncopation of writing about how 'the snow was falling on the playing fields of Shropshire' in the sticky Caribbean.[58] Of all the authors of the *novela de la selva*, it is Carpentier who has been most explicit about the importance of language for the postcolonial writer. He argues that the Spanish brought to South America by the conquistadors was transformed by Amerindians and African slaves, who appropriated 'sus acentos, sus inflexiones, sus sintaxis, su forma de concebir la función de la palabra dentro de modos de expresión que no eran necesariamente los de los conquistadores'.[59] Thus, the Spanish in current usage in Latin America has been appropriated and transformed to produce a language that is 'muchísimo más rico, más flexible que el de España'.[60]

Questions of linguistic essentialism are recurrent in the *novela de la selva*. To what extent can a culture be expressed in a language that is not its own? Can we truly gain access to Amerindian culture without understanding native languages? In *Canaima* the immersion of the Conde Giaffaro and Marcos Vargas in the jungle is signalled by their acquiring the sound patterns of Amerindian speech. Likewise, in *Los pasos perdidos* the narrator's lack of empathy for the tribes he meets in the forest is evidenced by the absence of native words in the novel – an absence which is conspicuous given the inclusion of English, Latin, German, and French in the novel, and the widespread use of glossed foreign words in Carpentier's *Ecué-Yamba-O* and *El reino de este mundo*, for example. In *Green Mansions* Abel laments his inability to comprehend his lover Rima, who is the last speaker of an extinct language:

> from her lips came a succession of those mysterious sounds which had first attracted me to her, swift and low and bird-like [...]. Ah, what feeling and fancies, what quaint turns of expression, unfamiliar to my mind, were contained in those sweet, wasted symbols! I could never know – never come to her when she called, or respond to her spirit. (p. 72)

Although they communicate in 'Spanish', Rima insists that this is 'not speaking' (p. 119). In the novel, words cease to be just a means of communication. They are carriers of culture and, in the case of Rima, a way of nurturing, rather than dispelling, unknowability.[61] The fact that the dialogue between Rima and Abel – which purports to be in Spanish – is written in English adds one more layer to the multiple decodings the reader is forced to make in the novel. It is noteworthy that Hudson does include a few Spanish expressions in *Green Mansions*, such as a song and the epitaph on Rima's urn. Likewise, when searching for an adjective to describe Rima's appearance Abel comes up with '*waspish*', only to reject it for '*avispada*' – 'literally the same word in Spanish, not having precisely the same meaning nor ever applied contemptuously' (p. 51). Hudson was caught up in his own dilemma over language, as Jason Wilson has discussed.[62] Although his literary output was in English he was bilingual and, notably, continued to use Spanish to communicate with his sister back in Argentina after he moved to England. It is no coincidence, Wilson argues, that given Hudson's associations of Spanish with emotion and spirituality, the name of the novel's fairylike heroine should be Rima – Spanish for 'rhyme'.[63]

Given the importance of language to identity, it is little wonder that the narrators of the *novela de la selva* frequently resort to Amerindian words when describing indigenous tribes or the unfamiliar jungle topography. In *Green Mansions* Abel refers to a 'zabatana' (p. 28) (a blowgun), a 'Curupitá' (p. 31) (an Amazonian forest demon), and a 'queyou' (p. 47) (an apron made from bark or seeds) – to give just some examples – without providing a translation for the reader. *Canaima* is replete with Amerindian words, including one that has not yet been identified.[64] They appear frequently throughout the novel, especially after Marcos has entered the forest, and are sometimes followed by an internal gloss. As part of Marcos's introduction into tribal life, for example, an Amerindian tries to teach him 'el acaribisi, su lengua cadenciosa': 'la vereda, la escopeta y el cuchillo: azarú, sarají, aracabusa y mariyá – le refirió que un día tuna y apoc – el agua y el fuego, la lluvia y eu [sic] rayo – destruyeron su churuata y mataron a baruchí, que significa hermana' (p. 155). Amerindian and Spanish words are juxtaposed with startling frequency in this section, with translations for the Spanish reader. Nevertheless, it is significant that one of the apparent nativisms in the quotation above – 'aracabusa', which is a type of gun – derives from Spanish or Portuguese, an etymology which suggests the interpenetrability of the two linguistic and cultural spheres.[65]

La vorágine, which is likewise replete with indigenous words, is the only *novela de la selva* to contain an internal glossary. This appendix was first introduced in the fifth edition in 1928 and prior to that specialist and indigenous words were italicized in the text. While the motives for the introduction of this glossary are uncertain, it is probable that it was included to make the text more accessible for readers outside Colombia. Carpentier has discussed how the monolingual appendix aided his reading of Rivera's novel:

> Tuve que acudir [...] al glosario, como se acude a un diccionario. Aquel idioma usado por José Eustasio Rivera era algo singular, por no decir bárbaro. Auténtico, sí. Exacto, sí. Pero localista, harto localista, y por lo mismo, digamos la palabra, exótico.[66]

These built-in lexicons are a common feature of the *novela de la selva*, as they are in postcolonial literature more generally. Although glossaries are evocative of the travel writing tradition, they serve a very different purpose in these post-independence texts, where they often occasion a feeling of semantic dislocation, thereby stressing the lack of transparency between the imperial language and the colonized space. The need for a monolingual appendix in *La vorágine* – despite the fact that the novel is written in Castilian – stresses the hermeticism of the tropical environment. The unglossed words and phrases in the novel, what have been called 'metonymic gaps' in postcolonial studies, destabilize the dominant language and synecdochically come to represent native culture, at the same time highlighting the lacunae in the reader's knowledge.[67] This is also the effect of the orthographic reproduction of the colloquialisms of the *llaneros* or *caucheros* in *La vorágine* and *Canaima*, the inclusion of which stresses the rich diversity of regional cultures throughout South America. The proliferation of dialogue in these novels not only heightens the sense of immediacy but also, via the use of provincialisms, embodies an affirmation of regional identity, which was so important in Spanish-American literature in the 1920s and 30s.[68]

The inclusion of indigenous words and regional expressions in the *novela de la selva* can be attributed to the novels' wider strategy of defamiliarization. Bill Ashcroft has argued that such moments of inaccessibility in the postcolonial text disrupt 'notions of "infinite transmissibility" to protect [...] difference from the incorporating universalism of the centre'.[69] They also destabilize the idea of the novel as being an inherently metropolitan form. The primacy of voices of the rural poor or of Amerindians in the *novela de la selva* prefigures the later popularity of testimonial literature throughout Central and South America.

In the *novela de la selva* the reader's total comprehension of Amerindian culture, like the narrators', is consistently stymied by unfamiliar vocabulary and unknown cultural practices. In *Canaima* the narrator describes how, when their working day was over, the Amerindians would withdraw into the forest, 'y allí, silenciosos y taciturnos o apenas cambiando entre sí breves frases, pasábanse las horas sentados uno al lado del otro' (pp. 155–56). Abel in *Green Mansions* also laments the 'sullen silence' (p. 167) of the tribe. Silence and unknowability – two tropes of colonial discourse – here function counter-intuitively. The indigenous tribes remain hermetic, despite all of the narrators' efforts to reduce them to a series of colonial stereotypes.

Even though indigenous words were commonly included in European descriptions of Amerindians, from the early colonial accounts of ethnographers such as Fray Ramón Pané to nineteenth- and twentieth-century adventure fiction, their presence in the *novela de la selva* is, paradoxically, one of the principal ways in which indigenous culture evades representation. The inclusion of indigenous words in the *novela de la selva* often gives rise to a sense of dislocation, forcing the reader to turn either to an appended lexicon or to accept a hiatus in his or her comprehension of the text. This, as Sommer has observed, is a feature of 'particularist fictions', in which a 'variety of rhetorical moves can hold readers at arm's length [...] in order to propose something different from knowledge. Philosophers have called it acknowledgement. Others call it respect'.[70] In the case of the *novela de la selva* the lack of complete textual penetrability disturbs not only the reading process but also, and more significantly, the writing process of the first-person narrators. Their inclusion of native words draws attention to the difference of indigenous culture and its refusal to be neatly translated into another cultural paradigm.

★ ★ ★

Clifford Geertz has argued that the credibility of ethnographers is dependent upon their ability to impress upon the reader their reliability as witness:

> Ethnographers need to convince us [...] not merely that they themselves have truly 'been there', but [...] that had we been there we should have seen what they saw, felt what they felt, concluded what they concluded.[71]

The aspiring ethnographies of the protagonists of the *novela de la selva* achieve quite the opposite. Their recourse to stale racial stereotypes, often flagrantly literary, not only severs the bond of complicity between narrator and reader but also suggests that the former had not 'been there' at all. The dynamics of representation – in this instance those governing the inscription of the racial Other – are once again seen to be of central concern to the authors of the *novela de la selva*. As is the case with topographical descriptions of the tropics, ethnography is revealed in these novels as a discipline deeply implicated in the preservation of imperial categories such as Self and Other or Them and Us. Nevertheless, the desire for textual mastery on the part of the narrators is constantly thwarted by the object of representation, the Amerindian, who, like the jungle in which he or she resides either evades the gaze of the outsider or implacably returns it. Such a strategy corresponds to Stanley Diamond's definition of anthropology as 'the study of men in crisis by men in crisis', which identifies the Self rather than the Other as the hidden subject of anthropology.[72] It is this repressed subject – the crisis of the urban traveller both inside and outside the boundaries of civilization – which will be explored in the final two chapters of this book.

Notes

1 Henri Baudet, *Paradise on Earth: Some Thoughts on European Images of Non-European Man*, trans. Elizabeth Wentholt (New Haven: Yale University Press, 1965), has argued that European views of the 'primitive' function around a 'fundamental ambivalence' (p. 5).

2 For a classic discussion of this debate see Lewis Hanke, *Aristotle and the American Indians: A Study in Race Prejudice in the Modern World* (London: Hollis & Carter, 1959).

3 Colón, *Textos y documentos completos*, p. 30.

4 For a discussion of the iconography of the Amerindian in Jean de Léry, Hans Burgkmair, and others see, William C. Sturtevant, 'First Visual Images of Native America', in Fredi Chiappelli (ed.), *First Images of America: The Impact of the New World on the Old*, 2 vols (Berkeley: University of California Press, 1976), I, pp. 417–54.

5 Todorov, *Conquest of America*, p. 42.

6 See René Prieto, 'The Literature of *Indigenismo*', in González Echevarría and Pupo-Walker (eds.), *Cambridge History of Latin American Literature*, II, pp. 138–63 (p. 140).

7 Carmelo Virgillo, 'Primitivism in Latin American Fiction', in A. Owen Aldridge (ed.), *The Ibero-American Enlightenment* (Urbana, IL: University of Illinois Press, 1971), pp. 243–55 (p. 247).

8 Robert F. Berkhofer, *The White Man's Indian: Images of the American Indian from Columbus to the Present* (New York: Knopf, 1978), p. 3.

9 Mario Vargas Llosa, *La utopía arcaica: José María Arguedas y las ficciones del indigenismo* (México: Fondo de Cultura Económica, 1996), p. 60.

10 See, for instance, Neale-Silva, *Horizonte humano*, pp. 232–60, for an account of Rivera's first-hand encounter with Amazonian tribes when he travelled to the south-east of Colombia as part of a delegation to establish the border between Colombia and Venezuela.

11 José Carlos Mariátegui, *Siete ensayos de la interpretación de la realidad peruana* (Lima: Empresa Editora Amauta, 1965), p. 292.

12 Linda Hutcheon, *A Poetics of Postmodernism: History, Theory, Fiction* (London: Routledge, 1988), p. 230.

13 Jorge Marcone, 'Jungle Fever: Primitivism in Environmentalism; Rómulo Gallegos's *Canaima* and the Romance of the Jungle', in Erik Camayd-Freixas and José Eduardo González (eds.), *Primitivism and Identity in Latin America: Essays on Art, Literature, and Culture* (Tucson: University of Arizona Press, 2000), pp. 157–72 (p. 157).

14 Frantz Fanon, *Black Skin, White Masks* [1952], trans. Charles Lam Markmann (London: Pluto Press, 1986), p. 192.

15 Discussing Lacan's theory of the 'Mirror Stage' in *Black Skin*, Fanon notes: 'the real Other for the white man is and will continue to be the black man. And conversely. Only for the white man The Other is perceived on the level of the body image, absolutely as the not-self – that is, the unidentifiable, the unassimilable' (p. 161).

16 Fanon, *Black Skin*, p. 157.

17 Frantz Fanon, *The Wretched of the Earth* [1961], trans. Constance Farrington (London: Penguin, 2001), p. 33.

18 Spurr, *Rhetoric of Empire*, p. 78.

19 Julia Kristeva, *Powers of Horror: An Essay on Abjection*, trans. Leon S. Roudiez (New York: Columbia University Press, 1982), p. 2.

20 John Block Friedman, *The Monstrous Races in Medieval Art and Thought* (Cambridge, MA: Harvard University Press, 1981), p. 27.

21 This description is by the Dominican friar Tomás Ortiz, and is cited in Todorov, *Conquest of America*, p. 151. This is mirrored by, for example, the description of a Jesuit who related how the Xixime of northern Mexico gorged themselves 'from dawn until dusk [...] without a qualm, rats, snakes, locusts and worms', cited in Anthony Pagden, *The Fall of Natural Man: The American Indian and the Origins of Comparative Ethnology* (Cambridge: Cambridge University Press, 1982), p. 87.

22 Jonathan Swift, *Gulliver's Travels* [1726] (London: Penguin, 1994), p. 294. It is noteworthy that this ironic recourse to *Gulliver's Travels* is repeated by Jorge Luis Borges in his story 'El informe de Brodie'.

23 Pagden, *Fall of Natural Man*, p. 87.

24 See Claude Rawson, '"Indians" and Irish: Montaigne, Swift, and the Cannibal Question', *Modern Language Quarterly*, 53 (1992), pp. 299–363 (p. 308).

25 Peter Hulme, *Colonial Encounters: Europe and the Native Caribbean 1492–1797* (London: Routledge, 1992), p. 14.

26 Gareth Griffiths, 'The Myth of Authenticity: Representation, Discourse and Social Practice', in Chris Tiffin and Alan Lawson (eds.), *De-Scribing Empire: Post-Colonialism and Textuality* (London: Routledge, 1994), pp. 70–85 (p. 71).

27 Roger Célestin, *From Cannibals to Radicals: Figures and Limits of Exoticism* (Minneapolis: University of Minnesota Press, 1996), p. 12.

28 Marianna Torgovnick, *Gone Primitive: Savage Intellects, Modern Lives* (Chicago: University of Chicago Press, 1990), p. 82. See also Sally Price, *Primitive Art in Civilized Places* (Chicago: University of Chicago Press, 1989).

29 For example, Aristotle said that all trees were potentially chairs, an idea which regained popularity in the early modern period given the resurrection of Aristotelian ideas at this time. See Anthony Pagden, 'Shifting Antinomies: European Representations of the American Indian since Columbus', in Deborah L. Madsen (ed.), *Visions of America Since 1492* (London: Leicester University Press, 1994), pp. 23–34 (p. 23).

30 Pagden, *European Encounters*, has discussed this trope, p. 152.

31 Jean Jacques Rousseau, 'Discourse on the Origin and Foundations of Inequality Among Men or Second Discourse', in *The Discourses and Other Early Political Writings*, ed. and trans. Victor Gourevitch (Cambridge: Cambridge University Press, 2003), p. 111–222 (p. 143).

32 Johannes Fabian, *Time and the Other: How Anthropology Makes its Object* (New York: Columbia University Press, 1983), p. 63.

33 Ian Duncan, 'Introduction', in W. H. Hudson, *Green Mansions*, ed. Ian Duncan (Oxford: Oxford University Press, 1998), pp. vii–xxiii (p. xviii).

34 The connections between travel writing and ethnography are discussed in Joan-Pau Rubiés, 'Travel Writing and Ethnography', in Hulme and Youngs (eds.), *Cambridge Companion to Travel Writing*, pp. 242–60.

35 Potelet, 'Novela del Indio Caribe', has discussed the development of anthropology in Venezuela in the late nineteenth century, including how Gaspar Marcano, who is considered to have been the first anthropologist in Venezuela, reconstructed the cultures of the Amerindians of the middle Orinoco through archaeological evidence and 'una revisión de los cronistas' (p. 377).

36 Talal Asad, 'Introduction', in Talal Asad (ed.), *Anthropology and the Colonial Encounter* (London: Ithaca Press, 1973), pp. 9–19 (p. 17).

37 Clifford, 'Partial Truths', p. 9.

38 Bill Ashcroft, Gareth Griffiths and Helen Tiffin, *Key Concepts in Post-Colonial Studies* (London: Routledge, 1998), p. 96.

39 Clifford, 'Partial Truths', p. 9.

40 Beardsell, *Returning the Gaze*, p. 39.

41 Stephen Greenblatt, 'Learning to Curse: Aspects of Linguistic Colonialism in the Sixteenth Century', in Chiappelli, *First Images of America*, I, pp. 561–86.

42 This trope began with Columbus's description of the Native Americans swapping gold for trinkets. It is repeated numerous times in the *novela de la selva*, including, for example, by Cova in *La vorágine*, who describes how the Amerindians he meets in the jungle exchange their valuable goods for 'baratijas que valían mil veces menos' (p. 203).

43 Humboldt, *Personal Narrative*, p. 122.

44 Honour, *New Golden Land*, has discussed how, in the sixteenth century, Amerindians were routinely brought to Europe and paraded in front of royalty. When Henri II went to Rouen on a state visit in 1550, for example, a Brazilian jungle village was built 'on the banks of the Seine where some fifty natives were to be seen dancing, fighting, shooting at birds with bows and arrows, climbing trees, and paddling canoes' (p. 63). For further discussion of the exhibition of indigenous people in Europe, see, for instance, Alden T. Vaughan, *Transatlantic Encounters: American Indians in Britain, 1500–1776* (Cambridge: Cambridge University Press, 2006); Roselyn Poignant, *Professional Savages: Captive Lives and Western Spectacle* (New Haven: Yale University Press, 2004); Peter H. Hoffenberg, *An Empire on Display: English, Indian, and Australian Exhibitions from the Crystal Palace to the Great War* (Berkeley: University of California Press, 2001).

45 Célestin, *From Cannibals to Radicals*, p. 7.

46 This echoes a comment made by Carpentier, cited in Chao, *Conversaciones*: 'Este hombre civilizado, que es incapaz de encender una hoguera, de cazar un pájaro o de pescar un pez, si lo soltaran en medio de la selva con un arco o con una cerbatana sería víctima de los animales o moriría de hambre' (p. 159).

47 Claude Lévi-Strauss, 'The Structural Study of Myth', in *Structural Anthropology*, trans. Claire Jacobson and Brooke Grundfest Schoepf (London: Allen Lane, 1968), pp. 206–31 (p. 210).

48 For a discussion of indigenous cosmogonies in *Los pasos perdidos*, see Gordon Brotherston, 'The Latin American Novel and its Indigenous Sources', in John King (ed.), *Modern Latin American Fiction: A Survey* (London: Faber and Faber, 1987), pp. 60–77 (p. 72–73); Gordon Brotherston, 'Pacaraima as Destination in Carpentier's *Los pasos perdidos*', *Indiana Journal of Hispanic Literatures* 1. 2 (1993), pp. 161–180; Sá, *Rain Forest Literatures*, pp. 76–88.

49 Lévi-Strauss, *Structural Anthropology*, has discussed the 'astounding similarity between myths collected in widely different regions' (p. 208). Carpentier wrote at least two articles on Lévi-Strauss: 'Luz del Páramo irá a Venecia en Junio', *El Nacional*, April 18, 1952, p. 12, and 'El Kodachrome y la etnografía', *El Nacional*, October 30, 1956, p. 12. González Echevarría, *Alejo Carpentier*, p. 176, has discussed Carpentier's interest in Lévi-Strauss, and Eduardo G. González, 'El tiempo del hombre: huella y labor de origen en cuatro obras de Alejo Carpentier' (unpublished doctoral thesis, Indiana University, 1974), has traced some of the parallels between *Los pasos perdidos* and *Tristes Tropiques*.

50 Indeed, Sá, *Rain Forest Literatures*, has argued that the indigenous concept of 'canaima' gives coherence to the narrative as a whole. In a survey of anthropological accounts defining 'canaima' (also spelled 'kanaima'), she concludes that the term usually has

negative associations related to death and retaliation and is 'especially used to define the relationship between invaders and invaded'. In this way, she argues, the concept of 'canaima' links 'the social narrative to the psychological quest of the protagonist' (p. 76).

51 Theodor Adorno and Max Horkheimer, *Dialectic of Enlightenment* [1944], trans. John Cumming (London: Verso, 1997), p. 27.

52 See Chapter 2 of René Prieto, *Miguel Angel Asturias's Archaeology of Return* (Cambridge: Cambridge University Press, 1993), pp. 85–160.

53 Denis Tedlock (trans.), *Popol Vuh: The Mayan book of the Dawn of Life*, rev. edn (New York: Simon & Schuster, 1996), pp. 83–84.

54 Erik Camayd-Freixas, 'Narrative Primitivism: Theory and Practice in Latin America', in Camayd-Freixas and González (eds.), *Primitivism and Identity*, pp. 109–34, has described anthropomorphism and zoomorphism as the 'main conceptual elements of primitivist expression' (p. 119).

55 An obvious example is when Yannes, the Greek miner whose penchant for epic adventure is fulfilled vicariously by his reading of *The Odyssey*, is ironically the one to tell the narrator that Rosario is not the epic heroine he imagines when she takes a new lover during the narrator's brief absence from the jungle: 'Ella no Penélope' (p. 277).

56 Lévi-Strauss, *Structural Anthropology*, p. 209.

57 Ngugi wa Thiong'o, *Decolonising the Mind: The Politics of Language in African Literature* (London: Currey, 1986), p. 15.

58 Edward Kamau Brathwaite, *History of the Voice: The Development of Nation Language in Anglophone Caribbean Poetry* (London: New Beacon Books, 1984), p. 9.

59 Chao, *Conversaciones*, p. 27.

60 Chao, *Conversaciones*, p. 27.

61 George Steiner, *After Babel: Aspects of Language and Translation* (London: Oxford University Press, 1975), has said that 'languages conceal and internalize more, perhaps, than they convey outwardly' (p. 32).

62 Jason Wilson, *W. H. Hudson: The Colonial's Revenge* (London: University of London Institute of Latin American Studies, 1981).

63 Wilson, *Colonial's Revenge*, p. 10.

64 The word 'mariyá'. This is the only untranslated indigenous word in the glossary of Charles Minguet's 1991 edition of *Canaima*.

65 See the note in Minguet (ed.), *Canaima* [1996]: 'Aracabusa, o *Arakabusa*, s. *Arcabuz*, escopeta quaiquera. Etimología: del español o portugués' (p. 256).

66 Chao, *Conversaciones*, pp. 30–31.

67 Ashcroft, *Key Concepts*, pp. 137–38.

68 See Vicky Unruh, *Latin American Vanguards: The Art of Contentious Encounters* (Berkeley: University of California Press, 1994). She has described how the search for regional identities accelerated in the first decades of the eighteenth century under calls of 'Peruanicemos al Perú' or 'Abrasileirar o Brasil' (p. 128).

69 Bill Ashcroft, 'Constitutive Graphonomy: A Post-Colonial Theory of Literary Writing', *Kunapipi*, 11.1 (1989), pp. 58–73 (p. 72).

70 Sommer, *Proceed with Caution*, p. xi.

71 Clifford Geertz, *Works and Lives: The Anthropologist as Author* (Cambridge: Polity, 1988), p. 16.

72 Stanley Diamond, *In Search of the Primitive: A Critique of Civilization* (New Brunswick: Transaction Books, 1974), p. 93.

CHAPTER FOUR

Paradise Lost:
Wilderness and the Limits of Western Escapism

Nature is thoroughly mediate. It is made to serve. It receives the dominion of
a man as meekly as the ass on which the Saviour rode. It offers all its kingdoms
to man as the raw material which he may mould into what is useful.

Ralph Waldo Emerson, 'Nature'[1]

While chapters 2 and 3 have explored the *novela de la selva*'s engagement
with colonial tropes relating to tropical landscape aesthetics and Amerindian culture, this chapter will address how the genre engages with idealized
notions of 'going primitive' in the jungle in order to debunk the commodification of wild nature in European literature, particularly in Romanticism and
colonial adventure novels. Throughout the *novela de la selva* the urban travellers' meditations on the jungle are often predicated less on experience than on
literary antecedent and are infused with neocolonial views of wild nature as a
space in which to escape from urban conventions. In these novels the jungle
exercises on travellers what the anthropologist Renato Rosaldo has termed
'imperialist nostalgia'.[2] Almost without exception, the narrators allude to
previous adventurers in the wilds of North or South America, and often truss
up their own experiences in the rainforest in an antiquated, heroic style. Far
from being assimilated into native tribes during their travels in the jungle, the
protagonists of the *novela de la selva* almost always remain outsiders, consistently poeticizing their surroundings and self-styling as Romantic heroes or
intrepid explorers.

The idealization of primitive life in these texts lightly veils a consciousness
of the Hobbesian reality of the jungle as a milieu where life is 'nasty, brutish,
and short' – a fact which becomes self-evident when the narrators finally
succumb to the horrors of the wilderness.[3] As this chapter will explore, the
thwarting of the urban travellers' aspirations for immersion in spiritual truths
and adventure in the South American tropics destabilizes European narratives of primitivism and presents the tropical forest not as a commodity for
urban self-actualization, but as a menacing and potentially deadly, postcolonial space.

Inventing the Wilderness

In order to understand how the *novela de la selva* parodies literary constructions of wild nature as a source of unexploited riches, poetic inspiration,
or uncurbed masculine adventure, it will be useful to consider some of the
changing views of wilderness – particularly of the American wilderness
– within a Western literary tradition. One of the most dominant views of
American nature, especially during the colonial period, was its potential to be
exploited. This is a view which persists up to the present day in many parts
of the Amazon, for example, where the extraction of petroleum or the introduction of cattle ranches has led to the destruction of vast swathes of forest.
The exploitation of the rainforest, and of its indigenous population, is a major
concern in *La vorágine*, which records with marked historical accuracy the
period of the rubber boom in the Putumayo. In his description of the depleted
forests of Amazonia, Rivera displays a nascent ecological awareness:

> los caucheros que hay en Colombia destruyen anualmente millones de árboles.
> En los territorios de Venezuela el balatá desapareció. De este suerte ejercecen el
> fraude contra las generaciones del porvenir. (p. 298)

In general, however, the *novela de la selva* is interested in exploring less
obvious forms of exploitation, such as the way in which, within the tradition
of European travel writing on the tropics, the jungle is reduced to a kind of
tropological commodity, esteemed by travellers as a purveyor of exotic experience, adventure, or 'authenticity'.

From the earliest accounts of the New World, the Americas were viewed as
a space for the realization of European aspirations. Ovid's presentation of the
Golden Age of man as an eternal spring in which nature flourished untended,
streams ran with milk, and man lived in harmony with his fellow man seems
to have been the inspiration for many of Columbus's observations on the
New World.[4] His journals are characterized by unbounded enthusiasm for
the indigenous people and the landscape, although his remarks about both
are often related to questions of usefulness and profit. The Edenic thrust of
Columbus's narrative culminates in his conviction that he had discovered
earthly paradise at 'el fin del Oriente' – a belief which attempted to eschew
pre-Columbian history and culture, and to insert the Other into a familiar
discourse of Christianity.[5] The prelapsarian associations of the American
wilderness remained strong over the coming centuries. It is not an accident
that the growth of Utopian literature in early modern Europe coincided
with an era of transatlantic travel and the broadening of cultural horizons.
The discovery of peoples on the cusp of civilization, enjoying the primordial
pleasures of Adam and Eve, aroused feelings of nostalgia and cultural rejection throughout Europe. Many travellers to America expressed the feeling that
they had been transported back to a golden age, or to the very beginning of
time, a trope of travel literature from Joseph-Marie Degerando's *Considérations
sur les diverses méthodes à suivre dans l'observation des peuples sauvages* [1800] to
Los pasos perdidos. Indeed, there were even attempts to establish colonies in the

New World after the precepts of Thomas More's *Utopia*.[6] Escaping one's own age, ravaged by war and famine, no longer necessitated time travel, but a step westwards to the Americas.

To the early settlers of the colonial era, American nature soon ceased to be regarded as paradisiacal and came to be viewed as a challenge, both physically and conceptually, saturated with symbolic reverberations of uncurbed sexuality and the very real threats of lurking beasts and Native Americans. In his account of his travels in the American tropics Cabeza de Vaca personified the landscape as 'un enemigo frente al cual no es posible defenderse'.[7] Similarly, in North American pioneering writing, wild nature was seen as the nemesis of civilization and progress. These negative connotations were replaced in the eighteenth century by a Romantic veneration of wild nature, particularly forests. The writings of Burke and Kant on the sublime and Rousseau's formulation of 'natural man' led to the reevaluation of wilderness, which was increasingly associated with aesthetic pleasure and enhanced self-knowledge. In Book 8 of his *Confessions* Rousseau describes a trip he takes from Paris to the woods of Saint-Germain, where he spent his time 'wandering deep in the forest' and 'sought and [...] found the vision of [...] primitive times'.[8] Forests, even in Europe, provided a window onto a prelapsarian world where humans were happy and free. In the late eighteenth century the American poet Philip Freneau published a number of poems on the subject of wild nature and, in a series of essays entitled 'The Philosopher of the Forest' (1781–82), contrasted corrupt urban existence with the wholesome life of the woods. The North American Transcendentalists likewise lauded wilderness as a site of spiritual rebirth. 'I went to the woods because I wished to live deliberately', Henry David Thoreau wrote in *Walden*, his autobiographical account of a period spent living in a forest hut near Concord.[9] In Emerson's 'Nature' the forest is regarded as a space of rationality, where man finds something 'more dear and connate than in streets or villages', adumbrating modernism's yearning to unearth primal nature below the loamy underlay of the city.[10] In contrast to the puritanical belief that wild nature would promote moral decay, the Transcendentalists followed philosophers like Rousseau in their faith that the innate beneficence of humanity could be released by a spell in the forest.

In the nineteenth century wilderness continued to be coveted, this time as the source of that peculiar 'American Mind', which was an important feature of the heroes of the popular Wild West novel. Contrary to Romantic notions of nature as a calming influence, it was believed that the American frontier produced aggressive, hardy men capable of defeating wild animals with their bare hands.[11] The enduring popularity of scouting, hunting, and fishing in the United States are throwbacks to the early years of colonization, when nature was viewed as a space for the distillation of masculine values. The connections between wild nature and masculinity were further consolidated in the late nineteenth and early twentieth centuries in the imperial romance, a genre which tirelessly replayed a basic formula of a white man's violent conquest of wild nature, near brush with death and/or primitivism, and subsequent return to a newly invigorated civilization.

The changing representation of the American wilderness in travel writing from the early modern period to the twentieth century, when the *novela de la selva* emerged, reveals that it is often viewed as a space for the correction of urban and European values. Porter has observed that travel writing 'reminds us [...] of how dissatisfied most people are much of the time'.[12] From the first days of conquest the American landscape was credited with values lacking back home. For the war-torn early modern period, America was seen as a place of peace and innocence; in response to the eighteenth-century doctrine of rationalism and logic, the wilderness was thought to be a source of spiritual truths; in the nineteenth century, wild nature became a site of the adventure sadly lacking in the industrial city. Roderick Nash has observed that, in the case of North America, '[a]ppreciation of wilderness began in the cities'.[13] The fact that modernity's esteem for wild nature increased in tandem with its destruction of it corresponds with Rosaldo's schema of 'imperialist nostalgia', which he defines as operating 'around a paradox':

> A person kills somebody, then mourns the victim. [...] people destroy their environment, and then they worship nature. In any of its versions, imperialist nostalgia uses a pose of 'innocent yearning' both to capture people's imaginations and to conceal its complicity with often brutal domination.[14]

The writers of the *novela de la selva* recognized this paradox, inherent in European accounts of the tropics, almost a century before Rosaldo. Throughout the *novela de la selva* the jungle fulfils a similar function to the colonies in imperial literature, acting as a last bastion of escape and adventure for the urban traveller. As such, the self-posturing of the protagonists of the *novela de la selva* as Romantic poets, Noble Savages, or hardy adventurers, smacks of belatedness and often slips into parody.[15] Despite its structural and thematic complicity with occidental travel literature, the *novela de la selva* therefore emerges as 'counter' or 'meta' travel writing – a genre which demythologizes the urban traveller as an instrument of cultural imperialism and his journey through the South American tropics as a self-aggrandizing odyssey, from which he will emerge not spiritually and physically invigorated, but in a state of degeneration and terror.

Romantic Nature

In the penultimate paragraph of *Los pasos perdidos* the narrator observes mournfully: 'Hoy terminaron las vacaciones de Sísifo' (p. 279). The protagonist's comparison of his stultifying urban existence to the fruitless labours of Sisyphus reveals a man little changed in outlook from the one who set out to the jungle some time earlier. Not only is he employing the same worn classical metaphors but he seems resigned to return to a life of monotony, 'subiendo y bajando la cuesta de los días, con la misma piedra en el hombro' (p. 13). More telling, however, is his use of the noun 'vacaciones'. The notion of the narrator's stay in the jungle as a 'vacation' denotes not merely the transient nature of the trip but also its connections to leisure. Rather than being the personal quest for fulfilment that the narrator titivates it as – something to counteract his feeling of being '¡[...] vacío! ¡Vacío! ¡Vacío!' (p. 25) – his trip to the Venezuelan rainforest, itself born out of an empty promise, is revealed as something equally vacuous given the etymological derivation of 'vacación' from the Latin *vacāre*, 'to be empty'.

Carpentier's narrator is not alone in his lightly concealed estimation of the South American tropics as a quick fix to the ennui of city life – a sort of telluric anodyne to the ills of modernity. Throughout the *novela de la selva* the jungle is fashioned as a space of release from the conventions of everyday life. As I will discuss below, in *La vorágine* Cova dreams about escaping the city and settling down with his girlfriend, Alicia, in the wilds of Colombia, and in *Green Mansions* Abel renounces his previous life in Caracas, 'with its old-world vices, its idle political passions, its empty round of gaieties' (p. 87) and – as he seems conveniently to forget – his wife, in favour of the charms of wild nature. For many of the protagonists the jungle is held in direct contrast to urban living, a binary nicely captured in Carpentier's use of the terms *allá* and *acá*, according with the traditional definition of a forest as a wooded region beyond the city precincts. The idealized view of the jungle throughout the *novela de la selva* ironically engages with Romantic conceptions of nature as a fount of spiritual enlightenment, as well as Rousseau's outline of 'natural man'. The urban traveller's fetishism of the jungle as a source of 'the authentic' arguably commodifies nature in much the same way as rubber-tapping or gold-mining, perpetuating imperial motifs of the tropics as a space for European exploitation.

Romantic writing seems to be the single most important literary influence on the *novela de la selva*. In this Spanish-American tradition the protagonists often mediate their experiences in the rainforest through Romantic texts in order to mythologize their journeys (and, therefore, the products of those journeys – their travel accounts) as exemplary Romantic quests, revealing the egoism inherent in Romantic discourses of primitivism, which are often less about nature than its possible elevatory effects on the individual. One of the principal difficulties of discussing the parody of the Romantic hero in the *novela de la selva* is defining against exactly which strand of Romanticism the parody is directed. In a classic study, Enrique Anderson Imbert has defined the first Romantic Movement in Latin America as spanning the period 1825–1860, and as having particular affiliations with Byron and Chateaubriand. Second-generation Romanticism continued to pay homage to Byron and Chateaubriand, as well as to Victor Hugo, and included works such as Jorge Isaacs's novel *María* [1867] in which we can trace allusions to Rousseau and to Bernardin's *Paul and Virginia*.[16] The *novela de la selva* engages with motifs from the canonical texts of German, English, and French Romanticism (throughout there are echoes of Goethe's *Werther*, Chateaubriand's *Atala* and *René*, *Paul and Virginia*, and numerous works by Shelley, Byron, and

Wordsworth) to create a generalized parody of the Romantic exaltation of the self and of the venerated Noble Savage. The *novela de la selva* also occasionally alludes to Latin American Romanticism, especially the figure of the gaucho.

While Romantic heroes are often associated with a love of nature, genius, and an unfettered imagination, the *novela de la selva* draws the reader's attention to some of their less positive characteristics. In the late eighteenth and early nineteenth centuries the Romantic cult of the individual gave way to a wave of egotistical, self-indulgent, and hypersensitive individuals, who often approached wild nature as a pretext for protracted self-analysis. Throughout the *novela de la selva*, the protagonists' desire to go 'donde había árboles' (*Los pasos perdidos*, p. 17) is consistent with the Romantic view of forests as spaces of aesthetic stimulation and spiritual elevation. Likewise, the confessional mode of many of the novels, which purport to be first-person written or oral accounts of a journey, conform to the Romantic predilection for self-introspection in autobiographies such as Rousseau's *Confessions*.[17]

In Hudson's novel Abel's 'discovery' of the titular 'green mansions' and daily trip to them thereafter, is celebrated as a Romantic quest for aesthetic pleasure, redolent with clichés of 'sun-impregnated' (p. 24) clouds and sweetly chirping birds.[18] Several times in the novel Abel refers to his love of solitude, a staple theme of Romantic poetry and prose, and one which is at odds with Abel's craving for human contact in the woods, first among a number of Amerindian tribes, and then with Nuflo and Rima. A short spell in the forest precipitates an epiphany about the value of solitude, paradigmatic within the Romantic tradition of nature writing:

> And caring not in that solitude to disguise my feelings from myself, and from the wide heaven that looked down and saw me – for this is the sweetest thing that solitude has for us, that we are free in it, and no convention holds us – I dropped on my knees and kissed the stony ground, then casting up my eyes, thanked the Author of my being for the gift of that wild forest, those green mansions where I had found so great a happiness! (p. 41)

Abel's correlation of wilderness with freedom from convention intones a popular Romantic belief, expressed, among many, by Shelley:

> Away, away, from men and towns,
> To the wild woods and the dawns –
> To the silent wilderness
> Where the soul need not repress
> Its music.[19]

Abel's esteem for solitude is clumsily finalistic and is engendered out of his fidelity to the precepts of Romantic individualism, rather than a natural disposition to solitariness. When Abel finds himself truly alone in the forest in an 'endless desolate waste of nameless days' (p. 191) his idealized notions quickly fade and we find him talking to himself and, like that other self-styled lover of solitude in the *novela de la selva*, the narrator of *Los pasos perdidos*, 'a punto de capitular [...] para oír voces de hombres' (*Los pasos perdidos*, p. 166).

In the early sections of *Green Mansions* the jungle is also presented as a source of spiritual cleansing, consistent with the earliest definitions of travel as a pilgrimage. When Abel describes how he felt 'purified' by his spell in the tropics, he reiterates the myth of wild nature as a place of rebirth and as a baptismal font of poetry and aesthetic stimulation:

> Doubtless into the turbid tarn of my heart some sacred drops had fallen – from the passing birds, from that crimson disc which had now dropped below the horizon, the darkening hills, the rose and blue of infinite heaven, from the whole visible circle; and I felt purified and had a strange sense and apprehension of a secret innocence and spirituality in nature. (p. 16)

David Miller has noted how Hudson often employs imagery of light and darkness in the forest metaphorically, as in the passage above, exploiting their links to mysticism and spirituality.[20] Here he also draws upon Romantic religious pantheism. In this and many other sections of the novel, Abel correlates the sensation of being amid wild nature with religious experience: nature is credited animistically with the possession of arcane knowledge and God appears to be immanent in both the sunset and 'the darkening hills' – 'Himself in all, and all things in himself'.[21]

The protagonist of *La vorágine* also self-styles as a prototypical Romantic hero.[22] In the 'Fragmento de la carta' on the novel's second page, Cova portrays himself as an ill-fated poet, whose creative gifts cannot thwart his 'destino implacable' (p. 77).[23] This helplessness before fate recalls Chateaubriand's René, who, as Lilian R. Furst has argued, nurtures calamity as an integral part of the Romantic personality which 'welcomes even exceptional sorrow or dramatic misfortune if it will serve to foster the image he cherishes of himself as a creature singled out for the special attention of fate'.[24] The 'tragic' conclusion to *La vorágine* – Cova's death – could therefore be regarded as the pinnacle of his career as a Romantic hero and the fulfilment of a desire for self-annihilation. Cova's failure as a lover could also be regarded as a subconscious aspiration to follow in the path of asocial Romantic heroes such as René, who lament their inability to form relationships or to fall in love.

Cova's fantasy of moving from the city to the plains is one of many Romantic passages in the novel:

> tuve deseos de confinarme para siempre en esas llanuras fascinadoras, viviendo con Alicia en una casa risueña, que levantaría con mis propias manos a la orilla de un caño de aguas opacas, o en cualquiera de aquellas colinas minúsculas y verdes donde hay un pozo glauco al lado de una palmera. Allí de tarde se congregarían los ganados, y yo, fumando en el umbral, como un patriarca primitivo de pecho suavizado por la melancolía de los paisajes, vería las puestas de sol en el horizonte remoto donde nace la noche; [...] limitaría mis anhelos a cuidar de la zona que abarcaran mis ojos, al goce de las faenas campesinas, a mi consonancia con la soledad.
>
> ¿Para qué las ciudades? Quizá mi fuente de poesía estaba en el secreto de los bosques intactos. (p. 161)

Cova's storybook vision of himself and Alicia living in perfect harmony is, however, immediately destabilized by the fact that he has just admitted to no longer being in love with his girlfriend and of being unfaithful to her. His description of the landscape is equally myopic. His image of fertile rolling hills seems to bear little resemblance to the rough scrub land surrounding Franco's lodge and clashes with the reference to the rather unpastoral 'pozo glauco'. Cova's vision of retiring to a country retreat with his lover is typically Romantic and corresponds to at least two particular instances in European accounts of the tropics. The first is the description by the narrator of *Paul and Virginia*, who aspires to live in a 'cabin that I built in the forest at the foot of a tree, a small field cleared with my own hands and a river that flows past my own door, suffice for my needs and my pleasures'.[25] The second is Chactas's plea to the heroine of Chateaubriand's *Atala* that they 'build a hut on those shores and hide [themselves] away forever'.[26] In his *Confessions* Rousseau also describes how he longed to leave the city (Paris): 'in my disgust for that turbulent life I began to long ardently to live in the country and, seeing that my profession did not allow me to settle there, I hastened at least to spend the few hours that I had free away from the town'.[27]

In the passage above, Cova's view of the wilderness emerges as utilitarian and self-centred. Far from desiring a small field tantamount to his culinary needs, Cova's fantasy of being a wealthy landowner, proprietor of cattle and land as far as the eye can see, smoking on the porch of his house, is redolent with expansionist rhetoric and is reminiscent of North American pioneering literature. Cova's daydream also parodies the suppressed commodification of wilderness in Romantic literature via its reference to nature as a 'fuente de poesía'. The notion of wild natural spaces as a catalyst for creativity is a constant in the *novela de la selva*, from the narrator of *Los pasos perdidos* composing a threnody in the midst of the jungle to Abel's desire to write a novel in *Green Mansions*. What Cova, in common with the other narrators of the *novela de la selva*, attempts to conceal from the reader and from himself is that while nature might stimulate aesthetic production, its target audience is back in the metropolis. The narrator of *Los pasos perdidos* is explicit about this, recognizing that while the jungle might be a place of inspiration, 'la obra de arte se destina a los demás, y muy especialmente la música, que tiene los medios de alcanzar las más vastas audiencias' (p. 227). Cova's image of his life in the plains is not that of a peasant-poet, living a simple life marked by the risings and 'puestas de sol', but of a self-serving aesthete. Cova's appeal to the Romantic trope of pathetic fallacy in his aspired 'consonancia con la soledad' is another symptom of his introspection. In several passages in the novel Cova animates the jungle plants as sentient beings who communicate with him. Although, as Furst has explained, this tendency to envisage nature as a living being is a constant in German Romantics such as Novalis, it registers as belated in this twentieth-century text, augmenting the anachronistic overtones of Cova's journal and drawing attention to his desire for self-aggrandizement.[28]

Romantic individualism reaches its apogee in the *novela de la selva* in the figure of Marcos Vargas. As already discussed, Marcos's comportment during a tropical storm is typically Romantic, especially his pleasure in the sensorial assault of the wind and rain:

> Se quitó el sombrero y lo arrojó al monte, se abrió la camisa haciendo saltar los botones, ensanchó el pecho descubierto, irguió la frente, acompasó el andar a un ritmo de marcha imperiosa. Luego se descalzó y se desnudó por completo [...]. Quería encontrar la medida de sí mismo ante la Naturaleza plena. [...]
> '¿Se es o no se es?'
> El Marcos Vargas del grito alardoso ante el peligro, del corazón enardecido ante la fuerza soberana, otra vez como antes gozoso y confiado. (pp. 188–89)

The Shakespearian echoes in this episode are not insignificant given the dramatist's importance for the Romantic imagination. Marcos's fit of ire against nature in the midst of the storm cannot but recall King Lear's outburst:

> Blow, winds, and crack your cheeks! rage! blow!
> You cataracts and hurricanes, spout [...]
> Singe my white head! And thou, all-shaking thunder,
> Strike flat the thick rotundity o'th'world![29]

In *Canaima*, however, this aspiring Romantic hero tries too hard and his self-dramatization spills into parody and farce. Ripping off his clothes to experience the storm at its most abrasive, and roaring at the surrounding trees, Marcos does not elevate his experiences in the forest to the literary heights of Shakespeare or of his Romantic disciples, but produces bathos. The representation of the storm as an epic 'lucha' (p. 192) between man and the elements might have been convincing in Romantic poetry, but it registers as just another instance of mock-heroic in a text in which even the local store is called 'Los Argonautas'. The figure of hyperbole is one of the linchpins of these anti-Romantic texts. The 'wild' nature admired by the protagonists of the *novela de la selva* is often very tame indeed, as when we learn in Hudson's novel that the eponymous forest is a 'patch of woodland covering five or six square miles' (p. 22) – closer to the size of a park than a South American rainforest. Despite the characters' best efforts, then, the celebration of wild nature characteristic of Romanticism often slips into a more domesticated pastoral in the *novela de la selva*, and from here it is a short step to its parodic kindred – the bucolic, which as Peter V. Marinelli affirms, usually tends to comedy.[30]

Natural Man

The Romantic celebration of the Noble Savage, particularly as formulated in Rousseau's *Discourse on the Origin and Foundations of Inequality among Men* [1755] (also known as the *Second Discourse*) is an important source of parody in the *novela de la selva*, particularly in *Green Mansions* and *Los pasos perdidos*, which engage with Rousseau's formulation of 'natural man' only to demonstrate the discrepancy between philosophical views of primitivism and the reality of living in the jungle. The *Second Discourse* is mistakenly invoked by the protagonists of the *novela de la selva* as a handbook for a more authentic existence, without their comprehending that the Noble Savage extolled in this document is not located among the modern tribes of Amazonia but in some hazy prehistory. As such, their efforts to 'go native' in the jungle often lead to farce and irony, and reveal their vision of wild nature as a ludic space where they can play at being 'savages' while retaining the moral and ideological high ground of 'civilized' men.

Abel's determination to 'live the easy, careless life of the idle man, joining in hunting and fishing expeditions when in the mood; at other times enjoying existence [...], conversing with wild nature in that solitary place' (p. 20), marries Rousseau's celebration of primitivism with a view of leisured tourism, geared at gratification rather than survival. Abel's pastime of learning to hunt stresses the performative aspect of his return to nature and its connections to leisure:

> I tried to imagine myself a simple Guayana savage, with no knowledge of that artificial social state to which I had been born, dependent on my skill and little roll of poison-darts for a livelihood. By an effort of the will I emptied myself of my life experience and knowledge [...]; and if the pleasure I had in the fancy was childish, it made the day pass quickly enough. (p. 39)

His description of his role-playing as a 'savage', while peppered with philo-sophical references to an 'artificial social state' and 'knowledge', is presented as a mere pastime. The very faculties Abel draws upon – imagination and will – are in themselves contrary to Rousseau's belief that natural man is lacking in such characteristics and is motivated by the necessity of survival alone. His fleeting efforts at 'going native' are completely unsuccessful. His hunting expedition is pure diversion and yields not a single hit. The self-congratulatory tone of the following passage reveals Abel's distance from anything like a state of raw nature:

> Finally, I slung my hammock in its old corner, and placing myself in it in my favourite oblique position, my hands clasped behind my head, one knee cocked up, the other leg dangling down, I resigned myself to idle thought. I felt very happy. How strange, thought I, with a little self-flattery, that I, accustomed to the agreeable society of intelligent men and charming women, and of books, should find such perfect contentment here! But I congratulated myself too soon. The profound silence began at length to oppress me. [...] I could not commune with mud walls and an earthen pot. (pp. 86–87)

This passage is comical in the sudden switch from the narrator's professed consonance with his surroundings (although the verb 'resign' implies some reluctance) to his boredom at the silence and lack of cerebral activity. The noun 'contentment' is significant here given that Abel's mother tongue is Spanish, for in Spanish the adjective 'content' is used in conjunction with the verb *estar* as opposed to *ser*, denoting its ephemeral quality. As is the case with the narrator of *Los pasos perdidos*, Abel fails to comprehend one of the central tenets of Rousseau's *Second Discourse*, which is that 'the state of reflection is a state against Nature' – particularly the act of reflecting on the experience of primitivism.[31]

Abel's decision to relinquish the trappings of modernity, what he terms that 'old artificial life' (p. 87), in favour of the jungle does not amount to a rejection of civilization per se. It is significant that Abel's decision to remain in the forest comes only after he meets the sprite-like Rima and her guardian Nuflo, for life in their little hut, though simple, is by no means primitive. Abel's love for Rima is not presented as an inter-cultural relationship but as ultimate communion with nature. Her vegetarianism, her harmony with the forest animals, and her tunic made from the silk of gossamer spiders presents Rima as a Titania-like fairy queen, thus revealing Abel's continued ties to idealized, literary views of primitivism.

Abel is ultimately unable to divorce his aesthetic appreciation of nature from the materialistic view that has characterized European views of the tropics. His presentation of the rainforest not only celebrates nature as a spiritual asylum from the assaults of modernity but is infused with imperial motifs of ownership:

> What a wild beauty and fragrance and melodiousness it possessed above all forests, [...]. And it was mine, truly and absolutely – as much mine as any portion of earth's surface could belong to any man – mine with all its products. (p. 41)

Although Abel goes on to qualify this capitalistic reverie by stressing his intention to preserve the 'precious woods and fruits and fragrant gums' against traffickers, his delight in ownership, signalled by the threefold repetition of 'mine', signals his distance from primitive life and directly recalls the opening of the second part of Rousseau's *Second Discourse*: 'The first man who, having enclosed a piece of ground, to whom it occurred to say *this is mine* [...] was the true founder of civil society.'[32] Even in the midst of the rainforest Abel is unable to escape the urge to civilize his surroundings. Far from according to the precepts of primitivism, then, Abel continues to view the jungle through a utilitarian lens as a force to be channelled, not only as a source of material wealth but also as a spiritual commodity for the elevation of the urban traveller.

Some fifty years later *Los pasos perdidos* approaches the theme of 'going native' with the same ironic recourse to Rousseau, albeit occasionally filtered through novels such as *Paul and Virginia*.[33] Carpentier's narrator regards the jungle as a telluric time capsule – a place of refuge and escape where man 'puede ignorarse el año en que se vive' (p. 278). While listening to a mass being celebrated in the midst of the jungle the narrator experiences the feeling of travelling back through the ages:

> El tiempo ha retrocedido cuatro siglos. Esta es misa de Descubridores recién arribados a orillas sin nombre.[...] Pero no es cierto. Los años se restan, se diluyen, se esfuman, en vertiginoso retroceso del tiempo. No hemos entrado aún

en el siglo XVI. Vivimos mucho antes. Estamos en la Edad Media. Porque no es el hombre renacentista quien realiza el Descubrimiento y la Conquista, sino el hombre medieval. [...] Y he aquí que ese pasado, de súbito, se hace presente. Que lo palpo y aspiro. Que vislumbro ahora la estupefaciente posibilidad de viajar en el tiempo, como otros viajan en el espacio ... *Ite misa est, Benedicamos Dómino, Deo Gratias.* Había concluido la misa, y con ella el Medioevo. Pero las fechas seguían perdiendo guarismos. En fuga desaforada, los años se vaciaban, destranscurrían, se borraban, rellenando calendarios, devolviendo lunas, pasando de los siglos de tres cifras al siglo de los números. Perdió el Graal su relumbre, cayeron los clavos de la cruz, los mercaderes volvieron al templo, bórrase la estrella de la Natividad, y fue el Año Cero. (p. 180–82)

While many critics consider this passage to be one of the most original of Latin American narrative, the narrator's proto-literary journey back in time to the year zero and beyond (he continues to the Paleolothic age) is really a repetition of an overworked convention of travel writing. Fabian has observed that the '*persistent and systematic tendency to place the referent(s) of anthropology in a Time other than the present of the producer of anthropological discourse*' is one of the most pernicious tropes of anthropology.[34] Transplanting modern tribes to a mythical or historically removed setting is a familiar technique in Western discourses of the Other. Diderot, for instance, regarded the Tahitians as 'close to the origins of the world', espousing the coeval eighteenth-century perception of Tahiti as 'an "elysium" where "natural man" was born essentially good'.[35] In *Los pasos perdidos* the narrator's vision of the retrogressive centuries recalls, in particular, Degerando, who in 1800 wrote:

> The traveller-philosopher who sails to the farthest corners of the Globe, travels, in fact, along the road of time. He travels in the past. Every step he takes is a century passed. [...] The peoples whom our ignorant vanity despises are revealed to him like ancient and majestic monuments from the origins of time.[36]

It is also strongly reminiscent of a passage in *Heart of Darkness* when Marlow describes the sensation of 'travelling back to the earliest beginnings of the world' as he sails along the Congo.[37]

The narrator's alleged spiritual metamorphosis in the Venezuelan jungle, far from being a personal odyssey, is modelled on a number of literary antecedents, particularly the outline of the Noble Savage in Rousseau's *Second Discourse.* Within a week of setting out on his journey – significantly the number of days ascribed to the Genesis creation – the narrator redevelops 'la facultad de dormir a cualquier hora' (p. 85), identified by Rousseau as a primary trait of the savage. He is also keen to stress his loss of calendrical consciousness in the jungle, a fact which does not, however, explain his continued success at keeping a journal:

> Observo ahora que yo, maniático medidor del tiempo, atento al metrónomo por vocación y al cronógrafo por oficio, he dejado, desde hace días, de pensar en la hora, relacionando la altura del sol con el apetito o el sueño. (p. 114)

This is a first step to a more primitive life and recalls a similar description in *Paul and Virginia*:

> Paul and Virginia had no clocks or almanacs, no books of chronology, history or philosophy. They regulated their lives according to the cycles of Nature. They knew the hours of the day by the shadows of the trees, the seasons by the times when they flower or fruit, and the years by the number of their crops.[38]

Another important change undergone by the narrator in the tropical rainforest is increased sensuality. 'To perceive and to sense will be his first state, which he will have in common with all animals' Rousseau says of the ideal primitive, and this is mirrored by the narrator's heightened sensory perception.[39] His enjoyment of 'la primordial sensación de belleza, de belleza físicamente percibidas [sic], gozada igualmente por el cuerpo y el entendimiento' (p. 166), epitomizes his growing spiritual and corporeal harmony. Indeed, as Torgovnick has argued, within Western culture 'the idiom "going primitive" is in fact congruent [...] to the idiom "getting physical"'.[40] Conforming to this pattern of occidental discourse, the narrator relates how:

> No hay alarde, no hay fingimiento edénico, en esta limpia desnudez, muy distinta de la que jadea y se vence en las noches de nuestra choza, y que aquí liberamos con una suerte de travesura, asombrados de que sea tan grato sentir la brisa y la luz en partes del cuerpo que la gente *de allá* muere sin haber expuesto alguna vez al aire libre. [...] Y el sol me entra por las piernas, me calienta los testículos, se trepa a mi columna vertebral. (p. 200)

This passage is comically self-paradoxical. Despite the narrator's claims to the contrary, there is much Edenic affectation in his nudity and he is never able to escape fully from the Western correlation of nudity with sex. His description of how the sunlight heats up his testicles quickly spills into a sexual fantasy: 'cubre de sudor mi nuca, me posee, me invade' (p. 200), and bears no resemblance to Rousseau's presentation of a simplistic and unthinking primitive lifestyle. Despite the narrator's attempts to observe the precepts of primitive life, he always seems comically out of sync. Although, for instance, he is keen to stress the animalistic nature of his and Rosario's sexual relationship, thus complying with Rousseau's stipulation of the non-monogamous nature of primitive man, the portrait is unconvincing. His description of their impassioned first encounters as 'el tiempo del celo' seems crudely biological and is somewhat undermined by the fact that he tells us it falls out of season, 'a medio verano' (p. 159). From his discarding of the modern appurtenances of clothes and money, useless in a region where 'todo comercio se reduce a trueques de objetos simples y útiles' (p. 156), to his celebration of uncomplicated coupling with Rosario, the narrator follows Rousseau's tenets of the Noble Savage without realizing that his acquaintance with these codes embodies his single greatest infringement of them. In the preface to his *Second Discourse* Rousseau makes it clear that learning is, paradoxically, the greatest obstacle to knowledge:

since every progress of the human species removes it ever farther from its primitive state, the more new knowledge we accumulate, the more we deprive ourselves of the means of acquiring the most important knowledge of all, and that in a sense it is by dint of studying man that we have made it impossible for us to know him.[41]

It is the narrator-protagonist's insistent search for knowledge in the Venezuelan rainforest which, ironically, prevents him from understanding the peoples, cultures, and landscapes that he encounters there.

Throughout *Los pasos perdidos* the primitive is extolled not for its cultural simplicity but for its potential for improvement, its proximity to – rather than its remoteness from – modern society. As is the case in More's *Utopia*, El Adelantado's New World 'paradise' is very civilized indeed, boasting all the trappings of a city, including a government, commerce, clothes, music, and literature. The narrator's preference for this 'urbane' location over a truly primitive domain attests to his bookish view of Amerindian culture, mediated through a profusion of idealized travel accounts and the figure of the Noble Savage. His inability to conform to primitive life is exemplified by his statement: 'no estoy aquí para pensar. No debo pensar. Ante todo sentir y ver' (p. 213). The narrator's twofold repetition that he is not supposed to think suggests that this rule has become as restrictive as the conventions of his former lifestyle in the city. Rather than discovering an idyllic life among 'pre-modern' man, the narrator finds that his desire to compose music transforms the wilderness into a veritable straitjacket to his creativity. Not only is he bereft of ample writing materials but also, and perhaps more importantly, of an audience before which to perform. In this sense the narrator comes closer to Diderot's belief in the boredom of primitive life than the version espoused by Rousseau. The lack of osmosis between primitive and modern life not only leads to the narrator's flight from the rainforest but also prevents him from retracing the eponymous 'pasos perdidos'.

Wilderness and the Myth of Masculine Escape

One of the most important functions of the jungle in the *novela de la selva* is its potential to define and to consolidate masculinity.[42] With the exception of *Green Mansions*, in which Rima plays an important role, the *novela de la selva* is peopled almost entirely by male characters, and when women do appear they tend to act as pawns in the action, or as foils to masculine bravery.[43] The reasons for the relative absence of female protagonists in these novels could be attributed to the fact that the occupations central to the texts (tapping rubber, searching for diamonds, exploring) have historically been filled by men. Indeed, travel writing has tended to be dominated by male authors, since it is they who have traditionally left their homelands for adventures abroad. Throughout the *novela de la selva* the untamed nature of the tropical jungle is posited as foundational for the male traveller's personal growth, often acting as a rite of passage to a life of enhanced heroism and masculinity.[44] In particular, forests are presented as spaces beyond the pale of urban laws or morality, which explains why in *La vorágine* Cova elopes with his girlfriend to the outback of Colombia or in *Green Mansions* Abel flees to the forest after taking part in a failed *coup d'etat*.

Patrick Brantlinger has argued that the preponderance of nineteenth-century English novels in which the empire is seen as a 'shadowy realm of escape, renewal, banishment, or return for characters who for one reason or another need to enter or exit from scenes of domestic conflict' (a succinct description of the role of the jungle in the *novela de la selva*) is a consequence of the decline of British imperial hegemony.[45] Nevertheless, despite the superficial similarities between the British imperial romance and the Spanish-American *novela de la selva*, there is a conceptual void between the literary output of a waning empire and that of a burgeoning postcolonial nation. Far from lamenting the attenuation of male heroism in modern society, the *novela de la selva* debunks European adventure narratives, especially their tendency to locate the action in exotic locales such as tropical rainforests, as a manifestation of 'imperialist nostalgia'.

González Echevarría has failed to make this distinction between the British tradition of adventure stories and the *novela de la selva*. His inclusion of novels such as Sir Arthur Conan Doyle's *The Lost World* and H. Rider Haggard's *King Solomon's Mines* under the collective heading of *libros de la selva* overlooks a crucial switch in tone between the two traditions.[46] *King Solomon's Mines*, first published in 1885, and dedicated in a unapologetic flourish of machismo to 'all the big and little boys who read it', is a Victorian adventure novel which celebrates in a totally unambiguous fashion not only British colonial ambitions in Africa but also the misogyny and racism which often underpinned them.[47] *The Lost World* [1912] is certainly parodic, yet the parody in this novel is very different from that formulated in the *novela de la selva*, not least because it is both generated by, and aimed at, the English gentleman explorer. The self-parody of *The Lost World* conforms to a broader trend in twentieth-century travel writing, where parody affords, as Holland and Huggan have argued, 'both the amateur explorer [...] and the professional anthropologist [...] with nothing less than a strategy of survival. Parody functions as protective covering, as camouflage; it constitutes a necessary act of self-defence.'[48] The Spanish-American tradition departs from Holland and Huggan's definition in that here parody is employed not to shield the intrepid traveller from censure, but to actively encourage the demystification of this figure as an agent of cultural imperialism. Far from registering as well-meaning buffoons, such as Malone in *The Lost World*, the protagonists of the *novela de la selva* appear either as exploitative or singularly naïve. Throughout the *novela de la selva* the appeal to imperial motifs of adventure and masculine heroism registers as not just belated but as completely inconsistent with the novels' postcolonial credentials, becoming a hollow act of repetition – repetition which at once produces 'its slippage, its excess, its difference'.[49]

The patriarchal structures of jungle life in these novels, grounded in male prowess and female domesticity, are a parody of those prescribed in Western adventure novels such as *She* or *King Solomon's Mines*. Throughout the *novela de la selva* the authors demystify the protagonists' self-styling as masculine heroes as a manifestation of what Judith Butler has axiomatically termed 'gender trouble'.[50] Butler's theory of gender performativity – the assimilation of gender roles as 'an incessant and repeated action of some sort' – can be seen as analogous to Bhabha's definition of colonial mimicry.[51] Gender role-play becomes one of many repetitions in the novels, all of which serve to excavate the hidden meaning of worn-out literary figures such as the 'Romantic hero' or the 'intrepid explorer', and unearth their complicity with a broader discourse of imperialism. The protagonists' overworked performance of machismo not only parodies the upbeat jingoism of the hardy explorers who fill the pages of British Victorian travel literature, but also reveals the suppressed commodification of the wilderness in these texts. The tropical jungle, traditionally seen as just another exotic space against which the Western (male) traveller can test his mettle, becomes in the *novela de la selva* a spot of ridicule, as heroic escapades turn into farce and machismo is undermined as a symptom of acute gender anxiety.

In *La vorágine* Cova's physical displacement from Bogotá to the Colombian plains and jungle is matched by his psychological transformation from a sensitive poet to a man wedded to machismo – a violent outlaw who assaults (and even murders) anyone who obstructs his path to self-actualization. In the novel, the South American wilderness is depicted as a last bulwark of patriarchy, where traditional codes of masculinity can be revitalized and reaffirmed. Cova's self-posturing as a masculine hero begins almost as soon as he leaves the city, although this might be explained by the benefit of hindsight, given that the opening section of the novel was composed later on in the jungle. For example, when he encounters a drunken man who makes lewd comments to Alicia, Cova spits on him and, 'lanzando al hombre contra el tabique, lo acomet[ió] a golpes de tacón en el rostro y en la cabeza' (p. 88). Likewise, when Alicia is abducted by Barrera later in the novel, Cova regards it as an attack on his masculinity: '¡Me robé una mujer y me la robaron! ¡Vengo a matar al que la tenga!' (p. 337). His macho pursuit of Barrera into the jungle to reclaim his 'woman' appeals to an honour code which is both antiquated and unsophisticated and which seems a crude counterweight to the narrator's worry of being perceived as unmanly beyond the precincts of the city.[52]

Despite his efforts to appear macho when he reaches the plains, as a middle-class intellectual Cova continues to form a sort of androgynous middle ground between the hardy cattle farmers and the women. On several occasions he describes how he is excluded from the rodeo and is left indoors in a domestic and feminized space. On one such occasion, the maid who serves him breakfast comments: 'Don Rafo y los hombres montaron y las mujeres tán bañándose' (p. 112), heightening his feeling of liminality. Instead of joining the men, Cova stands with the women to admire the cowboy's feats 'por entre los claros del palo a pique' (p. 118) – a barrier both physical and conceptual. When Cova finally breaches the masculine domain of the plains, his attempts at rounding up cattle are less than successful:

> Montaba yo, alegremente, un caballito coral, apasionado por las distancias [...]. Adiestrado por la costumbre, diose a perseguir a un toro barcino, y era de verse con qué pujanza le hacía sonar el freno sobre los lomos. Tiraba yo el lazo una y otra vez, con mano inexperta. (p. 176)

Cova's inexperience at rodeo leads to the goading of his horse and indirectly causes the death of a cowherd, who is horrifically beheaded by a bull. Contrary to Cova's aspiration to seem macho riding on horseback, his introduction to rodeo is, in reality, a profoundly emasculating experience.[53] His horse, a diminutive 'caballito', is beyond his equestrian skill, and his having to be rescued by the other workers places him in a position of subjection and dependence comparable to that of the women in the novel. The association of Cova with femininity in this passage is accentuated by the crude phallic imagery: the bull, a symbol of raw male power, succeeds in sinking 'ambos cuernos en la verija' (p. 176) of his mount – horns which, just a short while earlier, he admires as 'enormes' (p. 152).

In the jungle Cova's desire for enhanced masculinity is even more pronounced, and is instantiated by his fantasy of fostering a macho appearance – 'cierto descuido en el traje, los cabellos revueltos, el rostro ensombrecido de barba, aparentando el porte de un macho almizcloso y trabajador' (p. 164). The verb 'aparentar' is telling here, denoting the performative nature of Cova's machismo.[54] His definition of masculinity, from stubble to a musky scent, is comically stereotyped – an effect heightened by the use of the generic term 'macho'. Gender stereotypes are also parodied through Cova's wooing of Zoraida Ayram, especially when he tries to establish his dominance over her by biting her cheek, 'una sola vez, porque en [sus] dientes quedó un saborcillo de vaselina y polvos de arroz' (p. 329). Although Cova admits that he plays this role 'con ilusoria teatralidad' (p. 329), he seems to revel in this performance of masculine aggression, finally reducing her to tears. It is significant that Cova alludes to the theatricality of his performance of male aplomb. James Eli Adams has observed that there is an 'intractable element of theatricality in all masculine self-fashioning, which inevitably makes appeal to an audience, real or imagined', yet, as usual, Cova's performance is comically overworked.[55] In the same way that the repetition of colonial tropes succeeds in denaturalizing them, the recourse to stereotyped gender identities in the *novela de la selva* serves only to highlight the arbitrariness of such roles. The demystification of male identity as a performance in these novels is matched by the singularly unfeminine female characters, such as Zoraida Ayram, who is described by Cova as a '¡Mujer singular, mujer ambiciosa, mujer varonil!' (p. 324).

Eric J. Leed has argued that travel allows people to 'become "someone else," to recreate identity, to assume disguises and personae that would be forbidden or impossible at home'.[56] Cova's outmoded perception of the

South American wilderness as a space of unimpeded adventure for the white male traveller harks back to colonial times, thus problematically negating the successful pro-independence movements that spanned Latin America during the nineteenth century. Cova's violence throughout the novel is often no more excessive than that of the protagonists of imperial adventure literature. Nevertheless, in this postcolonial novel Cova's display of masculine brawn is not only ridiculed but rebuked. Far from assimilating him into life on the plains, his overworked display of aggression elicits shocked responses, such as that of the deadpan Griselda: 'usté tá loco, usté tá loco' (p. 117). Likewise his murder of Barrera is portrayed in grimly realistic terms, and departs from the more sterile deaths of most villains in adventure fiction:

> le agrandé con mis dientes las sajaduras, lo ensangrenté, y, rabiosamente, lo sumergí bajo la linfa para asfixiarlo como a un pichón.
> [...] millones de caribes acudieron sobre el herido, entre un temblor de aletas y centelleos, y aunque él manoteaba y se defendía, lo descarnaron en un segundo. (p. 382)

The eventual disintegration of Cova's gallant exterior, culminating in the terrified final line of his journal, '¡En nombre de Dios!' (p. 384), finally reveals a sensitive side to Cova, who we last glimpse tending to his premature baby. In this novel at least, the path to enhanced masculinity and adventure leads only to death.

In many regards Cova's vision of the jungle as a site for the distillation of masculinity is a direct precursor to that of Marcos Vargas in *Canaima*, who has been described by one critic as a 'paradigma del Hombre Macho'.[57] Six years before the publication of *Canaima*, Gallegos had demonstrated his interest in the symbolic use of male and female roles in *Doña Bárbara*, yet the later novel eschews the feminine for a prolonged examination of normative masculine values, particularly through the hero Marcos.

Despite its designation as a *novela de la selva*, the jungle as physical backdrop does not feature until almost two-thirds of the way through *Canaima*. Marcos's initiation into the forest takes place only after he has 'portado como un hombre, a riesgo de [su] vida' (p. 149) – that is, only after he has avenged his brother's murder by shooting the killer, and thus proving himself capable of survival in a world beyond the codes of Western 'civilization'. The notion of the jungle as a frontier to a life of masculine adventure (and, by extension, to barbarism and savagery) is signalled insistently throughout the novel. 'Quienes trasponen sus lindes ya empiezan a ser algo más o algo menos que hombres' (p. 150), states the third-person narrator, and the use of 'algo' implies the reification of man in the wilds of nature – a sort of dehumanization achieved by the 'selva inhumana'. The noun *linde* is telling. Sharing the same Latin root as the English 'liminal', *līmen* meaning 'threshold', the forest is shown to be a boundary, and this is made explicit throughout the novel. For instance, when Marcos first meets the Amerindian Ponchopire, who dons Western clothes and visits Ciudad Bolívar, his mood is described as being 'en el umbral del misterio' (p. 17), and his eventual penetration of the jungle is presented as a physical breaching of a frontier: 'Arteaguita se quedó al margen de la aventura y Marcos Vargas se vio lanzado a ella' (p. 150).[58]

The view of the wilderness as a frontier to enhanced masculinity is a literary stereotype not only of the British imperial adventure novel but also of Latin American gaucho literature. In Sarmiento's *Facundo* the wild expanses of jungle and pampa are credited as being outside the moral and ideological bounds of the city and ruled by the 'Gaucho Malo' – 'un *outlaw*, un *squatter*, un misántropo particular. Es el *Ojo del Halcón*, el *Trampero* de Cooper.'[59] It is ironic that, in his definition of the Argentine gaucho as a unique national icon, Sarmiento should not only employ English terms but also rely upon foreign literary texts to explicate the figure. In *Canaima*, Gallegos's allusions to the gaucho retain what might be called, with the benefit of hindsight, Sarmiento's somewhat Borgesian inversion, where life imitates art, imitating life. The episode in which Marcos murders his brother's assassin is stylized as a stereotyped gaucho exchange and lacks the psychological depth that characterizes the novel as a whole, adding to the sense of a ritualized 'coreografía del macho' which Alfredo Villanueva-Collado has noted in the novel.[60] The description of the victim entering the bar where he is to be murdered – an 'inconfundible silueta gigantesca' (p. 144) – not only transforms him into a faceless monster (an anonymity accentuated by the confusion over his real name) but also adopts the typical hero/villain binary of the gaucho novel. Nevertheless, the description of the dying man marks a departure from convention and reminds us of Barrera's grotesque death in *La vorágine*: 'dio un pujido y balbució, ya desplomándose, cenicienta la faz sombría' (p. 146). The remote anonymity of the 'asesino ambidextro' (p. 145) – here the alliterative 'a' underlying the comic literary status of Parima Cholo – is exchanged for a strangely haunting picture of a dying man reduced to physical impotence. Gallegos's novel seems intent on demystifying the conduct of the 'Hombre Macho' as an overworked performance of male power. Although Marcos's friends excuse his murder as a boyish peccadillo – as him having 'portado como un hombre, pero con sacrificio de [su] tranquilidad de conciencia' (p. 148) – it sits uneasily with the carefree youth we are first introduced to in the novel. Likewise, the contrast between the well-intentioned mordacity of Marcos's early encounters with Aracelis and his vicious treatment of her later in the novel is denotative of the pernicious effects of his manly escapades.[61] His uncouth proposal that Aracelis elope with him 'Para el Cuyuni, para Rionegro. ¡Para donde yo quiera llevarte!' (p. 212), marks the zenith of his misogyny and compounds the sense of futile self-destruction that pervades the novel.

Despite Gallegos's allusions to the literary mystification of the jungle as a place of unlimited masculine adventure, this vision is destabilized when Marcos finally enters the forest and learns to his disappointment that 'no era, por lo menos, como se lo había imaginado. [...] "¿Y esto era la selva?" se preguntó. "¡Monte tupido y nada más!"' (p. 150). The demystification of the term *selva*, synonymous in the novel with uncurbed adventure and legend, to prosaic 'monte tupido' mirrors the other demystifications which take place in *Canaima*. The oxymoronic 'hermosos peligros' (p. 61) of jungle life are revealed as far from gratifying, and the 'heroic' deeds of the 'hombre macho' as acts of desperation and cruelty. Marcos's 'vehementes inclinaciones hacia la aventura' (p. 61), which impel him to discharge the shibboleth of proving himself a 'man', are revealed by the end of the novel to be foolish aspirations, fed on the yarns of the rubber workers who perpetuate orally the long tradition of discursive violence against the Other that has characterized travel writing on tropical South America.

The destabilizing of machismo in *Canaima* is not, however, without a nostalgic backward glance, and might not achieve the total symbolic victory of civilization over barbarism it first appears to. Throughout *Canaima* Gallegos dramatizes the Latin American binary of civilization and barbarism, the former embodied by Gabriel Ureña, the latter by Marcos Vargas. While Ureña comes across sympathetically in the novel, Marcos is a much more compelling character.[62] Just as the novel takes its title from the malignant god of the forest, Marcos's spiralling brutality is the mainstay of the novelistic interest and it is noteworthy that Gallegos's dramatization of the struggle between civilization and barbarism in *Doña Bárbara* followed a similar pattern, with the male hero Santos Luzardo much less complex than the eponymous villain. If *Canaima* does not mark the total victory of civilization over barbarism, it does substitute uncurbed admiration for masculine escapades with an appreciation for more understated forms of heroism, such as Marcos's rescue of an orphaned monkey during a storm. The arrival of Marcos's son in the city at the end of the novel clearly denotes a compromise of sorts, although the reader is left uncertain as to whether his education at the hands of Ureña will have any greater effect than his father's teenage years in an English boarding school in Trinidad. If Marcos in *Los pasos perdidos* is offered by way of a sequel to *Canaima*, as González Echevarría has suggested, then it comes as no surprise to learn that he returns to his jungle home disillusioned and embittered after a short stay in the city.[63]

The parodic engagement with the masculine hero of the imperial romance continues in Carpentier's late *novela de la selva*, although it is only within the past few decades that critics have begun to interrogate the 'bluntly sexist [...] pronouncements' of the narrator, his discourse of female subjugation, and the concomitant 'machista gender economy' operative in the text.[64] The jungle in *Los pasos perdidos*, like that in the two earlier *novelas de la selva*, is presented by the narrator as a stage for the consolidation of traditional gender roles, where he renounces the modern world and nostalgically assimilates the misogynistic values of jungle-dwellers such as El Adelantado – a man who 'nunca prestaba atención a lo que decían las mujeres' (p. 139). The division of the sexes in the jungle of *Los pasos perdidos* is characterized by wildly overdetermined male and female roles, as the characters leave the 'modern' world and enter a seat of patriarchy where 'parecía que el hombre fuera más hombre' (pp. 116–17), and woman is suitably deflated to a position of meek admiration of masculine feats:

> Volvía a ser dueño de técnicas milenarias que ponían sus manos en trato directo con el hierro y el pellejo, le enseñaban las artes de la doma y la monta, desarrollando destrezas físicas de que alardear en días de fiesta, frente a las mujeres admiradas de quien tanto sabía apretar con las piernas, de quien tanto sabía hacer con los brazos. (p. 117)

The strict gender hierarchy embraced by the narrator in the novel augments the tone of belatedness which pervades his travel journal as a whole and is an important aspect of the more generalized parody of Western constructions of wilderness in the novel.

As Wyers reminds us, despite the narrator's visionary retrogression along the lost steps of Latin American history, his movement back in time does not predate the patriarchal kinship formations of the Upper Palaeolithic and therefore never transcends the heterosexual matrix of Western culture: life in the jungle functions along strict patriarchal lines, which prescribe 'la fidelidad al varón, el respeto a los padres' (p. 152), and an honour code which rivals that of Golden Age Spain.[65] In *Los pasos perdidos* the narrator employs a theatrical metaphor to describe the bifurcated male and female roles, which not only foregrounds the division of the sexes but is also invested with allegorical overtones:

> Como en los más clásicos teatros, los personajes eran, en este gran escenario presente y real, los tallados en una pieza del Bueno y el Malo, la Esposa Ejemplar o la Amante Fiel, el Villano y el Amigo Leal, la Madre digna o indigna. Las canciones ribereñas cantaban, en décimas de romance, la trágica historia de una esposa violada y muerta de vergüenza, y la fidelidad de la zamba que durante diez años esperó el regreso de un marido a quien todos daban por comido de hormigas en lo más remoto de la selva. (p. 152)

This stock dramatis personae epitomizes the narrator's predisposition towards simplistic gender binaries: the female is esteemed only through her relationship to the male as wife, mother, or faithful lover, whereas men are portrayed beyond the domestic sphere as founders of cities, diamond hunters, and explorers.

Despite the narrator's self-styling as an 'hombre macho' in the jungle, his gender identity is more precarious than that of any other character in the novel. Although he criticizes his wife's theatrical tendencies, he admits to responding to Mouche's suspected infidelity with another woman 'como un marido de melodrama' (p. 73). His stylized fight with Yannes later in the novel, which involves him and his opponent brawling on a floor covered with shards of broken glass, reads more like an episode from a Wild West novel than from the travel journal of a self-styled intellectual. Such public displays of male prowess correspond to David D. Gilmore's definition of the 'manly man' as 'one who performs': 'His role-playing is manifested in "foregrounded" deeds, in actions that are seen by everyone and therefore have the potential to be judged collectively.'[66] Shortly after his quasi-anthropological observation that, in the outback of Venezuela, 'los hombres tratan a las mujeres con una suerte de rudeza irónica y desenfadada que parece agradarles' (p. 115), the narrator begins to conform to the stereotyped gender roles of this new milieu. After an argument with Mouche, which ends with her falling into a mucky pool filled with turtles, he unceremoniously strips off her clothes and sends her to bed like a naughty child:

> metí a Mouche en la habitación, le quité las ropas hediondas a cieno y la bañé de pies a cabeza con un grueso paño roto. Y luego de hacerles beber un gran trago de aguardiente la arropé en su catre y marché a la calle sin hacer caso de sus llamadas ni sollozos. (p. 128)

The narrator's display of male mastery and dominance extends to his relationship with Rosario. Almost every commentator on the novel has deemed Rosario a 'símbolo de la matriz original, de la Madre Tierra',[67] corresponding to Carpentier's description of her as 'una mujer que representa [...] la mujer elemental, la mujer verdadera, telúrica, profunda'.[68] However, there is an insurmountable paradox at the heart of the narrator's presentation of Rosario: as 'una mujer de tierra' (p. 183) who is immune to the concept of time and who does not have 'siquiera una noción muy clara de la redondez de la tierra' (p. 110), surely she should transcend the arbitrary gender stereotypes of Western society. In fact, Rosario does not offer eternal truths about femininity, but is a projection of masculine desire – what Donald Shaw has described rather cavalierly as a 'man's ideal of a woman when he is in certain moods'.[69] The narrator's descriptions of Rosario exemplify his desire for mastery over her – a mastery that he was unable to achieve with Mouche or his wife:

> Me rodea de cuidados, trayéndome de comer, ordeñando las cabras para mí, secándome el sudor con paños frescos, atenta a mi palabra, mi sed, mi silencio o mi reposo, con una solicitud que me hace enorgullecerme de mi condición de hombre: aquí, pues, la hembra 'sirve' al varón en el más noble sentido del término, creando la casa con cada gesto. (p. 156)

This hyperbolic description of Rosario moving hastily from one domestic task to the next is highly parodic, not least in its ironic evocation of the idealized Victorian 'Angel of the House', 'creando la casa con cada gesto', despite the fact that the couple are residing in a jungle hut. The anaphoric use of the personal pronoun 'mi' reveals the narrator's characteristic self-absorption. This is less a celebration of female domesticity than male power and despite the narrator's euphemistic bracketing of the verb 'servir', it is clear that there is nothing 'noble' about Rosario's self-effacing servility: the narrator's perception of happy slavery is born only out of his condition as master.

In response to Simone de Beauvoir's criticism of him as having 'subscribed rather unthinkingly to the current myths about primitive life and femininity' in *Los pasos perdidos*,[70] Carpentier has acknowledged his propensity to exaggerate 'en un sentido o en otro'.[71] Nevertheless, the overdetermination of gender roles in the novel appears to far exceed Carpentier's penchant for allegory and universalism. The narrator's mystification of the feminine and the concomitant subtext of male hegemony are a source of much of the novel's irony, cleaving a rift between the narrator and the author which biographical criticism has not been able to bridge convincingly. The narrator's misplaced view of the jungle as a final bulwark of patriarchy follows a pattern initiated much earlier in *La vorágine* and *Canaima*, and issues the coup de grâce against urban myths of the South American tropics as a locus for the consolidation of masculine values.

★   ★   ★

The projection of the jungle as an exotic space for the bolstering of the urban individual – through the provision of spiritual truths or the distillation of heroism – posits nature as a reserve for outsiders, thereby discounting its role as home and habitat to indigenous tribes, plants, and animals. Far from being a mere resource, however, wild nature in the *novela de la selva* resists literary paradigms and challenges at every turn the conventions of Romantic poetry or imperial adventure literature. Although many of the novels central to this study are structurally consistent with the quest romance, they depart from the conventions of the genre in their tracing of the debilitation, rather than the coming of age, of the protagonist. Throughout the *novela de la selva* the narrators' idealized and literary expectations of wilderness are consistently thwarted. Far from succeeding in their performances as Romantic poets, Noble Savages, or masculine heroes, the comportment of these belated imperial travellers registers as inauthentic and out of place in the postcolonial jungle. In fact, in many of the *novelas de la selva*, the idealization of jungle life is in itself predicated on a misreading of Western discourses on primitivism, as we have seen with regard to the rather loose recourse to Rousseau in *Green Mansions* and *Los pasos perdidos*. In a later novel set in the jungle, *El hablador* [1987] by Mario Vargas Llosa, the first-person narrator reflects on the inauthenticity of the figure of the Noble Savage, despite its enduring and inexorable influence on European and Latin American travel writing on the tropics:

> Todas mis intentos culminaban siempre en un estilo que me parecía tan obviamente fraudulento, tan poco persuasivo como aquellos en los que, en el siglo XVIII, cuando se puso de moda en Europa el 'buen salvaje', hacían hablar a sus personajes exóticos los filósofos y novelistas de la Ilustración.[72]

The narrator's use of the term 'vacation' in *Los pasos perdidos*, discussed earlier in the chapter, is textually consistent, therefore, with the attempted commodification of nature by the protagonists of all of the *novelas de la selva* discussed in this book. Nevertheless, the view of the jungle as a space of festive release from the conventions of everyday life is, by definition, a transitory condition and one which does not have the ideological elasticity to cater for the very real dangers of the forest. It is noteworthy that in the *novela de la selva* characters are immersed gradually in nature and their romanticized view of their surroundings is often precipitated by early contacts with the countryside, rather than with the jungle itself. As I will discuss in the final chapter, when the travellers reach the rainforest the Romantic overtones of their narratives quickly yield to a horrified apprehension of the dystopian potential of nature, not just that of the jungle flora and fauna, but of their own humanity.

Notes

1 Ralph Waldo Emerson, 'Nature', in *Selected Essays*, ed. Larzer Ziff (Harmondsworth: Penguin, 1985), pp. 35–82 (pp. 57–58).
2 See Rosaldo, *Culture and Truth*, pp. 68–87. I follow Patrick Holland and Graham Huggan, *Tourists with Typewriters: Critical Reflections on Contemporary Travel Writing* (Ann Arbor, MI: University of Michigan Press, 1998), who draw upon Rosaldo's concept of 'imperial nostalgia' to unearth the complicity of travel writing with imperialism (pp. 29–30).
3 Thomas Hobbes, *Leviathan* [1651], ed. Richard Tuck (Cambridge: Cambridge University Press, 1996), p. 89.
4 Ovid, *Metamorphoses*, trans. A. D. Melville (Oxford: Oxford University Press, 1987), pp. 3–4.
5 Colón, *Textos y documentos completos*, p. 132.
6 Vasco de Quiroga established two experimental towns along the principles of More's *Utopia*. See Todorov, *Conquest of America*, pp. 194–95.
7 Cabeza de Vaca, *Naufragios*, p. 98.
8 Jean Jacques Rousseau, *The Confessions*, trans. J. M. Cohen (New York: Penguin, 1953), p. 362.
9 Henry David Thoreau, *The Portable Thoreau*, ed. Carl Bode (Harmondsworth: Penguin, 1982), p. 343.
10 Emerson, *Selected Essays*, p. 39.
11 See, for instance, Arthur K. Moore, *The Frontier Mind*, 2nd edn (New York: McGraw-Hill, 1963), pp. 86–87.
12 Porter, *Haunted Journeys*, p. 13.
13 Roderick Nash, *Wilderness and the American Mind*, rev. edn (New Haven: Yale University Press, 1973), p. 44.
14 Rosaldo, *Culture and Truth*, pp. 69–70.
15 Holland and Huggan, *Tourists with Typewriters*, have discussed the connections between belatedness and farce, particularly in recent British travel literature. They argue that the appeal to 'imperial nostalgia' is self-conscious and self-deprecating, when writers 'are aware [...] that their gestures are belated, and the result in their narratives is a turn to comedy – particularly farce' (p. 30).
16 Enrique Anderson Imbert, *Historia de la literatura hispanoamericana*, rev. edn (México: Fondo de Cultura Económica, 1957). See, in particular, chapters 7–9.
17 Olivera, 'El romanticismo de *La vorágine*', draws a parallel between Rousseau's *Confessions* and Cova's diary (pp. 260, 264).
18 Fletcher, 'Creator of Rima', and Macpherson, *Spirit of Solitude*, have both discussed the influence of Romantic literature on Hudson.
19 Percy Bysshe Shelley, 'To Jane. The Invitation', in *Shelley's Poetry and Prose*, ed. Donald H. Reiman and Sharon B. Powers (New York: Norton, 1977), p. 443.
20 David Miller, *W. H. Hudson and the Elusive Paradise* (London: Macmillan, 1990), p. 138.

21 Samuel Taylor Coleridge, 'Frost at Midnight', in *The Major Works*, ed. H. J. Jackson (Oxford: Oxford University Press, 2000), pp. 87–89 (p. 88).

22 Oscar Collazos, *Textos al margen* (Bogotá: Instituto Colombiano de Cultura, 1978) describes Cova as 'un héroe romántico, pese al contexto de la novela' (p. 180).

23 Olivera, 'El romanticismo de *La vorágine*', has argued that these words (from the 'Fragmento de la carta de Arturo Cova') 'no son otra cosa que un torrente de apasionado sentimentalismo romántico' (p. 259).

24 Lilian R. Furst, *Romanticism in Perspective: A Comparative Study of Aspects of the Romantic Movements in England, France and Germany*, 2nd edn (London: Macmillan, 1979), p. 103. My reading of Cova as Romantic hero owes much to Furst's commentary on René. Olivera, 'El romanticismo de *La vorágine*', has discussed the parallels between Cova and René (p. 260).

25 Jacques-Henri Bernardin de Saint Pierre, *Paul and Virginia* [1787], trans. John Donovan (London: Owen, 1982), p. 97.

26 François René Chateaubriand, *Atala. René* [1801], trans. Irving Putter (Berkeley: University of California Press, 1952), p. 43.

27 Rousseau, *Confessions*, p. 363.

28 Furst, *Romanticism in Perspective*, p. 84.

29 William Shakespeare, *King Lear*, ed. Kenneth Muir (London: Methuen, 1986), pp. 99–100.

30 Peter V. Marinelli, *Pastoral* (London: Methuen, 1971), p. 8.

31 Rousseau, *Discourses*, p. 138.

32 Rousseau, *Discourses*, p. 161.

33 Bernardin was a close friend of Rousseau, and *Paul and Virginia* reflects many of the philosopher's central tenets.

34 Fabian, *Time and the Other*, p. 31; emphasis in original.

35 Dorinda Outram, *The Enlightenment* (Cambridge: Cambridge University Press, 1995), p. 67.

36 Cited and translated by Pagden, *European Encounters*, p. 118.

37 Conrad, *Heart of Darkness*, p. 35.

38 Bernardin, *Paul and Virginia*, p. 70.

39 Rousseau, *Discourses*, p. 142.

40 Torgovnick, *Gone Primitive*, p. 228.

41 Rousseau, *Discourses*, p. 124.

42 González Echevarría, '*Canaima*', also recognizes the role of the forest in the *novela de la selva* as a testing-ground for masculinity, where characters such as Marcos Vargas and the narrator of *Los pasos perdidos* 'se internan en la espesura para someterse a pruebas de valor, audacia, resistencia y pericia' (p. 507).

43 The parody of adventure fiction in *Green Mansions* is largely confined to Abel's self-styling as a conquistador, as when he echoes Columbus's notorious thirst for gold: 'These Indians wore necklets, like nearly all the Guayana savages; but one, I observed, possessed a necklet unlike that of the others, which greatly aroused my curiosity. It was made of thirteen gold plates [...]. When questioned about it they said it was originally obtained from the Indians of Parahuari [...]. Every man and woman in that place, they assured me, had such a necklet. This report inflamed my mind to such a degree that I could not rest by night or day for dreaming golden dreams' (p. 13).

44 James S. Duncan, 'The Struggle to be Temperate: Climate and "Moral Masculinity" in mid-Nineteenth century Ceylon', *Singapore Journal of Tropical Geography*, 21 (2000), pp. 34–47, has described how in settlers' writings the jungle is posited as 'an adversary that presented a moral test of the planters' manhood, race and class' (p. 34).

45 Patrick Brantlinger, *Rule of Darkness: British Literature and Imperialism, 1830–1914* (Ithaca, NY: Cornell University Press, 1988), p. 12.

46 González Echevarría, 'Canaima', p. 510. Sá, Rain Forest Literatures, has also criticized
    González Echevarría's grouping of these novels as 'jungle books' – a definition which
    she considers reductive and unhelpful (p. 71).

47 H. Rider Haggard, King Solomon's Mines [1885] (Harmondsworth: Penguin, 1994),
    p. v.

48 Holland and Huggan, Tourists with Typewriters, p. 77.

49 Bhabha, Location of Culture, p. 86.

50 Judith Butler, Gender Trouble: Feminism and the Subversion of Identity (London: Routledge,
    1990).

51 Butler, Gender Trouble, p. 112.

52 Evelyn P. Stevens, 'Marianismo: The Other Face of Machismo in Latin America', in
    Ann Pescatello (ed.), Female and Male in Latin America: Essays (Pittsburgh: University
    of Pittsburgh Press, 1973), pp. 89–101, has shown how Latin American 'machismo' is
    particularly concerned with notions of honour (p. 91).

53 Alistair Hennessy, The Frontier in Latin American History (London: Arnold, 1978), helps
    to elucidate the significance of Cova's inability to ride when he describes how, in the
    plains, an 'effete townsman who cannot ride or compete with the equestrian skills of the
    cowboy is beneath contempt' (p. 114).

54 This seems to correspond to Butler's understanding of gender in Gender Trouble where
    she argues that the 'gendered body [...] has no ontological status apart from the various
    acts which constitute its reality' (p. 136).

55 James Eli Adams, Dandies and Desert Saints: Styles of Victorian Masculinity (Ithaca, NY:
    Cornell University Press, 1995), p. 11.

56 Eric J. Leed, The Mind of the Traveler: From Gilgamesh to Global Tourism (New York: Basic
    Books, 1991), p. 107.

57 María del Carmen Porras, 'Entre los peligros de la desmesura y las limitaciones de la
    normalidad: Canaima de Rómulo Gallegos', Alpha, 18 (2002), pp. 43–62 (p. 46).

58 Porras, 'Canaima de Rómulo Gallegos', has argued that 'Si, según la ya clásica defin-
    ición de Anderson, una nación es "una comunidad política imaginada como inherente-
    mente limitada y soberana" [...], en esta novela la selva y quienes viven de ella o en sus
    alrededores son imaginados como esos límites de la nación' (p. 50).

59 Domingo F. Sarmiento, Facundo: civilización y barbarie [1845] (México: Editorial
    Porrúa, 1998), p. 27.

60 Alfredo Villanueva-Collado, 'El macho, la historia y la otredad: Canaima, de Rómulo
    Gallegos', Alba de América: Revista Literaria, 13 (1995), pp. 105–13 (p. 110).

61 Marvin Goldwert, 'Mexican Machismo: The Flight from Femininity', Psychoanalytic
    Review, 72 (1985), pp. 161–69 (p. 163), has included the trait of disdain or indiffer-
    ence to women, except the mother, as a prime characteristic of machismo. Marcos's
    contempt for Aracelis and love for his mother is therefore consistent with the stereotype
    of the Latin American macho.

62 Porras, 'Canaima de Rómulo Gallegos', has described Ureña as 'un ser más bien gris y
    diríamos que hasta mediocre' (p. 59).

63 González Echevarría, 'Canaima', p. 503.

64 Kutzinski, Against the American Grain, p. 3; Mark I. Millington, 'Gender Monologue
    in Carpentier's Los pasos perdidos', Modern Language Notes, 111 (1996), pp. 346–67 (p.
    356).

65 Wyers, 'Carpentier's Los pasos perdidos', p. 91.

66 David D. Gilmore, Manhood in the Making: Cultural Concepts of Masculinity (New Haven:
    Yale University Press, 1990), p. 36.

67 Harrs, Los nuestros, p. 70.

68 Chao, Conversaciones, p. 152.

69 Donald L. Shaw, *Alejo Carpentier* (Boston: Twayne, 1985), p. 50.
70 Simone de Beauvoir, *Force of Circumstance*, trans. Richard Howard (London: Deutsch, 1965), p. 347.
71 Chao, *Conversaciones*, p. 155.
72 Mario Vargas Llosa, *El hablador* (Barcelona: Seix Barral, 1997), p. 152.

CHAPTER FIVE

Jungle Fever:
Degeneration as a Trop[olog]ical Disease

> It was the jungle, the endless, all-embracing, fearful jungle, that overwhelmed my mind. No shipwrecked mariner driven to madness by long tossing on a raft at sea ever conceived such hatred and horror of his surroundings as that which now came upon me for the fresh, perpetual, monotonous green of the interminable forest.
>
> F. W. Up de Graff, *Head Hunters of the Amazon*[1]

In the introduction to his 1845 biography, *Facundo*, Domingo Sarmiento characterized the future of Argentina as 'una lucha [...] entre los últimos progresos del espíritu humano y los rudimentos de la vida salvaje, entre las ciudades populosas y los bosques sombríos'.[2] This view of South America as an epic struggle between civilization and barbarism – a barbarism which finds its fullest expression in 'los bosques sombríos' – reinvigorated a motif that can be traced from the very beginnings of Spanish-American literature in the early modern chronicle, which regarded the Spanish colonization of the New World as a battle between culture and nature, Christianity and paganism. It also anticipated a debate which was to reach fruition in the late nineteenth and early twentieth centuries regarding Latin America's destiny as a 'continente enfermo' (the title of a 1899 pamphlet by the Venezuelan César Zumeta) – a land enervated by its 'unhealthy' ethnic and telluric make-up.[3] This debate often focused on climate, particularly on the influence of the tropics on health and national prosperity.

In the first decades of the twentieth century, literature continued to be one of the principal ways in which Latin Americans explored the civilization/barbarism question. In the *novela de la tierra*, in particular, writers such as Gallegos and Quiroga dramatized the struggle between the barbarous forces of nature and the civilizing influences of the city. While telluric novels such as *Doña Bárbara* might be seen to reconcile these opposing forces, this is not the case in the *novela de la selva*, where the harnessing of wild nature lacks any sense of moderation. Indeed, as Jean Franco has incisively concluded of the quintessential *novela de la selva*: 'If *La vorágine* has a message, it is that nature is more powerful than civilization in Latin America.'[4] Far from establishing a balance between civilization and barbarism, the *novela de la selva* presents the tropics as a space of uncurbed degeneration. The previous chapter traced myths of wild nature as a playground for the urban traveller – a space for the buttressing of selfhood and of masculinity. This chapter will show how, in the *novela de la selva*, travel to the jungle leads only to self-disintegration, with the traveller's tenuous mask of urbanity slipping to reveal the underbelly of civilization – the forces of barbarism and irrationalism which, as Foucault has argued in *Madness and Civilization*, have been stifled but not expelled by the institutions of modernity.[5] Beyond the 'holy terror of scandal and gallows and lunatic asylums', the innate savagery of civilized man is unleashed, resulting in unrestrained atavism.[6] Unlike Rousseau's model of the Noble Savage, those who 'go native' in the *novela de la selva* end up at best tattered, stammering, and tenuously clinging to their sanity, at worst driven mad by the 'heavy mute spell of the wilderness', yelling at trees, stripping off their clothes, laughing hysterically, and engaging in heinous crimes.[7]

This chapter will position the urban traveller's slip into savagery in the *novela de la selva* within the context of nineteenth- and early twentieth-century debates about tropical degeneration. The theme of the double will be of particular interest, especially how it relates to the idea of civilization and barbarism not as dichotomous forces but as co-existing in every human being. In his discussion of Brazilian geography, R. M. Morse has argued that:

> We must [...] speak not of a frontier but of multiple complex frontier experiences, transactions and mutations. We can draw no fixed line between white man and Indian, civilization and primitivism, settled and unsettled areas, imperial outpost and autonomous community.[8]

This assertion – a less philosophical rendering of Walter Benjamin's statement that 'there is no document of civilization which is not at the same time a document of barbarism' – can also be applied to the figure of the urban traveller in the jungle, whose outer semblance of insuperable civility time and again gives way to barbarism.[9]

In some respects, the *novela de la selva*'s engagement with the theme of tropical degeneration might appear to revitalize the colonialist tropes of the early modern chronicle, the English imperial romance, or the discourses of tropical pathology which dominated views of the tropics in the late nineteenth and early twentieth centuries. Nevertheless, while European stereotypes of tropical degeneration instantiated an anxiety about the precariousness of European civilization and its potential to slip into barbarism (a pessimism which only increased in the twentieth century when the dissolution of European imperialism was all but inevitable, and reached its peak in Oswald Spengler's *The Decline of the West*) many Latin Americans were drawing upon the notion of the innate savagery of tropical nature counter-intuitively. As early as 1823, for example, the European soldier and merchant, Gaspard Théodore Mollien, noted in his *Travels in the Republic of Colombia* how Colombians actively encouraged perceptions of some of the country's regions as unhealthy, believing that disease would act as a disincentive to European invasion.[10]

The tendency for characters to 'go native' in the *novela de la selva* is an important aspect of the genre's wider parody of European discourses of the tropics. Just as the Brazilian modernists drew ironically upon the imperial trope of cannibalism in their 'Anthropophagous Manifesto', the authors of the *novela de la selva* recognized not only the urgent need to reconstruct the tropics from a Latin American perspective but also the potential to exploit Western fears of the degenerative influence of the rainforest to this very end. In chapters 2 and 3 I explored how the *novela de la selva* invested the colonial trope of 'Otherness' with new meaning in relation to landscape aesthetics and anthropology. In this chapter it will be shown that the urban traveller's slip into savagery in the tropical jungle issues the mortal blow to the leitmotif of Otherness. Although the urban protagonists describe the forest and its indigenous inhabitants in narratives replete with imperial tropes, in these novels the colonial gaze is returned and it is they who register as conspicuously exotic. Throughout the *novela de la selva* the notion of savagery is intensified and transformed into a powerful postcolonial rejoinder, with the tropical jungle refashioned not as a place of self-discovery, but of self-disintegration and corruption.

Tropical Degeneration

The precariousness of civilization and the ease with which Europeans could revert to primitivism outside the so-called temperate zone were abiding concerns in Europe and its imperial outposts from the middle of the nineteenth century. While in the eighteenth century it was generally believed that Europeans living or travelling in the tropics could acclimatize, during the nineteenth century, particularly after colonial campaigns in the Indian subcontinent and Africa, this optimism gave way to constructions of the tropics as pestilential and degenerate.[11] Africa, in particular, was conceived in the popular imagination as a 'dark continent' – a space not just of native savagery but where Europeans might unleash their repressed animal instincts. Tropical regions, with their sultry climate and luxuriant vegetation, were correlated with unbridled sexuality and savagery – conditions which were thought to lead to degeneration in settlers. In the late nineteenth century, the tropics were literally and figuratively mapped in terms of disease when the concentration of 'tropical' diseases such as malaria, yellow fever, and leprosy began to be represented schematically as part of the new discipline of Tropical Medicine.[12] It was widely held that the twin threats of climate and miscegenation would lead to an inexorable decline of Europeans in the tropics. Eugene Talbot in *Degeneracy: Its Causes, Signs and Results* [1898] followed on from the work of the Comte de Gobineau and F. W. Farrar's argument that the European traveller to the tropics could become indolent and destitute, and could 'accelerate the degenerative process by illicit relations which resulted in degenerative offspring'.[13] Benjamin Kidd in his 1898 *The Control of the Tropics* was most explicit in his call for the abandonment of colonial projects in tropical regions:

the attempt to acclimatize the white man in the tropics must be recognized to be a blunder of the first magnitude. [...] In climatic conditions which are a burden to him; in the midst of races in a different and lower stage of development; divorced from the influences which have produced him, from the moral and political environment from which he sprang, the white man does not in the end, in such circumstances, tend so much to raise the level of the races amongst whom he has made his unnatural home, as he tends himself to sink slowly to the level around him.[14]

In fin de siècle colonial fiction the tropics was viewed not only as a space of masculine adventure but also of disease and pathology. A panoply of fictional travellers testifies to the dangers of tropical travel: in *Heart of Darkness* Kurtz goes mad and dies in the jungle, and in Evelyn Waugh's *A Handful of Dust* Tony is taken captive by a mad Englishman, Mr Todd, in the wilds of Brazil, and is forced to remain there reading aloud the works of Charles Dickens. European travel literature on the tropics from the late nineteenth and early twentieth centuries also stresses the hardships and potential hazards of journeys in the 'torrid zone'. In his 1914 travel account, *The Upper Reaches of the Amazon*, the English traveller Joseph F. Woodroffe describes the Amazon as overrun with diseases, flea-infested wild pigs, and Europeans, such as the Englishman in the passage below, who had 'gone native' in the tropics:

> an Englishman appeared, seated in a crazy boat, almost square, and made apparently out of a biscuit box or other similar packing-case. The man was almost naked, his clothes worn to shreds, and his skin burned to the colour of a boiled lobster.[15]

Another traveller to the Amazon in the same period is described as having emerged from the forest as 'an emaciated fever-wreck, placing one foot before the other only with much exertion'.[16]

Spanish-American intellectuals in the tropics were also concerned with theories of racial and environmental determinism.[17] In the decade from 1899 to 1909 a number of fundamental texts on degeneration were published in Latin America, including Agustín Alvarez's *Manual de patología política*, Manuel Ugarte's *Enfermedades sociales*, and Carlos Octavio Bunge's *Nuestra América* – a book which classified the different races of South America and concluded with the belief that 'the mestizo tends to reproduce a kind of primitive man, or, at least an ancient and pre-Christian man'.[18] Although in this period many Latin American thinkers attributed the 'barbarism' of the continent's political unrest to racial mixing, encouraging immigration from Europe to counteract the Indian influence, a growth in nationalism from the 1920s onwards produced works such as the Mexican José Vasconcelos's *La raza cósmica*, which argued for 'constructive miscegenation', believing that *mestizaje* could help to forge a hybrid race congenitally suited to America's hostile physical environment.[19]

Far from distancing themselves from European views of the tropics as a place of moral lassitude and disease, the authors of the *novela de la selva* appeared to intensify tropes of tropical degeneration. A spell in the Amazon rainforest in the *novela de la selva* leads to mental and physical degeneration among many of the white characters. In *Green Mansions*, Abel's trip to the jungle reduces him 'almost to a skeleton by fever and misery of all kinds' (p. 4); in *La vorágine,* Cova disappears without a trace; and in *Canaima* we learn of Mr Davenport's imported American livestock which 'no resitían el clima' (p. 121), and of the Italian Count given to 'internarse [...] en las selvas del Cuyuni' (p. 127), and who one day did not return. Although the narrator of *Los pasos perdidos* is reluctantly 'rescued' from the jungle by a search party led by his hysterical wife, other urban travellers in the novel do not fare so well: Mouche contracts malaria, Fray Pedro is discovered 'atrozmente mutilado' (p. 263) at the hands of Amerindians, and El Adelantado's village is frequented by a leper, a former *buscador de oro*, who attempts to rape a young child. His decaying face – 'un residuo, una piltrafa de semblante, una escoria de carne que aún se sujeta en torno a un agujero negro, abierto en sombras de garganta, cerca de dos ojos sin expresión' (p. 228) – seems a fittingly didactic symbol for the jungle's degenerative influence, especially on those who attempt to exploit it. The workers of *La vorágine* and *Canaima* suffer a similar fate, their dreams of quick riches lost in the reality of peonage in the eternal jungle gloom, where we witness them dying of fever or being tortured by their overseers.

A repeated motif in many European narratives of tropical degeneration is the representation of the jungle as a point of no return, which draws the traveller into its dark heart only to hinder all future attempts at escape. This is a theme which seems to be at odds with the arrogant assurance of uncontaminated travel that drives the European adventure narrative. The possibility that the traveller might not emerge from his or her trip to the tropics stresses the very real dangers of the jungle and modifies exploration as less a case of filling in the empty spaces on colonial maps, or testing one's mettle, than a matter of life and death. *Heart of Darkness* exemplifies the motif of the brooding forest swallowing up all traces of the traveller:

> The reaches opened before us and closed behind, as if the forest had stepped leisurely across the water to bar the way for our return. We penetrated deeper and deeper into the heart of darkness. (p. 37)

The personification of the forest stepping 'leisurely' behind Marlow's boat not only adumbrates the superfluity of anthropomorphic imagery in the *novela de la selva* but also initiates the theme of man as a plaything of the wilderness. Throughout *Heart of Darkness*, Marlow intimates the notion of a ludic combativeness on the part of the jungle, which begins with 'playful paw-strokes' (p. 43) and 'prodigious peal[s] of laughter' (p. 49), before moving on to drive the traveller raving mad. Almost all of the narrators of the *novela de la selva* allude to the concept of an animate 'selva enemiga' (*La vorágine*, p. 213). Cova, in the midst of a cataleptic fit, echoes Kurtz's parting shot at the wilderness – 'Oh, but I will wring your heart yet' (p. 67) – when he directly defies the forest to kill him, 'si quieres, que estoy vivo aún' (p. 229), and in *Los pasos perdidos* the narrator styles a succession of terrifying experiences navigating along the Orinoco River as 'pruebas' issued by the jungle as a rite of passage to primitivism.[20] Nevertheless, in this novel and in the *novela de la selva* more generally, characters quickly come to realize the futility of struggling against tropical nature. As the soldiers of Carpentier's *El siglo de las luces* recognize as they emerge fatigued and grimy from an unsuccessful mission in the jungle: 'Esto no es guerra. [...] Se puede pelear con los hombres. No se puede pelear con los árboles.'[21]

The trope of the forest as a point of no return is invoked throughout the *novela de la selva*. In *Canaima* the American settler, Mr Davenport, meditates on the case of the dying English engineer, Mr Reed, who typifies the propensity for Westerners to become 'marooned' in the jungle:

'Puede que esté tuberculoso, como dicen, pero su enfermedad más grave, su enfermedad incurable, tiene otro nombre. Se llama chinchorro, que es la enfermedad más traidora de esta tierra. La madre de ese muchacho es rica, [...] y ya varias veces le ha escrito que se vaya a un sanatorio de Suiza, el mejor que quiera elegir para su curación; pero ya él ha cogido gusto al chinchorrito de moriche y de ahí nadie lo arranca ni con una yunta de bueyes.'[...]

'También tiene un catre de campaña que no es producto de esta tierra' objeta Néstor Salazar.

'Sí.¡Pero el chinchorrito, el chinchorrito! Cuando yo digo esta cosa quiero decir todo lo que significa el trópico para los hombres que no hemos nacido en él. Tú decides marcharte, porque ves que por dentro de ti ya no anda bien la cosa, y el trópico te dice, suavecito en la oreja: "Deja eso para después, musiú. Hay tiempo para todo."' (p. 126)

The comic neologism, the malady 'el chinchorrito', becomes a synonym of 'el mal de la selva' – a strain of jungle fever that coaxes the traveller to remain amid the miasmic vegetation despite all of its pernicious effects. Mr Reed's malady can be related to the popular belief in 'tropical inertia' – a tendency to indolence that was thought to afflict many travellers to lowland forests. A 1915 work by the Yale geographer Ellsworth Huntington, *Civilization and Climate*, describes the classic symptoms of 'tropical inertia':

After a long sojourn in the tropics it is hard to spur one's self to the physical effort of a mountain climb, and equally hard to think out the steps in a long chain of reasoning. The mind, like the body, wants rest.[22]

Mr Davenport himself suffers from tropical inertia, being 'uno de los extranjeros que, yendo a aquella tierra en plan temporal de negocio o de aventura, luego se "quedan varados" en ella' (p. 121). In a placid acceptance of his fate, Mr Davenport names his ranch 'El varadero' – the dry dock – which, as he explains to Marcos, is a fitting symbol for the tropics: 'El varadero es el trópico, chico. Esta cosa sabrosa de contester a todo lo que te proponen: "Déjalo para mañana, chico. Del apuro no queda sino el cansancio"' (p. 121).

In the Amazon jungle this tendency to inertia among white travellers becomes even more pronounced. In *La vorágine* it is likened to bewitchment – the 'embrujamiento de la selva':

> La selva los aniquila, la selva los retiene, la selva los llama para tragárselos. Los que escapan, aunque se refugien en las ciudades, llevan ya el maleficio en cuerpo y en alma. Mustios, envejecidos, decepcionados, no tienen más que una aspiración: volver, volver, a sabiendas de que si vuelven perecerán. Y los que se quedan, los que desoyen el llamamiento de la montaña, siempre declinan en la miseria, víctimas de dolencias desconocidas, siendo carne palúdica de hospital, entregándose a la cuchilla que les recorta el hígado por pedazos, como en pena de algo sacrílego que cometieron contra los indios, contra los árboles. (p. 355)

Throughout the *novela de la selva* the jungle is not only presented as an insidious degenerative force, debilitating to mind and body, but also as powerfully animate – 'un ser sensible' (*La vorágine*, p. 297), capable of luring men to their death. The so-called 'mal de la selva' emerges as an illness which does not afflict those native to the jungle, but rather outsiders who attempt to exploit the forest, particularly rubber workers. These workers seem doubly trapped in *Canaima* and *La vorágine*, both by the malignant forest and the cycle of debt bondage from which many of them will never escape. The use of the verb 'tragar' in the above passage corresponds to an extended metaphor throughout *La vorágine*, which presents the jungle as a vortex capable of ingesting all traces of the traveller. This is not only the infamous fate of the novel's protagonist, who is 'devoured' by the jungle, but also that of two native oarsmen, who are drowned in a whirlpool: 'el embudo trágico los sorbió a todos. [...] Los sombreros de los dos náufragos quedaron girando en el remolino' (p. 233). Throughout the *novela de la selva* the forest is compared over and over again to a prison, an abyss, a purgatory, and a hell. Like the metaphor of the jungle as a vortex, these images emphasize the potential irreversibility of any journey to the tropics – a space which can engulf the traveller, mentally and physically, and inhibit his return back home.

The Double

The concern with tropical degeneration in late nineteenth- and early twentieth-century travel writing is closely related to the concept of the double – the glimpse of the Self in the Other, or of the Other in the Self – which is an all-pervasive motif of the *novela de la selva*. Chronologically this concords with the popularity of the doppelgänger in British fin de siècle literature, represented by pairs such as Holmes/Moriarty, Van Helsing/Dracula, Marlow/Kurtz, and Jekyll/Hyde. William Greenslade has argued that these duos were 'emblematically figured for a post-Darwinian culture as the beast in man' – a product of what would have been the rather unnerving breakdown of boundaries between humans and animals precipitated by nineteenth-century theories of evolution.[23] The theme of the 'beast in man' is present in much late nineteenth- and early twentieth-century British imperial literature. In Rider Haggard's *She*, for example, the protagonist is described as closely resembling a gorilla:

> he was shortish, rather bow-legged, very deep chested, and with unusually long arms. He had dark hair and small eyes, and the hair grew right down on his forehead, and his whiskers grew right up to his hair, so that there was uncommonly little of his countenance to be seen. Altogether he reminded me forcibly of a gorilla.[24]

Likewise, in Conan Doyle's *The Lost World*, the urban travellers encounter a race of apemen in the Jurassic forest, the leader of which bears more than a passing resemblance to one of their party, Professor Challenger:

> In all things he was [...] the very image of our Professor, save that his colouring was red instead of black. [...] Only above the eyebrows, where the sloping forehead and low, curved skull of the ape-man were in sharp contrast to the broad brow and magnificent cranium of the European, could one see any marked difference. At every other point the king was an absurd parody of the Professor.[25]

This description is crudely evolutionist in its evocation of the physical parallels between the rather simian scientist and the apeman, and seems to predicate the final distinction between the two not on their adhesion to the category of human or animal but on racial grounds. It is only Professor Challenger's 'magnificent' European skull which ultimately sets him apart from his savage ancestor.

The theme of the 'beast in man' is present in each of the novels under consideration here and is often occasioned by the narrators' reflections on the proximity of their culture to that of the indigenous people they meet in the jungle. Their encounters with 'primitive' doubles often precipitate a sensation of the uncanny, as defined in Sigmund Freud's 1925 essay 'Das Unheimliche'. If we eschew the standard translation of *unheimlich* as 'uncanny' for the more literal equivalent of 'unhomely', its pertinence to travel literature and, as Bhabha has argued, to colonialism and postcolonialism, becomes apparent.[26] In his seminal essay Freud defines the term not only in contradistinction to the homely, but to the indigenous, given the etymological intersections between *heimlich* and *heimisch* (native). This means that, in many respects, foreign accounts of the New World constitute a literature of the *unheimlich*, sated with glimpses of exotic and frightening Otherness that leads us back 'to what is known of old and long familiar'.[27] When Cova observes a tribal dance in *La vorágine*, for example, he is gradually drawn in by its uncanny familiarity:

> miraba yo la singular fiesta, complacido de que mis compañeros giraran ebrios en la danza. [...] Mas, a poco, advertí que gritaban como la tribu, y que su lamento acusaba la misma pena recóndita [...]. Su queja tenía la desesperación de las razas vencidas, y era semejante a mi sollozo, ese sollozo de mis aflicciones que suele repercutir en mi corazón aunque lo disimulen los labios: ¡Aaaaay... Ohé! ... (p. 211)

This mirrors an episode in *Heart of Darkness* when Marlow watches a dance and exclaims 'what thrilled you was just the thought of their humanity – like yours – the thought of your remote kinship with this wild and passionate uproar. Ugly.' (pp. 37–38) – one of many passages in Conrad's novella which led Achebe to disclaim the author as 'a thoroughgoing racist'.[28] Marlow's use of the ambiguous verb 'thrill' denotes, on the one hand, longing and, on the other hand, fear and trepidation – a response which is shared by Cova. In Gallegos's 1935 novel, Marcos experiences a similar feeling when he witnesses a 'danza lúbrica, sin arte alguno, bestia pura' (p. 182). While the other white spectators titter at the drug-induced anguish of the tribe, Marcos is transfixed by the dance and eventually joins in on the chanting. This scene cannot be said to share the same impulses of the uncanny as those described above. For one thing, Marcos does not look upon the Amerindians through the same lens of solipsism as Marlow or Cova, and therefore is not so hostile to the idea of a common bond of humanity uniting the tribesmen and himself. In both *Heart of Darkness* and *La vorágine* the narrators prefer to believe that they 'were cut off from the comprehension of [their] surroundings' (*Heart of Darkness*, p. 37), rather than run the risk of ancestral recognition.

Many characters in the *novela de la selva* share this antagonistic response to the Other, as if they sense, in all the horror of primitivism, their own potential to degenerate in the jungle. Carpentier's narrator is perhaps the least open to the notion of a common core of humanity linking himself to the Amerindians he meets in the forest. During one visit to an Amerindian village he describes 'perros anteriores a los perros', women 'cuyos senos son ubres fláccidas', and children 'que se estiran y ovillan con gestos felinos' (p. 185). The proliferation of animal imagery testifies to what the narrator perceives to be a sharp descent down the evolutionary ladder, the nadir of which comes when El Adelantado directs him, in true anthropological fashion, to 'un hueco fangoso', where he sees:

> las más horribles cosas que mis ojos hayan conocido: son como dos fetos vivientes, con barbas blancas, en cuyas bocas belfudas gimotea algo semejante al vagido de un recién nacido; enanos arrugados, de vientres enormes, cubiertos de venas azules como figuras de planchas anatómicas, que sonríen estúpidamente, con algo temeroso y servil en la mirada [...]. Tal es el horror que me producen esos seres, que me vuelvo de espaldas a ellos, movido, a la vez, por la repulsión y el espanto. [...] Siento una suerte de vértigo ante la posibilidad de otros escalafones de retroceso, al pensar que esas larvas humanas, de cuyas ingles cuelga un sexo eréctil, como el mío, no sean todavía *lo último*. (pp. 185–86)

This is a paradigmatic instance of the *unheimlich*. While the narrator vociferously denies any parallels between himself and these 'larvas humanas', it is clear that his 'espanto' and 'horror' derive from just such a realization. While the above description draws heavily upon Aristotelian theories of imperfection, widespread at the time of the Spanish conquest of the New World, and thereby fitting with the narrator's self-styling as a conquistador, the narrator is not able to offset completely his fear that these 'entes' might hold the seeds of his own physiology, just as the village dogs have 'ojos de zorros y de lobos' (p. 185). The social alienation of the physically deformed has been well documented in medieval and early modern writing. Augustus is reputed to have detested dwarfs as aberrations of nature and portents of evil,[29] and in Book Seven of his *Ethics* Albertus Magnus associates the physically disabled with 'bestial men'.[30] The narrator's appeal to these dusty banalities, and to colonial tropes of native stupidity, sexual lasciviousness, and unsavoury dietary norms lightly conceals his horrified recognition of the similarities between the dwarfs and himself – of their 'sexo eréctil, como el mío' (p. 186).

The sensation of the *unheimlich*, Freud argues, is not produced by something 'new or alien, but something which is familiar and old-established in the mind and which has become alienated from it only through the process of repression'.[31] In their discussion of imagery surrounding 'the double' in British imperial literature, Peter Brooker and Peter Widdowson have noted the persistent references to pits or abysses, which correspond to the repressed or the unconscious in a Freudian model of the psyche.[32] In the *novela de la selva* the jungle is the symbolic equivalent of the abyss – a comparison which D. H. Lawrence also makes when he metaphorically describes how 'our feelings are the first manifestations within the aboriginal jungle of us. Till now, in sheer terror of ourselves, we have turned our backs on the jungle, fenced it in with an enormous entanglement of barbed wire and declared it did not exist.'[33] For the protagonists of the *novela de la selva*, too, travel in the tropics is likened to a journey through the unconscious mind, which succeeds in awakening 'forgotten and brutal instincts' (*Heart of Darkness*, p. 65), long lulled to sleep by urban torpor.

Dressing to Impress

In much travel literature, minutiae relating to clothes and grooming acquire added significance as markers of the struggle between civilization and barbarism – between urban man and his primitive double. Telling references to apparel were present from the very earliest chronicles on the New World, when Columbus set the tone in his relentlessly voyeuristic descriptions of the Amerindians' nudity. In the first decades of the Spanish conquest the New World was a site of cultural uprooting and replanting, a locus of radical *mestizaje* and hybridity, which Pratt has referred to as a 'contact zone'.[34] Such cultural fusion led to disquiet about the rapid breakdown of visual boundaries between urban travellers and indigenous peoples, an example of which can be found in Bernal Díaz's *Historia verdadera de la conquista de la Nueva España*, when he describes the appearance of a Spanish man who had lived among the Indians for many years:

> ¿qué es del Español? aunque iba allí junto con él, porque le tenian por Indio propio, porque de suyo era moreno, [...] y traia un remo al hombro, y una cotara

vieja calzada, y la otra en la cinta, y una manta vieja muy ruin, é un braguero
peor, con que cubria sus vergüenzas, y traia atada en la manta un bulto, que eran
Horas muy viejas.[35]

The disorientation of Cortés's men is accentuated by the fact that the 'Spaniard'
speaks in broken Castilian and squats down before them 'á manera de Indio
esclavo'.[36] This figure becomes a textual metonym for the cultural syncretism
which characterized the conquest of Mexico. While his physical appearance
(dark skin; untidy hair) conforms to native typology, the loincloth and prayer
book tenuously connect him to Western culture. Throughout Díaz's narrative, references to apparel are a gauge of allegiance to Spanish society. For
example, the atavism of the Spaniard Gonzalo Guerrero, who marries a native
woman and masterminds an attack on Cortés's fleet, is signalled principally
via his penchant for tattoos and piercings. Likewise, when the troops' indigenous interpreter flees, Díaz informs us tellingly that he had left his Spanish
clothes hanging in a tree. Perhaps the most famous early modern traveller to
'go native' was Cabeza de Vaca, who recounts in *Naufragios* his epic travels
through the American wilderness. This text epitomizes the gradual erosion of
Western cultural artefacts before the exigencies of survival: Cabeza de Vaca
and his crew kill their horses, destroy their guns, and rip up their clothes in
an attempt to construct new boats, thus being materially reduced to the level
of the Native Americans – naked and technologically defenceless. Although
Cabeza de Vaca seems unruffled in his admission of enforced naturism, he
does record the consternation it causes among onlookers, including among
a group of Native Americans who had befriended Cabeza de Vaca's ill-fated
men, and who flee in terror when they see them naked.[37] The theme of misrec-
ognition in the anecdotes of Cabeza de Vaca and Bernal Díaz reveals how,
during the first years of European colonization in the Americas, propriety of
dress was regarded as an important marker of the wearer's ongoing adherence
to European values and morality.

Writers of fiction quickly adapted the correlation between 'going native'
and the shedding of clothes. In Henry Neville's 1668 desert island utopia *The
Isle of Pines*, the English inhabitants quickly abandon the custom of wearing
clothes, yet it is implicit throughout the text that this is the first step in the
islanders' slide into uncurbed sexuality and lawlessness. In Daniel Defoe's
Robinson Crusoe [1719], clothes are presented as fundamental to the stability
of the subject as a shield against the maladies of primitivism. Despite being
stranded on an island for over two decades, the eponymous hero clings to
English mores, especially those relating to dress, long after they have become
merely gestural:

> The Weather was so violent hot, that there was no need of Cloaths, yet I could
> not go quite naked; no, tho' I had been inclin'd to it, which I was not, nor could
> not abide the thoughts of it, tho' I was all alone.[38]

The syntactical confusion of this sentence accentuates the sense of futility in
Crusoe's continuing compliance with Western customs. His intense disgust

at the idea of nudity, although fitting with the puritanical precepts of the work, smacks of overcompensation and seems to reflect his growing proclivities towards atavism. By the late nineteenth and early twentieth centuries, the recourse to clothes as a symbol of civilization or barbarism had become a hackneyed trope of travel literature and imperial fiction. Erskine Childers's 1903 spy novel *The Riddle of the Sands* opens with the lines: 'I have read of men who, when forced by their calling to live for long periods in utter solitude – save for a few black faces – have made it a rule to dress regularly for dinner in order to maintain their self-respect and prevent a relapse into barbarism', and this is a motto which resonates throughout travel literature, from the accountant in *Heart of Darkness* who continues to wear a 'high, starched collar, white cuffs, a light alpaca jacket, snowy trousers, a clean necktie, and varnished boots' (p. 21), to André Gide's attention to the niceties of dress throughout *Travels in the Congo*.[39] In Chapter 4 I discussed the turn to self-parody in Conan Doyle's *The Lost World*. The tendency in this novel to deflate the tropes of travel literature (which, as I have shown, fulfils a very different function in the late imperial romance than in the *novela de la selva*) is manifest in the narrator's amazement at his and his companions' rapid descent in the forest from 'the highest product of modern civilization to the most desperate savage[s] in South America' (p. 144) – a change which is principally signalled by their 'unshaven grimy faces' (p. 154) and 'bedraggled' (p. 154) clothes. The idea of appearance as somehow intrinsic to selfhood is supported, in particular, by Malone's description of Lord John:

> It was he – and yet it was not he. I had left him calm in his bearing, correct in his person, prim in his dress. Now he was pale and wild-eyed, gasping as he breathed like one who has run far and fast. His gaunt face was scratched and bloody, his clothes were hanging in rags, and his hat was gone. I stared in amazement. (pp. 136–37)

'It was he – and yet it was not he': this is a classic statement in imperial adventure literature on the tropics, echoed years later by Bhabha's description of the colonist as '*less than one and double*'.[40] While Lord John's murdering of an Amerindian guide earlier in the novel evinces little surprise or sympathy in the narrator, his dishevelment seems a major blow to the adventurer's status as an archetypal English gentleman.

It is no surprise that the *novela de la selva*, a genre which at every turn mimics and destabilizes European travel writing on the tropics, should engage with sartorial motifs. Throughout these novels the narrators communicate day-to-day facts relating to dress and grooming not only as a way to maintain a grip on reality but also as metonyms of their continued ties to the city. Clothes (or lack of clothes) are also an important symbol of degeneration. In *La vorágine*, Pipa, a white man who 'errante y desnudo vivió en las selvas más de veinte años' (p. 197), is a stark memento of the ease of atavism. Cova's demonization of Pipa as a paradigm of the worst excesses of primitivism is based largely on the latter's physical appearance, particularly his 'prurito de desnudarse' (p. 212), and his tattoos and scarification. Throughout the *novela de la selva* clothes are revealed as flimsily inadequate against tropical nature. More commonly the protagonists are defeated by the incipient forces of barbarism, symbolized by merciless climatic damp and grime. In *Los pasos perdidos* the tropics radically alters Mouche's appearance:

> El cutis, maltratado por aguas duras, se le había enrojecido, descubriendo zonas de poros demasiado abiertos en la nariz y en las sienes. El pelo se le había vuelto como de estopa, de un rubio verde, desigualmente matizado, revelándome lo mucho que debía su cobrizo relumbre habitual al manejo de inteligentes coloraciones. Bajo una blusa manchada por resinas raras caídas de las lonas, su busto parecía menos firme. (p. 125)

Despite her efforts to disguise the ill-effects of the climate, the narrator describes how '[e]n pocos días, una naturaleza fuerte, honda y dura, se había *divertido* en desarmarla, cansarla, afearla, quebrarla, asestándole, de pronto, el golpe de gracia' (p. 152: my emphasis). Although the narrator may well be shifting the referent of the verb from himself to the jungle in this passage, the use of 'divertirse' is significant. The reference to the jungle's 'enjoyment' animates the natural milieu as a spritish observer of the urban traveller's misfortunes in its midst, and recalls the Conradian notion of the 'playful paw-strokes' (p. 43) of the wilderness discussed above. In *La vorágine* Cova also struggles against his tendency to dishevelment in the jungle. He is outraged when Zoraida Ayram calls him 'mugroso', leading him to exclaim angrily, 'A ver si vuelve a decirme mugroso. [...] Esta noche lavaremos nuestros vestidos y los secaremos a la candela' (p. 324).

The fact that whiteness came to be associated with health in discourses of tropical pathology elucidates the importance of images of dirt in these novels. The narrator of *Los pasos perdidos* describes the typical appearance of those who live in the jungle as 'sucios, pringosos; las camisas ensombrecidas desde adentro por el sudor' (p. 165), and in *Canaima* Juan Solito is said to have an 'aspecto selvático' (p. 32) – 'barbudo, greñudo' and dirty. The darkening of the travellers' skin, whether via grime or a suntan, synecdochically hints at their greater brush with moral darkness in the jungle and can be related to late nineteenth-century concerns with racial degeneration. Nevertheless, unlike imperial travel accounts, where the disarray of the traveller is easily corrected with a bath and a change of clothes, these postcolonial novels suggest that the onset of barbarism is much more irreversible. In the *novela de la selva* the tropical travellers' misplaced assurance in their immunity to the forces of the jungle is mocked by their rapid physical degeneration in the forest.

Of all the references to apparel in the *novela de la selva*, it is Abel in *Green Mansions* who exemplifies the futile struggle of the urban traveller to remain neat and tidy in the midst of the tropical forest. Catching a glimpse of his unkempt reflection in a forest pool, he describes how:

> [...] it showed me a gaunt, ragged man with a tangled mass of black hair falling over his shoulders, the bones of his face showing through the dead-looking,

sun-parched skin, the sunken eyes with a gleam in them that was like insanity.

To see this reflection had a strangely disturbing effect on me. A torturing voice would whisper in my ear: 'Yes, you are evidently going mad. By-and-by you will rush howling through the forest, only to drop down at last and die [...].'

[...] I cut from a tree a score of long, blunt thorns, tough and black as whalebone, and drove them through a strip of wood in which I had burnt a row of holes to receive them, and made myself a comb, and combed out my long, tangled hair to improve my appearance.

'It is not the tangled condition of your hair,' persisted the voice, 'but your eyes, so wild and strange in their expression, that show the approach of madness. Make your socks as smooth as you like, [...] but the crazed look will remain just the same.' (pp. 186–87)

Here, Hudson proffers a revised narrative of the urban traveller's experience of wilderness – one of the many tales of transgression that have been edited out of European travel accounts of America. This scene resonates with imagery of the doppelgänger, from the schizophrenic voices echoing in Abel's head to the pervasive mirror imagery – an aspect further intensified when Abel throws a stone into the pool, shattering his reflection into a million fragments. Abel refers to his reflection as though disembodied, offsetting his connections to the 'gaunt, ragged man' by the use of the third person, and the generic 'the'.[41] Just as Cova and Marlow negate any parallels between themselves and the chanting tribesmen, so does Abel refuse to acknowledge the forces of wildness welling up within. His attempt to propitiate the schizophrenic voices which taunt him in the forest by improvising a comb is futile and serves only to highlight the connection between his external and internal savagery.

In many respects, this episode is not only paradigmatic of the pervasive anti-pastoralism of the *novela de la selva* as a whole, but of Freud's understanding of the *unheimlich* as all that is 'concealed and kept out of sight': man's repressed primitive instincts, kept at bay by the ebb of city living.[42] Macpherson has explained that within Romantic literature mirror images tend to refine one's reflection, often providing an image which is more beautiful or perfect than the original.[43] Despite the obvious self-styling of the protagonists of the *novela de la selva* after Romantic heroes, in this instance Abel's repulsive reflection strikes a darker note and is suggestive of the alter ego, corresponding to contemporary discussions of the precariousness of Western civilization and of the fragility of the rational mind. Henry Maudsley in his 1895 *The Pathology of Mind* referred directly to the significance of mirrors as a means of glimpsing the internal 'double':

Now and then a person may detect in his own face in the looking-glass a momentary flash of expression of the sort which he will find formal in the portrait of an ancestor [...]. Beneath every face are the latent faces of ancestors, beneath every character their characters.[44]

Hudson's rewriting of the Narcissus myth, which hinges on Abel's horrified rejection of his image, might be explained by what Michael Parker and Roger Starkey regard as the intertextual tendency of postcolonial literature to engage with the mythologies of classical Europe and to reinscribe them 'into new contemporary complexities of alienation'.[45] The explicit invocation of the Narcissus legend (bear in mind also that the Arabic root of Abel means 'vanity') serves only to undermine the pertinence of myths of Western integrity to a colonial world which is predicated on the precarious distinction between Self and Other, and on 'a doubling, dividing and interchanging of the self'.[46] Abel and the other belated travellers of the *novela de la selva* should not, after all, expect to recognize their reflections at a time when, in the words of Bhabha, '[t]he displacement from symbol to sign creates a crisis for any concept of authority based on a system of recognition: colonial specularity, doubly inscribed, does not produce a mirror where the self apprehends itself; it is always the split screen of the self and its doubling, the hybrid.'[47]

Dietary Taboos

In many respects the urban travellers who slip into savagery in the jungle resemble the medieval Wild Man, a figure which, as Richard Bernheimer has argued in his classic study, sprang from an unrelenting 'psychological urge [...] to give external expression and symbolically valid form to the impulses of reckless physical self-assertion which are hidden in all of us, but are normally kept under control'.[48] Roger Bartra has developed Bernheimer's thesis in his observation that the representation of the Wild Man in the Middle Ages seems to have been motivated by the need to negotiate the boundaries between man and beast and, more broadly, those between nature and culture.[49] As Hayden White has observed, the particular menace of the Wild Man was his role both 'as nemesis and as a possible destiny, both as enemy and as representative of a condition into which an individual man, having fallen out of grace or having been driven from his city, might degenerate'.[50]

There are many parallels between the medieval image of the Wild Man and the urban travellers who slip into savagery in the *novela de la selva*. Often referred to as *Homo sylvaticus*, the Wild Man was a denizen of the woods. He was notoriously hairy and unkempt, rather like Abel in the above description, he lacked sexual inhibition, he lived outside time, and he was solitary. What is more, he lived off the grubs and plants in the forest, he was unfamiliar with fire, and he consumed meat raw. The association of the Wild Man with the transgression of Western dietary taboos adheres to long-established ethnographical patterns. Edith Hall has discussed how Greek writers forged a particular vocabulary for the barbarian predicated on his 'animal nature or appetites', thus intimating the connection between cultural Otherness and transgressive eating.[51] Such a view was perpetuated in early modern accounts of the Amerindians (for instance, in Columbus's description of the Caribs as man-eaters) and persisted in ethnography and travel writing well into the twentieth century.

Nevertheless, in many travel accounts the violation of dietary taboos, especially through cannibalism, took place not only among the indigenous population but also among the urban travellers who had 'gone native' in the tropics. Díaz and Cabeza de Vaca both admit to eating dogs and raw meat during their travels, and in *Naufragios* the only instances of cannibalism mentioned take place not among Native Americans but European travellers, a fact that outrages the former.[52] Fictional travellers, too, have not infrequently engaged in cannibalism, induced both by hunger and the onset of savagery. The 'strange rumours' (p. 34) surrounding Kurtz in *Heart of Darkness* – one of the unspeakable 'horrors' in the novel – is surely the spectre of cannibalism, which not only threatens Marlow as he sails upriver in the form of his ravenous cannibal crewmen, but also hovers insistently over Kurtz. Marlow appeals to the reader to make the leap from insinuation to certainty:

> But this must have been before his – let us say – nerves went wrong and caused him to preside at certain midnight dances ending with unspeakable rites, which – as far as I reluctantly gathered from what I heard at various times – were offered up to him – do you understand – to Mr. Kurtz himself. (p. 50)

Like the travellers in the *novela de la selva*, Kurtz's mask of civility has slipped to reveal the beast in man. As E. N. Dorall has argued, 'he tore down the façade behind which the other colonialists sheltered, and converted metaphor into brutal fact, not only devouring Africa, as they did, but, very specifically, devouring Africans'.[53]

Green Mansions is replete with references to transgressive eating, especially during Abel's struggle to allay starvation while he is living alone in the forest. Rima's vegetarianism is foregrounded in the novel and her disapproval of killing animals has the effect of demonizing meat-eating in general as 'unclean'. Prior to Rima's death, Abel tries to desist from eating meat. However, when he is on an arduous trip with Rima's guardian, Nuflo, he finally gives in to temptation:

> at length one of the dogs fell lame, and Nuflo, who was very hungry, made its lameness an excuse for despatching it [...]. He cut up and smoke-dried the flesh, and the intolerable pangs of hunger compelled me to share the loathsome food with him. We were not only indecent, it seemed to me, but cannibals to feed on the faithful servant that had been our butcher. (p. 161)

Although travellers have not infrequently eaten dog in times of dearth, within a Western tradition this meat has been considered unclean and has been associated with the unselective diets of the cultural Other, including Native Americans.[54] In *Green Mansions* the eating of dog seems particularly transgressive given that, firstly, the creature was a pet and, secondly, that it is described by Abel as a person – a 'servant' and a 'butcher' – figures who do, significantly, normally provide food.

Later on in the novel descriptions of Abel hunting for lizards or frogs and foraging for grubs and insects transgress all sorts of biblical taboos and closely align him to the figure of the Wild Man and to the Amerindians. In *Green Mansions* the consumption of meat is always correlated with animality. For example, a description of how Abel killed a sloth and 'crunched the bones and sucked the marrow, feeding *like some hungry carnivorous animal* (p. 196; my emphasis), explicitly connects him to dogs. This episode also has overtones of cannibalism given that, after the repast, Abel describes how he glances around and sees 'fragments scattered on the floor'. Hulme has shown that 'the primal scene of "cannibalism" as "witnessed" by Westerners is of its aftermath rather than its performance'.[55] Abel's postprandial vision of the scattered remnants of the sloth seems to allude to the tropological discovery of the cannibal feast in European travel accounts, except that, crucially, in this postcolonial rendering of it the traveller, and not the indigenous population, is responsible for the carnage.

In *Canaima*, the narrator attributes Marcos's slip into savagery not only to 'el mal de la selva' but also to 'la bárbara experiencia de alimentarse con el trozo de la presa cazada por el acarabisi, sin sal y apenas pasada por el fuego, mientras tuvo fósforos, [...] y últimamente crudo y sangrante' (p. 174). From the ancient Greeks to the present day, raw meat has been associated with cultural simplicity, demonstrating, as Pagden has explained, 'the barbarian's inability to modify significantly his environment'.[56] Lévi-Strauss develops the binary of the raw and the cooked into a more generalized 'culinary triangle', which extrapolates contrasts between nature and culture, processed and non-processed foods. Although the narrator of *Los pasos perdidos* is keen to stress the highbrow nature of his 'primitivism' in the jungle, telling details suggest that he comes close to the bone-chewing bestiality that he so abhors in the Amerindian dwarfs. When he first enters the jungle he observes how the raw inner organs of a tapir that is about to be roasted 'atiza [...] el desaforado apetito que suele atribuirse a los salvajes' (p. 158) – a statement which not only crudely draws upon imperial tropes of the inordinate appetite of the 'savage' but is also imbued with undertones of cannibalism, given that the Latin etymology of the past participle 'desaforado' means 'outside the law'. By alluding to the lighting of the fire, the skewers, and the raw meat, the narrator fashions this feast not, as he professes, after an ancient Mediterranean tradition but as a primal scene of cannibalism. The fact that the travellers decide to roast the meat is also significant, given Lévi-Strauss's discussion of roast meat in *The Origin of Table Manners*:

> on two counts, the roast can be placed on the side of nature, and the boiled on the side of culture. Literally, since boiled food necessitates the use of a receptacle, which is a cultural object; and symbolically, in the sense that culture mediates between man and the world, and boiling is also a mediation, by means of water, between the food which man ingests and that other element of the physical world: fire.[57]

There is also a rather strange 'affinity of the roast with the raw' given that roast meat is often not uniformly cooked.[58] It is not surprising, therefore, that Aristotle – that great arbiter of civilization, who is so often invoked by the narrator of *Los pasos perdidos* – should prefer boiling over roasting, 'roast meat being *rawer* [...] than boiled meat'.[59] The proclivity for categorizing the Other according to diet is challenged throughout *Los pasos perdidos* and the *novela de la selva* more generally, as the will to survive forces the traveller to infringe all kinds of urban niceties. The reversal of tropes of cannibalism, gluttony, and animality throughout the novels, habitually employed in Western travel narratives to debase native populations, proves a powerful rejoinder to imperial clichés.

Tropical Pathology

In *Civilization and Its Discontents* Freud argues that man has an innate tendency to aggression and cruelty: '*Homo homini lupus*'.[60] It follows that 'civilized society is constantly threatened with disintegration. [...] Civilization has to make every effort to limit man's aggressive drives.'[61] Hannah Arendt develops this view of the city as a stopper against savagery when she describes how the cogs of nineteenth-century colonial enterprises were turned by men who 'had escaped the reality of civilization':

> Outside all social restraint and hypocrisy, against the backdrop of native life, the gentleman and the criminal felt [...] the impact of a world of infinite possibilities for crimes committed in the spirit of play, for the combination of horror and laughter, that is for the full realization of their own phantom-like existence. Native life lent these ghostlike events a seeming guarantee against all consequences.[62]

Savagery and madness emerge, once again, as suppressed but intrinsic tendencies of human beings, which can develop outside the constraints of the city. The belief that 'el hombre en perpetuo contacto con esa naturaleza salvaje, llega a ser tan salvaje como ella', expressed in this instance by a Colombian traveller, Joaquin Rocha, who travelled to the country's wild southern jungles at the beginning of the twentieth century, is a commonplace of travel literature.[63] While Conrad created the prototype for this tendency – Kurtz in *Heart of Darkness* – there are many other fictional and factual explorations of the theme, as in, for instance, Werner Herzog's films *Aguirre: Wrath of God* and *Fitzcarraldo*. In Spanish-American literature the short stories of Quiroga and Uribe Piedrahita's *Toá* also correlate internal with external wildness.

The theme of the jungle as a catalyst for pathology is omnipresent in the *novela de la selva*. In *Green Mansions* Abel admits to a 'secret dark chapter [...] of moral insanity' (p. 179) in the forest; in *La vorágine* Cova experiences the classic symptoms of catalepsy and 'depersonalization' – defined by Armando R. Favazza as the sensation that the body is 'unreal, that time and the environment have mysteriously changed, and that [you] are becoming insane';[64] and in *Canaima* Marcos converses with trees and runs through the forest howling. The *novela de la selva* insistently makes explicit the link between *silva* and savagery – between the forest and its etymological origin as something which lies 'beyond'.

The two principal embodiments of madness in the *novela de la selva* are torture and self-mutilation. Instances of torture are most acute in *La vorágine* in Rivera's descriptions of the abuses of the rubber industry. In Chapter I of this book I refuted the critical tendency to regard *La vorágine* simply as a *documento de denuncia*, exposing the widespread enslavement, torture, and murder of Amerindian rubber workers in the forests of the Putumayo in the first decade of the twentieth century. Rather, I argued, Rivera's use of historical material provokes important questions about literary authority, especially the reliability of the transcendent narrator of European travel literature. Nevertheless, it is noteworthy that the debate about the Putumayo atrocities, which raged in Peru, Colombia, and Britain in the decade from 1910 to 1920, engaged with the question of tropical degeneration, specifically on the relationship between jungles and pathology. In an official report for the Peruvian government published in 1911, Dr Rómulo Paredes attributed the cruelty of the overseers of the Peruvian Amazon Company to a condition known as 'la enfermedad de la montaña', which he describes as a 'moral and spiritual malady', afflicting those living in the Amazon, where 'life resolved itself into a dreary round of criminal excess and murder'.[65] In *La vorágine* Clemente Silva, a rubber worker who had been to the Putumayo, echoes Paredes's assessment in his description of how 'la selva trastorna al hombre, desarrollándole los instintos más inhumanos: la crueldad invade las almas como intrincado espino' (p. 245). Clemente Silva describes some of the tortures sanctioned by the Peruvian Amazon Company, and the sadistic pleasure of the perpetrators:

> me decretaron una novena de veinte azotes por día y sobre las heridas y desgarrones me rociaban sal. A la quinta flagelación no podía levantarme; pero me arrastraban en una estera sobre un hormiguero de congas, y tenía que salir corriendo. Esto divirtió de lo lindo a mis victimarios. (p. 264)

Arendt has defined different kinds of torture in the Nazi concentration camps. One type 'since it pursues a definite, rational aim, has certain limitations: either the prisoner talks within a certain time, or he is killed'.[66] Another type is much more pernicious, and involves the manipulation of the body 'in such a way as it makes it destroy the human person'.[67] For Arendt, this kind of prolonged torture results in victims who 'are more effectively cut off from the world of the living than if they had died, because terror enforces oblivion'.[68] Arendt's analysis explicates the sentiment of another traveller to the Putumayo in the first decade of the twentieth century: 'It is a horror to go to the Putumayo. I should prefer to go to hell.'[69] Death is often preferable to life in this 'mundo abismático' (*Canaima*, p. 152). As Cova asserts when he contemplates murdering his fellow travellers 'por compasión': '¿Para qué la tortura inútil, cuando la muerte era inevitable?' (p. 216).

There are also descriptions of extreme cruelty in *Canaima*. As in *La vorágine*, the 'influencia deshumanizante de la soledad salvaje' (p. 184) brutalizes the jungle workers and drives them to acts of sadism and torture:

> Crímenes y monstruosidades de todo género, referidos y comentados con sádica minuciosidad, constituían el tema casi exclusivo de las conversaciones, y cuando

se hallaban solos empleaban las horas muertas en la torva complacencia silenciosa de darles tortura lenta y atroz a los insectos o bestezuelas inofensivas que para ello capturaban, arrancándoles las alas, vaciándoles los ojos, descuartizándolos calmosamente, atentos a las mínimas manifestaciones del sufrimiento animal, mientras una horrible insensibilidad petrificaba sus rostros. (pp. 184–85)

In *Canaima* the concept of 'horas muertas' is literalized into a terrifying reality, filled with ghoulish dissections and slow torture. What is particularly interesting about this description is the unnatural calm of the jungle workers and their growing 'insensibilidad', recalling Arendt's description of the 'ghost-like' feeling surrounding the atrocities perpetrated in the 'phantom world of colonial adventure'.[70] The description of the workers' faces 'petrifying' not only points to their growing lack of feeling but also suggests an extreme form of tropical inertia. In some respects it is the jungle workers' detachment from their actions, and not the actions themselves, which is the most terrifying aspect of their degeneration in the forest.

The protagonist of *Canaima* is also driven to savagery amid the jungle. In the chapter 'Tormenta', which marks the apex of his madness in the forest, he stumbles upon a horrible scene: a rubber worker prepares to cut off his gangrenous finger with a machete while another watches on calmly. What happens next is horrific, and is unaccountably breezed over in the remainder of the novel and in the critical literature on *Canaima*. Marcos rushes over to stop the man:

pero con un arrebato colérico que por primera vez se adueñaba de su espíritu. Desarmó la mano sanguinaria, [...] y blandiendo a su vez el machete lo descargó de plano, sin darle descanso, sobre las espaldas del hombre acuchillado, que allí mismo rodó por tierra retorciéndose de dolor, [...] y luego arremetió contra el espectador impasible – [...] y del mismo modo lo castigó, totalmente *fuera de sí*. (pp. 187–88; my emphasis)

The description of Marcos as 'fuera de sí' once again denotes the double and the latent animal instincts that well up beyond the city. The passage is very ambiguous. Marcos and the men are not named throughout, giving an impression of interchangeable identity, and it is not altogether clear in what physical state Marcos leaves the rubber workers. Neither is it clear how the reader ought to respond to Marcos's actions for, despite his brutality, the attack might be seen as a gesture against savagery – that which drives a man to self-mutilate, while another watches on in fascination.

Instances of self-mutilation occur throughout the *novela de la selva*, and to an even greater extent than torture these represent the splitting and disintegration of the subject. Among the indigenous tribes of the Amazon, self-mutilation (tattoos, piercings, and the various self-inflicted tortures which constitute initiation rites) is sanctioned by the community, thus symbolizing a sense of belonging. In contrast, the self-harming of the enslaved peons or urban travellers in the jungle attests to frustration and despair, terror and neurosis. In *La vorágine*, in the oft-cited lament of the *cauchero*, the rubber worker exclaims: '¡A menudo, al clavar la hachuela en el tronco vivo sentí deseo de descargarla contra mi propia mano, que tocó las monedas sin atraparlas [...]!' (p. 287) In *Canaima* the narrator refers to the prevalence of parasitosis among the jungle workers, who self-mutilate under the pretext of having to 'extraerse espinas o extirparse las niguas o los "gusanos de monte" que bajo la piel les sembraban ciertas moscas cuyas larvas se crían en carne viviente' (p. 185). Favazza has described the skin as 'a border between the outer world and the inner world, the environment and the personal self'.[71] As has been explored, the jungle, above all other topographical spaces, manages to dissolve the boundaries of selfhood. In psychological terms, skin mutilation can be considered an attempt to reverse this dissolution: 'cutting causes blood to appear and stimulates nerve endings in the skin. When this occurs cutters [...] are able to focus attention on their skin border and to perceive the limits of their bodies.'[72] Self-harming in the *novela de la selva* thus embodies the pinnacle of the jungle's degenerative influence on the outsider, and of his desperate efforts to reestablish the imagined borders between civilization and savagery, Self and Other.

★ ★ ★

The theme of degeneration in the *novela de la selva* has implications not only for the mental stability of the urban traveller but also for the reliability of the narrative as a whole. Swift, who some two hundred years before the *novela de la selva* had illustrated in *Gulliver's Travels* the potential for travellers to go mad, exemplifies this gap in perception between the reader and the traveller in his description of Gulliver's return from the land of the giants:

> As I was on the road, observing the littleness of the houses, the trees, the cattle, and the people, I began to think myself in Lilliput. I was afraid of trampling on every traveller I met, and often called aloud to have them stand out of the way. [...] This I mention as an instance of the great power of habit and prejudice.[73]

Throughout the *novela de la selva*, textual authority is diminished, then, not only via the belated recycling of the tropes of travel literature, or by the insistent unknowability of the landscape and the native people, but also through the protagonists' slip into savagery or madness in the jungle. Yet this shift of perspective is surely true of any travel account. Topographical and ethnological descriptions of the exotic are always tantamount to an act of cultural transgression. Foreign spaces not only challenge the traveller's capacity to comprehend and to describe his or her surroundings but also vitiate a world view which places the home culture confidently in the centre. Tropical nature, in particular, has tended to challenge European norms regarding landscape aesthetics, as well as dress, diet, and comportment. Almost every travel document on the jungle – fictional or factual – refers to ways in which the traveller makes a break with his or her habitual self back home, whether that be through growing a beard, eating raw meat, shooting game, or – not infrequently – murdering indigenous people. Many travel accounts also refer to the danger of contracting 'jungle fever' or of 'going native'.

The writers of the *novela de la selva* not only intensify imperial projections of the jungle as a terrifying, hypnotic space but also engage with coeval fears of degeneration by illustrating the ease with which the traveller can fall into barbarism. This, however, is very different from similar motifs in European travel writing. Atavism in the *novela de la selva* is not a tropological exigency – a fleeting brush with the dark side of the Self before the traveller returns home to domestic and mental stability – but irredeemable and, occasionally, fatal. We need only think of Cova, Alicia, and their newborn child, forever lost in the jungle, or Count Giaffaro, self-exiled in the wilderness, who is described with his head rocking back and forth mechanically, and who is no longer able to talk. Those who do escape from the jungle are no more fortunate. In *Green Mansions*, for example, Abel remains scarred from his brush with primitivism. When asked by the frame narrator about his experiences in the jungle, we are told that Abel's expression 'would change, becoming hard and set' (p. 5).

Travel writing is ultimately revealed to be as much about the Self as the Other – and especially about the Otherness of the Self. Taussig has discussed the metaphorical significance of the savagery ascribed to the South American jungle in anthropology and travel writing: 'the brutal destructiveness imputed to the natural world serves to embody even more destructive relations in human society'.[74] The jungle itself, then, might not be regarded as a space of inherent cruelty: savagery in the *novela de la selva* always springs from the urban traveller and is a direct response to the lack of social restraints in the wilderness. In his discussion of the barbarity of the Spanish soldiers during the conquest of Mexico, Todorov has also dismissed the notion of savagery as having anything 'atavistic or bestial about it':

> it is quite human [...]. What the Spaniards discover is the contrast between the metropolitan country and the colony, for radically different moral laws regulate conduct in each: massacre requires an appropriate context.[75]

In its representation of the traveller's easy slide from civilization into barbarism and sanity into madness, then, the *novela de la selva* comments less on the innate savagery of South American nature than on that of the urban traveller, and especially of the society which engendered him.

Notes

1 F. W. Up de Graff, *Head Hunters of the Amazon; Seven Years of Exploration and Adventure*, ed. R. B. Cunninghame Graham (London: Jenkins, 1923), p. 306.
2 Sarmiento, *Facundo*, p. 2.
3 For a further discussion of this debate see Chapter 2 of Stabb, *In Quest of Identity*.
4 Jean Franco, *An Introduction to Spanish-American Literature* (Cambridge: Cambridge University Press, 1969), p. 210.
5 Michel Foucault, *Madness and Civilization: A History of Insanity in the Age of Reason*, trans. Richard Howard (London: Tavistock, 1967).
6 Conrad, *Heart of Darkness*, p. 49.
7 Conrad, *Heart of Darkness*, p. 65.

8   Cited in Hennessy, *Frontier in Latin American History*, p. 17.

9   Walter Benjamin, 'Theses on the Philosophy of History', in *Illuminations*, trans. Harry Zorn and ed. Hannah Arendt (London: Pimlico, 1999), pp. 245–55 (p. 248).

10 See Benigno Trigo, *Subjects of Crisis: Race and Gender as Disease in Latin America* (Hanover, NH: Wesleyan University Press, 2000), p. 31.

11 For general discussions of the association of the tropics with disease in the nineteenth century see: Warwick Anderson, 'Disease, Race and Empire', *Bulletin of the History of Medicine*, 70 (1996), pp. 62–67; Rod Edmond, 'Returning Fears: Tropical Disease and the Metropolis', in Felix Driver and Luciana Martins (eds.), *Tropical Visions in an Age of Empire* (Chicago: University of Chicago Press, 2005), pp. 175–94; and Nancy L. Stepan, 'Biology and Degeneration: Races and Proper Places', in J. Edward Chamberlin and Sander L. Gilman (eds.), *Degeneration: The Dark Side of Progress* (New York: Columbia University Press, 1985), pp. 97–120. It should be noted that the association of the tropics, or at least of hot places, with degeneration and disease was current much earlier. In Montesquieu's 1748 *The Spirit of the Laws*, for instance, he describes the ill-effects of life outside the northern climates: 'The heat of the climate can be so excessive that the body there will be absolutely without strength. So, prostration will pass even to the spirit; no curiosity, no noble enterprise, no generous sentiment; inclinations will all be passive', cited in Shawn William Miller, *An Environmental History of Latin America* (Cambridge: Cambridge University Press, 2007), p. 107.

12 Stepan, *Picturing Tropical Nature*, p. 163.

13 Cited in Stepan, 'Biology and Degeneration', p. 113.

14 Benjamin Kidd, *The Control of the Tropics* (London: Macmillan, 1898), pp. 48–51.

15 Joseph F. Woodroffe, *The Upper Reaches of the Amazon* (London: Methuen, 1914), p. 22.

16 Lange, *In the Amazon Jungle*, p. v.

17 See Miller, *Environmental History*, pp. 105–135, for a discussion of 'tropical determinism'.

18 Cited in Stabb, *In Quest of Identity*, p. 17.

19 See, for instance, Nancy Stepan, *'The Hour of Eugenics': Race, Gender, and Nation in Latin America* (Ithaca, NY: Cornell University Press, 1991), pp. 138–39.

20 In the manuscript version of *Heart of Darkness*, Kurtz says '"Oh! But I will make you serve my ends."' See Conrad, *Heart of Darkness*, p. 67 (n).

21 Alejo Carpentier, *El siglo de las luces*, Obras completas de Alejo Carpentier (México: Siglo Veintiuno Editores, 1984), V, p. 390.

22 Ellsworth Huntington, *Civilization and Climate* (Hamden, CT: Archon, 1971), p. 69.

23 William Greenslade, *Degeneration, Culture, and the Novel 1880–1940* (Cambridge: Cambridge University Press, 1994), p. 72.

24 H. Rider Haggard, *She*, ed. Patrick Brantlinger (London: Penguin, 2001), p. 12.

25 Arthur Conan Doyle, *The Lost World* [1912], ed. Ian Duncan (Oxford: Oxford University Press, 1998), p. 144.

26 Bhabha, *Location of Culture*, has defined the 'unhomely' as 'a paradigmatic colonial and post-colonial condition' (p. 9).

27 Sigmund Freud, 'The Uncanny', in *Art and Literature: Jensen's 'Gradavia', Leonardo da Vinci and Other Works*, ed. Albert Dickson, trans. Alix Strachey, The Penguin Freud Library (Harmondsworth: Penguin, 1990), XIV, pp. 335–76 (p. 340).

28 Achebe, *'Hopes and Impediments'*, p. 8.

29 Friedman, *Monstrous Races*, has cited one description of Augustus: 'he abhorred dwarfs, cripples, and everything of that sort, as freaks of nature and of ill omen' (p. 179).

30 Pagden, *Fall of Natural Man*, has quoted Albertus Magnus: 'Bestial men, however, are rare, since it is a rare man who has no spark of humanity. It does, however, occur, and

usually from two causes: physical handicap and deprivation, or from disease causing deprivation' (p. 21).

31 Freud, 'The Uncanny', p. 363.
32 Peter Brooker and Peter Widdowson, 'A Literature for England', in Robert Colls and Philip Dodd (eds.), *Englishness: Politics and Culture 1880–1920* (London: Croom Helm, 1986), pp. 116–63 (p. 142).
33 D. H. Lawrence, 'The Novel and the Feelings' [1923], cited in Greenslade, *Degeneration*, p. 66.
34 Pratt, *Imperial Eyes*, has used the term 'contact zone' to 'refer to the space of colonial encounters, the space in which peoples geographically and historically separated come into contact with each other and establish ongoing relations, usually involving conditions of coercion, radical inequality, and intractable conflict' (p. 6).
35 Bernal Díaz del Castillo, *Historia verdadera de la conquista de la Nueva España* (México: Rafael, 1854), I, p. 76.
36 Díaz, *Historia verdadera*, p. 76.
37 Cabeza de Vaca, *Naufragios*, p. 123.
38 Daniel Defoe, *Robinson Crusoe* [1719], ed. J. Donald Crowley (Oxford: Oxford University Press, 1998), p. 134.
39 Erskine Childers, *The Riddle of the Sands* (Harmondsworth: Penguin, 1995), p. 15.
40 Bhabha, *Location of Culture*, p. 97.
41 Lacan's description of the 'Mirror Stage', when a child catches a glimpse of his or her image for the first time, intersects interestingly with Abel's alienation in this episode. As Malcolm Bowie has explained in *Lacan* (London: Fontana, 1991), 'the child, itself so recently born, gives birth to a monster: a statue, an automaton, a fabricated thing. [...] The self-division of the subject, first revealed to Freud by dreams, is here being re-imagined by Lacan as nightmare' (p. 26).
42 Freud, 'The Uncanny', p. 345.
43 Macpherson, *Spirit of Solitude*, p. 81.
44 Cited in Greenslade, *Degeneration*, p. 73.
45 Michel Parker and Roger Starkey, 'Introduction', in Michael Parker and Roger Starkey (eds.), *Postcolonial Literatures: Achebe, Ngugi, Desai, Walcott* (Basingstoke: Macmillan, 1995), pp. 1–30 (p. 20).
46 Freud, 'The Uncanny', p. 356.
47 Bhabha, *Location of Culture*, p. 114.
48 Richard Bernheimer, *Wild Men in the Middle Ages: A Study in Art, Sentiment, and Demonology* (Cambridge, MA: Harvard University Press, 1952), p. 3.
49 Roger Bartra, *Wild Men in the Looking Glass: The Mythic Origins of European Otherness*, trans. Carl T. Berrisford (Ann Arbor: University of Michigan Press, 1994), p. 85.
50 White, *Tropics of Discourse*, p. 166.
51 Edith Hall, *Inventing the Barbarian: Greek Self-definition through Tragedy* (Oxford: Clarendon Press, 1991), p. 126.
52 Cabeza de Vaca, *Naufragios*, p. 102.
53 E. N. Dorall, 'Conrad and Coppola: Different Centres of Darkness', in Conrad, *Heart of Darkness*, ed. Kimbrough, pp. 301–11 (pp. 305–06).
54 Pagden, *Fall of Natural Man*, has argued that, for the conquistadors, the unselective eating habits of the Amerindians 'was a sure sign of their barbarism', and an 'indication of their failure to respond to the presence of pollution' (p. 87).
55 Peter Hulme, 'Introduction: The Cannibal Scene', in Francis Barker, Peter Hulme, and Margaret Iverson (eds.), *Cannibalism and the Colonial World* (Cambridge: Cambridge University Press, 1998), pp. 1–38 (p. 2).
56 Pagden, *Fall of Natural Man*, p. 89.

57 Claude Lévi-Strauss, *Introduction to a Science of Mythology: The Origin of Table Manners*, trans. John and Doreen Weightman, 3 vols (London: Cape, 1978), III, p. 480.

58 Lévi-Strauss, *Origin of Table Manners*, p. 481.

59 Lévi-Strauss, *Origin of Table Manners*, p. 482; my emphasis.

60 Sigmund Freud, *Civilization and Its Discontents*, trans. David McLintock (London: Penguin, 2002), p. 48.

61 Freud, *Civilization and Its Discontents*, p. 49.

62 Hannah Arendt, *The Origins of Totalitarianism* (London: Deutsch, 1990), p. 190.

63 Joaquin Rocha, *Memorandum de viaje* (Bogotá: Editorial El Mercurio, 1905), p. 29. For further discussion of Rocha and of the relationship between savagery and jungles, see Taussig, *Shamanism, Colonialism, and the Wild Man*, pp. 74–92.

64 Armando R. Favazza, *Bodies Under Siege: Self-Mutilation and Body Modification in Culture and Psychiatry*, 2nd edn (Baltimore: Johns Hopkins University Press, 1996), p. 274.

65 This report was cited (and translated) by Roger Casement, a British investigator sent to the Putumayo in 1910. See *Sir Roger Casement's Heart of Darkness: The 1911 Documents*, ed. Angus Mitchell (Dublin: Irish Manuscripts Commission, 2003), p. 705.

66 Arendt, *Origins of Totalitarianism*, p. 453.

67 Arendt, *Origins of Totalitarianism*, p. 453.

68 Arendt, *Origins of Totalitarianism*, p. 443.

69 Cited in W. E. Hardenburg, *The Putumayo: The Devil's Paradise; Travels in the Peruvian Amazon Region and an Account of the Atrocities Committed upon the Indians Therein*, ed. C. Reginald Enock (London: Unwin, 1912), p. 216.

70 Arendt, *Origins of Totalitarianism*, p. 190.

71 Favazza, *Bodies Under Siege*, p. 148.

72 Favazza, *Bodies Under Siege*, p. 148.

73 Swift, *Gulliver's Travels*, pp. 160–61.

74 Taussig, *Shamanism, Colonialism, and the Wild Man*, p. 75.

75 Todorov, *Conquest of America*, p. 145.

Conclusion

El último cable de nuestro Cónsul, dirigido al señor Ministro y relacionado con
la suerte de Arturo Cova y sus compañeros, dice textualmente:
'Hace cinco meses búscalos en vano Clemente Silva.
Ni rastro de ellos.
¡Los devoró la selva!' (p. 385).

These are the chilling final lines of *La vorágine* – a novel which, as I have
shown in the previous chapter, epitomizes the maleficent influence of the
tropical forest and its power to entrance, corrupt, and even annihilate the
urban traveller. The victims of this telluric ingestion are Cova, his girlfriend,
their premature baby, and their travelling companions, who disappear without
a trace in the midst of the jungle. The use of the verb 'devorar' (which shares
the same Latin etymology as 'vorágine', *vorare*) is significant. Replete with
overtones of excess and gluttony, the verb was commonly used in European
travel writing on the Americas to denote the immoderate dietary habits of
native populations. In *Robinson Crusoe*, for instance, the protagonist refers to
the 'Cannibals, or Men-eaters' who reside on the '*Savage* Coast between the
Spanish Country and *Brasils*', and who 'fail not to murther and devour all
the humane Bodies that fall into their Hands'.[1] Swift's Yahoos are likewise
'rendered [...] odious' for their 'undistinguishing appetite to devour every
thing that came in their way'.[2] Taken literally, then, the description of the
jungle 'devouring' Cova could be regarded as consistent with colonial views
of the jungle and its native inhabitants as irredeemably savage. Yet, as I have
been arguing throughout this book, such a reading would neglect the clearly
parodic intent of this novel. In fact, the forest's consumption of Cova (who
is, lest we forget, a writer) and of his offspring (writing?) clearly marks the
culmination of the novel's ironic engagement with European discourses of
tropicality, and can be taken as a metatextual instantiation for what takes
place in the novel – and in the *novela de la selva* – as a whole. Cova is devoured
by the forest, which flourishes in his wake. Imperial accounts of the tropics
are 'cannibalized' by Spanish-American writers, who digest their merits and
through them construct a postcolonial literary identity.

Of course, the trope of the traveller being swallowed up by nature is not restricted to the *novela de la selva* but is a constant of the Spanish-American novel in the first decades of the twentieth century. As Carlos Fuentes has rather overstated in his classic analysis, *La nueva novela hispanoamericana*, the *novela de la tierra* is full of characters who are devoured by nature:

> '¡Se los tragó la selva!', dice la frase final de *La Vorágine* de José Eustasio Rivera. La exclamación es algo más que la lápida de Arturo Cova y sus compañeros: podría ser el comentario a un largo siglo de novelas latinoamericanas: se los tragó la montaña, se los tragó la pampa, se los tragó la mina, se los tragó el río.[3]

Although Fuentes overlooks the lightly concealed irony of many of these texts, mistakenly identifying them with a belated desire among early twentieth-century Latin American writers to align themselves with the 'grandes explora-dores del siglo XVI', he does identify one of the fundamental characteristics of this postcolonial genre: the representation of American nature as destructive, terrifying, and invincible.[4] The tendency for characters to be swallowed up by the jungle (or the mountain, or the *pampa*) throughout the *novela de la tierra* is always presented as a corrective to man's misplaced belief in his mastery over nature. The domesticating inclinations of a Santo Luzardo or an Arturo Cova are time and again rebuffed by an indomitable natural milieu.

It is, of course, of particular significance that in three out of the four novels central to this study the male travellers who are conquered by the jungle are also engaged in the attempt to represent it. In his 1948 prologue to *El reino de este mundo*, Carpentier discusses the case of another person who was 'devoured' by the jungle:

> cuando André Masson quiso dibujar la selva de la isla de Martinica, con el increíble entrelazimiento de sus plantas y la obscena promiscuidad de ciertos frutos, la maravillosa verdad del asunto devoró el pintor, dejándolo poco menos que impotente frente al papel en blanco. Y tuvo que ser un pintor de América, el cubano Wilfredo Lam, quien nos enseñara la magia de la vegetación tropical, la desenfrenada Creación de Formas de nuestra naturaleza – con todas sus metamorfosis y simbiosis.[5]

In the *novela de la selva*, being American is no guarantee of success in the search for a tropical aesthetic. Rather, writers and painters are obliged to confront the excessive, uncontainable qualities of the tropics – the 'desenfrenada Creación de Formas' – in order to represent it. When writing this prologue, Carpentier clearly had in mind Lam's most famous tropical painting, *La selva* [1943]. The Afro-Caribbean imagery of *La selva*, in which abstract bodies, with heads resembling African masks, merge with the limbs of the surrounding vegeta-tion, is a visual embodiment of the kind of synthetic postcolonial aesthetic that Carpentier was striving to achieve not just in his 1948 novel of the Haitian Revolution, but throughout his literary career. It is noteworthy that Carpen-tier's description of the jungle in *Los pasos perdidos* echoes the terms he had used about Lam's painting some years earlier:

La selva era el mundo de la mentira [...] allí todo era disfraz, estratagema, juego de apariencias, metamorfosis. Mundo del lagarto-cohombro, la castaña-erizo, la crisálida-ciempiés. (p. 169)

We might follow Lam's painting by adding to this list of hybrids the arm-trunk, the fruit-breast, the leaf-finger. Throughout the *novela de la selva*, nature ceases to be represented as separate from the urban traveller and becomes coextensive with his body as the genre moves away from a picturesque conception of landscape to one in which man and nature are fully integrated. It is this representational shift, among others, which necessitates a reconsideration of the effectiveness of European landscape aesthetics in the tropics.

This book has been about the rewriting of European historical and literary constructions of the tropics by Spanish-American authors in the first half of the twentieth century. As I have shown in the foregoing chapters, the relationship of the *novela de la selva* to the colonial past is not purely antagonistic. Rather, the genre exploited European discourses of the tropics to generate a powerful postcolonial counter-narrative, appropriating and re-semanticizing tropes from which they had 'been banished by means of the same trope carried over from the imperial into the new culture and adopted, reused, relived'.[6] The parodic rewriting of European discourses on the tropics was fundamental to the efforts of the *novela de la selva* to forge a postcolonial literary identity for the Spanish-American novel. While the genre's aping of certain stylistic and aesthetic conventions from, in particular, European travel writing, has led to misreadings of certain *novelas de la selva* as colonial adventure narratives or neo-Romantic celebrations of nature, these novels should not be placed at the end of a long line of colonial representations of the South American tropics, but at the beginning of a Latin American tradition of nature writing and ethnography predicated on a misidentification with its European forebears.

Throughout the *novela de la selva* there is an attempt not only to distance the Spanish-American novel from European accounts of the tropics but also to forge a postcolonial nature aesthetics – a kind of poetics of the jungle. As I have explored, these novels eschew the pictorial tendencies of eighteenth- and nineteenth-century travel writing by representing nature as something that can be experienced not just visually but on a number of sensory levels. Although these multidimensional descriptions of the jungle seem at first to heighten the realism of the novels by recreating the myriad sounds and smells of the tropical forest, the reader's knowledge, like that of the urban traveller, is only ever partial. The incommensurability of language with land throughout the *novela de la selva* produces a kind of fractured realism, where the jungle can only ever be glimpsed in a succession of snapshots. The same strategy can be seen at work in the genre's important revision of European ethnographic conventions. Heavily ironizing the stock colonial figures of the barbarian and the noble savage, the authors of the *novela de la selva* suggest new ways of writing about South America's indigenous people based not on the universalizing tendencies of European anthropology but on cultural impenetrability.

While much of this book has been concerned with the *novela de la selva*'s engagement with the colonial past, it is important to remember that the genre was also looking towards the future. Despite the fate of urban travellers such as Arturo Cova, life in the jungle is presented as ever-renewing, with both *Canaima* and *Los pasos perdidos* concluding with a reference to new birth – Rosario's forthcoming child, and Marcos's son. This second generation in the *novela de la selva* seems to fulfil a symbolic role as hybrids of nature and culture, of barbarism and civilization, and of the future possibilities of 'transcultura- tion', where two or more cultures collide and 'transforman los elementos que reciben prestados y los incorporan a una realidad cultural enteramente nueva e independiente'.[7] The unstoppable fecundity of the South American jungle in these novels gives rise to renewed optimism about the continent's future, and it is surely no coincidence that what comes to symbolize the vitality of postcolonial Spanish America in the *novela de la selva* – the forest – should also be the raw material of paper, of pencils, and of rubber.[8]

The jungle, then, both literally and metaphorically, provides the materials for writing and for erasure – a fact which is not lost on either the narrators or the authors of the *novela de la selva*. In *Green Mansions* Abel procures ink 'from the juices of some deeply coloured berries' (pp. 190–91) to decorate Rima's urn; in *La vorágine* Clemente Silva carves messages to his missing son on the bark of trees; and in *Los pasos perdidos* the narrator speculates that '[a]lguna materia debe haber en la selva, tan pródiga en tejidos naturales, yutas extrañas, yaguas, envolturas de fibra, en que se haga posible escribir' (p. 226). González Echevarría has described Carpentier's novel as the 'founding archival fiction': '*Los pasos perdidos* is an archive of stories and a storehouse of the master- stories produced to narrate from Latin America.'[9] It is a book obsessed with writing. Yet this preoccupation with writing, and the important intersections between textuality and the jungle, began, as I have shown throughout this book, much earlier in *Green Mansions*, *La vorágine*, and *Canaima*. In fact, in some respects, *La vorágine* might be seen as the paradigmatic 'archival fiction' – a novel which, in its first edition, consisted of a prologue by the editor, a manuscript of a first-person travel narrative, an epilogue citing the contents of a telegraph, and photographs of Cova, Zoraida Ayram, 'Un cauchero', and Clemente Silva. Nor should we forget that, while Cova disappears in the forest, his journal does not, but is placed – under his strict instructions – 'en manos del Cónsul' (p. 383), from whence it is sent to the fictional editor of the novel for publication.

Texts are endowed with incredible powers of survival in the *novela de la selva*, yet that is not to say that their meaning always remains inert. Meaning changes according to who reads them, and to our knowledge of who wrote them, when, and for whom. Colonial tropes in the *novela de la selva* likewise shift in significance, invested with an ironic edge absent in their original artic- ulation.

Notes

1 Defoe, *Robinson Crusoe*, p. 109.
2 Swift, *Gulliver's Travels*, p. 289.
3 Fuentes, *La nueva novela hispanoamericana*, p. 9. In fact, Fuentes slightly misquotes the last line of *La vorágine* here, but the point is the same.
4 Fuentes, *La nueva novela hispanoamericana*, p. 9.
5 Alejo Carpentier, *El reino de este mundo* (Madrid: Alianza Editorial, 2003), p. 9. Detail from Lam's painting is featured on the front cover of this edition.
6 Said, *Culture and Imperialism*, p. 254. Here Said is referring specifically to James Joyce's re-inscription of the quest motif in *Ulysses* – a trope which is also parodied throughout the *novela de la selva*.
7 Bronislaw Malinowski, 'Introducción', in Fernando Ortiz, *Contrapunteo cubano del tabaco y el azúcar*, ed. by Enrico Mario Santí (Madrid: Cátedra, 2002), pp. 123-33 (p. 127).
8 Alonso, *The Regional Novel*, has discussed this double function of rubber in the novel: 'the etymology of the word that refers to the substance whose exploitation Rivera condemned is allusive of its capacity to erase, to obliterate the trace of writing' (p. 162).
9 González Echevarría, *Myth and Archive*, p. 3.

Bibliography

Achebe, Chinua, '*Hopes and Impediments*': *Selected Essays, 1965–1987* (London: Heine-mann, 1988).

Adams, James Eli, *Dandies and Desert Saints: Styles of Victorian Masculinity* (Ithaca, NY: Cornell University Press, 1995).

Adorno, Theodor, and Max Horkheimer, *Dialectic of Enlightenment*, trans. John Cumming (London: Verso, 1997).

Almoina de Carrera, Pilar, '*Canaima*: Arquetipos ideológicos y culturales', in Rómulo Gallegos, *Canaima: edición crítica*, ed. Charles Minguet (Madrid: Archivos, CSIC, 1991), pp. 325–39.

Alonso, Carlos J., *The Spanish American Regional Novel: Modernity and Autochthony* (Cambridge: Cambridge University Press, 1991).

———, 'The *Criollista* Novel', in Roberto González Echevarría and Enrique Pupo-Walker (eds.), *The Cambridge History of Latin American Literature*, 3 vols (Cambridge: Cambridge University Press, 1996), II, pp. 195–211.

Anderson Imbert, Enrique, *Historia de la literatura hispanoamericana*, rev. edn (México: Fondo de Cultura Económica, 1957).

Anderson, Warwick, 'Disease, Race and Empire', in *Bulletin of the History of Medicine*, 70 (1996), pp. 62–67.

Añez, Jorge, *De 'La vorágine' a 'Doña Bárbara'* (Bogotá: Imprenta del Departamento, 1944).

Arendt, Hannah, *The Origins of Totalitarianism* (London: Deutsch, 1990).

Arnold, David, *The Problem of Nature: Environment, Culture and European Expansion* (Oxford: Blackwell, 1996).

Asad, Talal, 'Introduction', in Talal Asad (ed.), *Anthropology and the Colonial Encounter* (London: Ithaca Press, 1973), pp. 9–19.

Ashcroft, Bill, 'Constitutive Graphonomy: A Post-Colonial Theory of Literary Writing', *Kunapipi*, 11.1 (1989), pp. 58–73.

———, Gareth Griffiths, and Helen Tiffin (eds.), *The Post-Colonial Studies Reader* (London: Routledge, 1995).

———, Gareth Griffiths, and Helen Tiffin, *Key Concepts in Post-Colonial Studies* (London: Routledge, 1998).

Bachelard, Gaston, *The Poetics of Space*, trans. Maria Jolas (Boston, MA: Beacon Press, 1994).

Baker, Carlos A., 'The Source-book for Hudson's *Green Mansions*', *PMLA*, 61 (1946), pp. 252–57.

Bartra, Roger, *Wild Men in the Looking Glass: The Mythic Origins of European Otherness*, trans. Carl T. Berrisford (Ann Arbor: University of Michigan Press, 1994).

Bates, Henry Walter, *The Naturalist on the River Amazons* (London: Dent, 1969).

Baudelaire, Charles, *Les fleurs du mal* [1857], ed. Graham Chesters (London: Bristol Classical Press, 1995).

Baudet, Henri, *Paradise on Earth: Some Thoughts on European Images of Non-European Man*, trans. Elizabeth Wentholt (New Haven: Yale University Press, 1965).

Beardsell, Peter, *Europe and Latin America: Returning the Gaze* (Manchester: Manchester University Press, 2000).

Bello, Andrés, *Obra literaria*, ed. Pedro Grases, 2nd edn (Caracas: Biblioteca Ayacucho, 1985).

Benjamin, Walter, *Illuminations*, trans. Harry Zorn and ed. Hannah Arendt (London: Pimlico, 1999).

Berger, John, *About Looking* (London: Writers and Readers, 1980).

Berkhofer, Robert F., *The White Man's Indian: Images of the American Indian from Columbus to the Present* (New York: Knopf, 1978).

Berleant, Arnold, *The Aesthetics of Environment* (Philadelphia: Temple University Press, 1992).

Bernardin de Saint Pierre, Jacques-Henri, *Paul and Virginia*, trans. John Donovan (London: Owen, 1982).

Bernheimer, Richard, *Wild Men in the Middle Ages: A Study in Art, Sentiment, and Demonology* (Cambridge, MA: Harvard University Press, 1952).

Bertens, Johannes Willem, *The Idea of the Postmodern: A History* (London: Routledge, 1995).

Bhabha, Homi K., *The Location of Culture* (London: Routledge, 1994).

Booth, Wayne C., *A Rhetoric of Irony* (Chicago: University of Chicago Press, 1974).

Borges, Jorge Luis, *El informe de Brodie* [1970] (Madrid: Alianza Editorial, 1999).

Bourassa, Steven C., *The Aesthetics of Landscape* (London: Belhaven Press, 1991).

Bowie, Malcolm, *Lacan* (London: Fontana, 1991).

Brantlinger, Patrick, *Rule of Darkness: British Literature and Imperialism, 1830–1914* (Ithaca, NY: Cornell University Press, 1988).

Brathwaite, Edward Kamau, *History of the Voice: The Development of Nation Language in Anglophone Caribbean Poetry* (London: New Beacon Books, 1984).

Brooker, Peter, and Peter Widdowson, 'A Literature for England', in Robert Colls and Philip Dodd (eds.), *Englishness: Politics and Culture 1880–1920* (London: Croom Helm, 1986), pp. 116–63.

Brotherston, Gordon, 'The Latin American Novel and its Indigenous Sources', in John King (ed.), *Modern Latin American Fiction: A Survey* (London: Faber and Faber, 1987), pp. 60–77.

——, 'Pacaraima as Destination in Carpentier's *Los pasos perdidos*', *Indiana Journal of Hispanic Literatures* 1. 2 (1993), pp. 161–80.

Buell, Lawrence, *The Environmental Imagination: Thoreau, Nature Writing and the Formation of American Culture* (Cambridge, MA: Belknap Press of Harvard University Press, 1995).

Bull, William E., 'Naturaleza y antropomorfismo en *La vorágine*', in Montserrat Ordóñez (ed.), *La vorágine: textos críticos* (Bogotá: Alianza Editorial Colombiana, 1987), pp. 319–34.

Burke, Edmund, *A Philosophical Enquiry into the Origin of our Ideas of the Sublime and Beautiful* [1757], ed. Adam Phillips (Oxford: Oxford University Press, 1990).

Butler, Judith, *Gender Trouble: Feminism and the Subversion of Identity* (London: Routledge, 1990).

Cabeza de Vaca, Álvar Núñez, *Naufragios* [1542], ed. Juan Francisco Maura (Madrid: Cátedra, 1989).

Calderón de la Barca, Frances, *Life in Mexico* (London: Dent, 1970).

Camayd-Freixas, Erik, 'Narrative Primitivism: Theory and Practice in Latin America', in Erik Camayd-Freixas and José Eduardo González (eds.), *Primitivism and Identity in Latin America: Essays on Art, Literature, and Culture* (Tucson: University of Arizona Press, 2000), pp. 109–34.

Carpentier, Alejo, *Ecue-Yamba-O: novela afro-cubana* [1933] (Buenos Aires: Editorial Xanandú, 1968).

——, *El siglo de las luces* [1962], *Obras completas de Alejo Carpentier* (México: Siglo Veintiuno Editores, 1984), V.

——, *Los pasos perdidos* [1953] (Madrid: Alianza Editorial, 1998).

——, *Visión de América* (Barcelona: Seix Barral, 1999).

——, *El reino de este mundo* [1948] (Madrid: Alianza Editorial, 2003).

Carreras González, Olga, 'Tres fechas, tres novelas y un tema: estudio comparativo de *La vorágine, Canaima y Los pasos perdidos*', *Explicación de Textos Literarios*, 2 (1974), pp. 169–78.

Carter, Paul, *The Road to Botany Bay: An Essay in Spatial History* (London: Faber and Faber, 1987).

Casement, Roger, *Sir Roger Casement's Heart of Darkness: The 1911 Documents*, ed. Angus Mitchell (Dublin: Irish Manuscripts Commission, 2003).

Castillo, Eduardo, '*La vorágine*', in Montserrat Ordóñez (ed.), *La vorágine: textos críticos* (Bogotá: Alianza Editorial Colombiana, 1987), pp. 41–43.

Célestin, Roger, *From Cannibals to Radicals: Figures and Limits of Exoticism* (Minneapolis: University of Minnesota Press, 1996).

Chao, Ramón, *Conversaciones con Alejo Carpentier* (Madrid: Alianza Editorial, 1998).

Chateaubriand, François-René, *Atala. René*, trans. Irving Putter (Berkeley: University of California Press, 1952).

Childers, Erskine, *The Riddle of the Sands* [1903] (Harmondsworth: Penguin, 1995).

Clifford, James, 'Introduction: Partial Truths', in James Clifford and George E. Marcus (eds.), *Writing Culture: The Poetics and Politics of Ethnography* (Berkeley: University of California Press, 1986), pp. 1–26.

Colebrook, Claire, *Irony* (London: Routledge, 1994).

Coleridge, Samuel Taylor, *The Major Works*, ed. H. J. Jackson (Oxford: Oxford University Press, 2000).

Collazos, Oscar, *Textos al margen* (Bogotá: Instituto Colombiano de Cultura, 1978).

Colón, Cristobal, *Textos y documentos completos: relaciones de viajes, cartas y memoriales*, ed. Consuelo Varela (Madrid: Alianza Editorial, 1984).

Conan Doyle, Sir Arthur, *The Lost World* [1912], ed. Ian Duncan (Oxford: Oxford University Press, 1998).

Connerton, Paul, *How Societies Remember* (Cambridge: Cambridge University Press, 1989).

Conrad, Joseph, *Heart of Darkness: An Authoritative Text; Backgrounds and Sources; Criticism*, ed. Robert Kimbrough, 3rd edn (New York: Norton, 1988).

Cudjoe, Selwyn R., *Resistance in Caribbean Literature* (Athens: Ohio University Press, 1980).

D'Allemand, Patricia, 'José Carlos Mariátegui: Culture and the Nation', in Robin

Fiddian (ed.), *Postcolonial Perspectives on the Cultures of Latin America and Lusophone Africa* (Liverpool: Liverpool University Press, 2000), pp. 79–102.

David, Elba R., 'El pictorialismo tropical de *La vorágine* y *El viaje* de Alexander von Humboldt', *Hispania*, 47 (1964), pp. 36–40.

de Beauvoir, Simone, *Force of Circumstance*, trans. Richard Howard (London: Deutsch, 1965).

De Chasca, Edmundo, 'El lirismo de *La vorágine*', in Montserrat Ordóñez (ed.), *La vorágine: textos críticos* (Bogotá: Alianza Editorial Colombiana, 1987), pp. 239–57.

Defoe, Daniel, *Robinson Crusoe* [1719], ed. J. Donald Crowley (Oxford: Oxford University Press, 1998).

Dewey, John, *Art as Experience* (London: Allen & Unwin, 1934).

Diamond, Stanley, *In Search of the Primitive: A Critique of Civilization* (New Brunswick: Transaction Books, 1974).

Díaz del Castillo, Bernal, *Historia verdadera de la conquista de la Nueva España* (México: Rafael, 1854).

Dorall, E. N., 'Conrad and Coppola: Different Centres of Darkness', in Joseph Conrad, *Heart of Darkness*, ed. Robert Kimbrough, 3rd edn (New York: Norton, 1988), pp. 301–11.

Duguid, Julian, *Green Hell: Adventures in the Mysterious Jungles of Eastern Bolivia* (New York: Century, 1931).

Duncan, Ian, 'Introduction', in W. H. Hudson, *Green Mansions*, ed. Ian Duncan (Oxford: Oxford University Press, 1998), pp. vii–xxiii.

Duncan, James S., 'The Struggle to be Temperate: Climate and "Moral Masculinity" in Mid-Nineteenth Century Ceylon', in *Singapore Journal of Tropical Geography*, 21 (2000), pp. 34–47.

Edmond, Rod, 'Returning Fears: Tropical Disease and the Metropolis', in Felix Driver and Luciana Martins (eds.), *Tropical Visions in an Age of Empire* (Chicago: University of Chicago Press, 2005), pp. 175–94.

Emerson, Ralph Waldo, *Selected Essays*, ed. Larzer Ziff (Harmondsworth: Penguin, 1985).

Eyzaguirre, Luis B., 'Arturo Cova, héroe patológico', in Montserrat Ordóñez (ed.), *La vorágine: textos críticos* (Bogotá: Alianza Editorial Colombiana, 1987), pp. 373–90.

Fabian, Johannes, *Time and the Other: How Anthropology Makes its Object* (New York: Columbia University Press, 1983).

Fanon, Frantz, *Black Skin, White Masks* [1952], trans. Charles Lam Markmann (London: Pluto Press, 1986).

——, *The Wretched of the Earth* [1961], trans. Constance Farrington (London: Penguin, 2001).

Favazza, Armando R., *Bodies Under Siege: Self-Mutilation and Body Modification in Culture and Psychiatry*, 2nd edn (Baltimore: Johns Hopkins University Press, 1996).

Fernández de Oviedo y Valdés, Gonzalo, 'Sumario de la natural historia de las Indias', in *Historiadores primitivos de Indias*, ed. Don Enrique de Vedia (Madrid: Atlas, 1946), I, pp. 473–515.

Fiddian, Robin, 'Locating the Object, Mapping the Field: The Place of the Cultures of Latin America and Lusophone Africa in Postcolonial Studies', in Robin Fiddian (ed.), *Postcolonial Perspectives on the Cultures of Latin America and Lusophone Africa* (Liverpool: Liverpool University Press, 2000), pp. 1–26.

Fiddian, Robin (ed.), *Postcolonial Perspectives on the Cultures of Latin America and*

Lusophone Africa (Liverpool: Liverpool University Press, 2000).

Fletcher, James V., 'The Creator of Rima, W. H. Hudson: A Belated Romantic', *Sewanee Review*, 41 (1933), pp. 24–40.

Ford, Richard, 'El marco narrativo de *La vorágine*', in Montserrat Ordóñez (ed.), *La vorágine: textos críticos* (Bogotá: Alianza Editorial Colombiana, 1987), pp. 307–16.

Foucault, Michel, *Madness and Civilization: A History of Insanity in the Age of Reason*, trans. Richard Howard (London: Tavistock, 1967).

Franco, Jean, 'Image and Experience in *La vorágine*', in *Bulletin of Hispanic Studies*, 41 (1964), pp. 101–110.

——, *An Introduction to Spanish-American Literature* (Cambridge: Cambridge University Press, 1969).

Fraser, Robert, *Lifting the Sentence: A Poetics of Postcolonial Fiction* (Manchester: Manchester University Press, 2000).

French, Jennifer L., *Nature, Neo-Colonialism, and the Spanish American Regional Writers* (Hanover, NH: Dartmouth College Press, 2005).

Freud, Sigmund, 'The Uncanny', in *Art and Literature: Jensen's 'Gradavia', Leonardo da Vinci and Other Works*, ed. Albert Dickson and trans. Alix Strachey, The Penguin Freud Library (Harmondsworth: Penguin, 1990), XIV, pp. 335–76.

——, *Civilization and its Discontents*, trans. David McLintock (London: Penguin, 2002).

Friedman, John Block, *The Monstrous Races in Medieval Art and Thought* (Cambridge, MA: Harvard University Press, 1981).

Fuentes, Carlos, *La nueva novela hispanoamericana* (México: Mortiz, 1969).

Furst, Lilian R., *Romanticism in Perspective: A Comparative Study of Aspects of the Romantic Movements in England, France and Germany*, 2nd edn (London: Macmillan, 1979).

Fusco, Coco, *English is Broken Here: Notes on Cultural Fusion in the Americas* (New York: New Press, 1995).

Gallegos, Rómulo, *Canaima* [1935], 12th edn (Madrid: Colección Austral, 1977).

——, *Canaima: edición crítica*, ed. Charles Minguet (Madrid: Archivos, CSIC, 1991).

——, *Canaima: edición crítica*, ed. Charles Minguet, rev. edn (Madrid: Archivos, CSIC, 1996).

——, *Doña Bárbara* [1929], ed. Domingo Miliani (Madrid: Cátedra, 2001).

García Márquez, Gabriel, *Cien años de soledad* [1967], ed. Jacques Joset (Madrid: Cátedra, 2004).

Geertz, Clifford, *Works and Lives: The Anthropologist as Author* (Cambridge: Polity, 1988).

Gide, André, *Travels in the Congo*, trans. Dorothy Bussy (New York: Knopf, 1930).

Gilmore, David, *Manhood in the Making: Cultural Concepts of Masculinity* (New Haven: Yale University Press, 1990).

Giunta, Andrea, 'Strategies of Modernity in Latin America', in Gerardo Mosquera (ed.), *Beyond the Fantastic: Contemporary Art Criticism from Latin America* (London: Institute of International Visual Arts, 1995), pp. 53–67.

Goldwert, Marvin, 'Mexican Machismo: The Flight from Femininity', *Psychoanalytic Review*, 72 (1985), pp. 161–69.

González, Eduardo G., 'El tiempo del hombre: huella y labor de origen en cuatro obras de Alejo Carpentier' (Unpublished doctoral thesis, Indiana University, 1974).

González Echevarría, Roberto, 'Ironía y estilo en *Los pasos perdidos*, de Alejo Carpentier', in Klaus Müller-Bergh (ed.), *Asedios a Carpentier: once ensayos críticos sobre el novelista cubano* (Santiago de Chile: Editorial Universitaria, 1972), pp. 134–45.

——, *Alejo Carpentier: The Pilgrim at Home* (Ithaca, NY: Cornell University Press, 1977).

——, *Myth and Archive: A Theory of Latin American Narrative* (Cambridge: Cambridge University Press, 1990).

——, 'Canaima y los libros de la selva', in Rómulo Gallegos, *Canaima: edición crítica*, ed. Charles Minguet, rev. edn (Madrid: CSIC, 1996), pp. 503–14.

Green, Joan R., 'La estructura del narrador y el modo narrativo de *La vorágine*', in Montserrat Ordóñez (ed.), *La vorágine: textos críticos* (Bogotá: Alianza Editorial Colombiana, 1987), pp. 269–77.

Greenblatt, Stephen, 'Learning to Curse: Aspects of Linguistic Colonialism in the Sixteenth Century', in Fredi Chiappelli (ed.), *First Images of America: The Impact of the New World on the Old*, 2 vols (Berkeley: University of California Press, 1976), I, pp. 561–86.

——, *Marvelous Possessions: The Wonder of the New World* (Oxford: Clarendon Press, 1991).

Greenslade, William, *Degeneration, Culture, and the Novel 1880–1940* (Cambridge: Cambridge University Press, 1994).

Griffiths, Gareth, 'The Myth of Authenticity: Representation, Discourse and Social Practice', in Chris Tiffin and Alan Lawson (eds.), *De-scribing Empire: Post-Colonialism and Textuality* (London: Routledge, 1994).

Guerrero, Gustavo, 'De las notas a la novela: el memorándum de Gallegos y la génesis de *Canaima*', in Rómulo Gallegos, *Canaima: edición crítica*, ed. Charles Minguet (Madrid: Archivos, CSIC, 1991), pp. 359–75.

Hall, Edith, *Inventing the Barbarian: Greek Self-definition through Tragedy* (Oxford: Clarendon Press, 1991).

Hanke, Lewis, *Aristotle and the American Indians: A Study in Race Prejudice in the Modern World* (London: Hollis & Carter, 1959).

Hardenburg, W. E., *The Putumayo: The Devil's Paradise; Travels in the Peruvian Amazon Region and an Account of the Atrocities Committed upon the Indians Therein*, ed. C. Reginald Enock (London: Unwin, 1912).

Harris, Wilson, 'The Frontier on which *Heart of Darkness* Stands', in Joseph Conrad, *Heart of Darkness*, ed. Robert Kimbrough, 3rd edn (New York: Norton: 1988), pp. 262–68.

Harrison, Dick, *Unnamed Country: The Struggle for a Canadian Prairie Fiction* (Edmonton: University of Alberta Press, 1977).

Harrs, Luis, *Los nuestros* (Buenos Aires: Editorial Sudamericana, 1966).

Henighan, Stephen, 'Caribbean Masks: Frantz Fanon and Alejo Carpentier', in Robin Fiddian (ed.), *Postcolonial Perspectives on the Cultures of Latin America and Lusophone Africa* (Liverpool: Liverpool University Press, 2000), pp. 169–90.

Hennessy, Alistair, *The Frontier in Latin American History* (London: Arnold, 1978).

Henríquez Ureña, Pedro, *Ensayos en busca de nuestra expresión* (Buenos Aires: Raigal, 1952).

Hirsch, Eric, 'Landscape: Between Place and Space', in Eric Hirsch and Michael O'Hanlon (eds.), *The Anthropology of Landscape: Perspectives on Place and Space* (Oxford: Oxford University Press, 1995), pp. 1–30.

Hobbes, Thomas, *Leviathan* [1651], ed. Richard Tuck (Cambridge: Cambridge University Press, 1996).

Hoffenberg, Peter H., *An Empire on Display: English, Indian, and Australian Exhibitions from the Crystal Palace to the Great War* (Berkeley: University of California Press, 2001).

Holland, Patrick, and Graham Huggan, *Tourists with Typewriters: Critical Reflections on Contemporary Travel Writing* (Ann Arbor: University of Michigan Press, 1998).

Honour, Hugh, *The New Golden Land: European Images of America from the Discoveries to the Present Time* (New York: Pantheon Books, 1975).

Hudson, W. H., *The Naturalist in La Plata* (London: Chapman and Hall, 1892).

——, *W. H. Hudson's South American Romances: The Purple Land; Green Mansions; El Ombu* (London: Duckworth, 1930).

——, *Far Away and Long Ago* [1918] (London: Eland, 1991).

——, *Green Mansions: A Romance of the Tropical Forest* [1904], ed. Ian Duncan (Oxford: Oxford University Press, 1998).

Hulme, Peter, *Colonial Encounters: Europe and the Native Caribbean 1492–1797* (London: Routledge, 1992).

——, 'Including America', *ARIEL: A Review of International English Literature*, 26.1 (1995), pp. 117–123.

——, 'Introduction: The Cannibal Scene', in Francis Barker, Hulme, and Margaret Iverson (eds.), *Cannibalism and the Colonial World* (Cambridge: Cambridge University Press, 1998), pp. 1–38.

Humboldt, Alexander von, *Views of Nature: The Sublime Phenomena of Creation*, trans. E. C. Otté and Henry G. Bohn (London: Bohn, 1850).

——, *Personal Narrative of a Journey to the Equinoctial Regions of the New Continent*, trans. Jason Wilson (Harmondsworth: Penguin, 1995).

Huntington, Ellsworth, *Civilization and Climate* (Hamden, CT: Archon Books, 1971).

Hussey, Christopher, *The Picturesque: Studies in a Point of View*, with a new preface (Hamden, CT: Archon Books, 1967).

Hutcheon, Linda, *A Poetics of Postmodernism: History, Theory, Fiction* (London: Routledge, 1988).

——, *Irony's Edge: The Theory and Politics of Irony* (London: Routledge, 1994).

Isaacs, Jorge, *María* [1867], ed. Donald McGrady (Madrid: Cátedra, 2001).

Kadir, Djelal, *Questing Fictions: Latin America's Family Romance* (Minneapolis: University of Minnesota Press, 1986).

Kant, Immanuel, *Critique of Judgement* [1790], trans. Werner S. Pluhar (Indianapolis: Hackett, 1987).

Kidd, Benjamin, *The Control of the Tropics* (London: Macmillan, 1898).

Klor de Alva, J. Jorge, 'The Postcolonization of the (Latin) American Experience: a Reconsideration of "Colonialism," "Postcolonialism," and "Mestizaje"', in Gyan Prakash (ed.), *After Colonialism: Imperial Histories and Postcolonial Displacements* (Princeton: Princeton University Press, 1995), pp. 241–275.

Kristeva, Julia, *Powers of Horror: An Essay on Abjection*, trans. Leon S. Roudiez (New York: Columbia University Press, 1982).

Kutzinski, Vera, *Against the American Grain: Myth and History in William Carlos Williams, Jay Wright, and Nicolás Guillén* (Baltimore: John Hopkins University Press, 1987).

Lacan, Jacques, *The Four Fundamental Concepts of Psychoanalysis*, ed. Jacques-Alain Miller, trans. Alan Sheridan (London: Norton, 1998).

Lange, Algot, *In the Amazon Jungle: Adventures in the Remote Parts of the Upper Amazon River, including a Sojourn among Cannibal Indians*, ed. J. Odell Hauser (London: Putnam's Sons, 1912).

Larsen, Neil, 'Foreword', in D. Emily Hicks, *Border Writing: The Multidimensional Text* (Minneapolis: University of Minnesota Press, 1991), pp. xi–xxi.

Leed, Eric J., *The Mind of the Traveler: From Gilgamesh to Global Tourism* (New York: Basic Books, 1991).

León Hazera, Lydia de, *La novela de la selva hispanoamericana: nacimiento, desarrollo y transformación* (Bogotá: Instituto Caro y Cuervo, 1971).

Lévi-Strauss, Claude, *Structural Anthropology*, trans. Claire Jacobson and Brooke Grundfest Schoepf (London: Allen Lane, 1968).

——, *Introduction to a Science of Mythology: The Origin of Table Manners*, trans. John and Doreen Weightman, 3 vols (London: Cape, 1978).

——, *Tristes Tropiques*, trans. John and Doreen Weightman (New York: Penguin, 1992).

Loomba, Ania, 'Overworlding the "Third World"', *Oxford Literary Review*, 13 (1991), pp. 164–91.

Lozano, Hernán, *La vorágine: ensayo bibliográfico* (Bogotá: Instituto Caro y Cuervo, 1973).

Macpherson, Jay, *The Spirit of Solitude: Conventions and Continuities in Late Romance* (New Haven: Yale University Press, 1982).

Magnarelli, Sharon, *The Lost Rib: Female Characters in the Spanish-American Novel* (Lewisburg: Bucknell University Press, 1985).

Maligo, Pedro, *Land of Metaphorical Desires: The Representation of Amazonia in Brazilian Literature* (New York: Lang, 1998).

Malinowski, Bronislaw, 'Introducción', in Fernando Ortiz, *Contrapunteo cubano del tabaco y el azúcar*, ed. Enrico Mario Santí (Madrid: Cátedra, 2002), pp. 123–33.

Marcone, Jorge, 'De retorno a lo natural: *La serpiente de oro*, la "novela de la selva" y la crítica ecológica', *Hispania*, 18 (1998), pp. 299–308.

——, 'Jungle Fever: Primitivism in Environmentalism; Rómulo Gallegos's *Canaima* and the Romance of the Jungle', in Erik Camayd-Freixas and José Eduardo González (eds.), *Primitivism and Identity in Latin America: Essays on Art, Literature, and Culture* (Tucson: University of Arizona Press, 2000), pp. 157–72.

Mariátegui, José Carlos, *Siete ensayos de la interpretación de la realidad peruana* (Lima: Biblioteca Amauta, 1965).

Marinelli, Peter V., *Pastoral* (London: Methuen, 1971).

Márquez Rodríguez, Alexis, *La obra narrativa de Alejo Carpentier* (Caracas: Ediciones de la Biblioteca, Universidad Central de Venezuela, 1970).

Menton, Seymour, '*La vorágine*: Circling the Triangle', *Hispania*, 59 (1976), pp. 418–34.

Mera, Juan León, *Cumandá o un drama entre salvajes* [1879], ed. Angel Esteban (Madrid: Cátedra, 1998).

Mignolo, Walter D., 'Colonial and Postcolonial Discourse: Cultural Critique or Academic Colonialism', *Latin American Research Review*, 28.3 (1993), pp. 120–134.

Miller, David, *W. H. Hudson and the Elusive Paradise* (London: Macmillan, 1990).

Miller, Shawn William, *An Environmental History of Latin America* (Cambridge: Cambridge University Press, 2007).

Millington Mark I., 'Gender Monolgue in Carpentier's *Los pasos perdidos*', *Modern Language Notes*, 111 (1996), pp. 346–67.

Minguet, Charles, 'Introducción', in Rómulo Gallegos, *Canaima: edición crítica*, ed. Minguet (Madrid: Archivos, CSIC, 1991), pp. xvii–xxii.

Minguet, Charles (ed.), Rómulo Gallegos, *Canaima: edición crítica* (Madrid: Archivos, CSIC 1991).

Miyazaki, Tieko Yamaguchi, '*Canaima* no Contexto dos Romances sobre a Selva', *Revista de Letras*, 20 (1980), pp. 75–87.

Molloy, Sylvia, 'Contagio narrativo y gesticulación retórica en *La vorágine*', in Montserrat Ordóñez (ed.), *La vorágine: textos críticos* (Bogotá: Alianza Editorial Colombiana, 1987), pp. 489–513.

Moore, Arthur K., *The Frontier Mind*, 2nd edn (New York: McGraw-Hill, 1963).

Morales, Leonidas, '*La vorágine*: un viaje al país de los muertos', in Montserrat Ordóñez (ed.), *La vorágine: textos críticos* (Bogotá: Alianza Editorial Colombiana, 1987), pp. 149–67.

More, Thomas, *Utopia* [1516], trans. Paul Turner (Harmondsworth: Penguin, 1968).

Moreno-Durán, R. H., 'Las voces de la polifonía telúrica', in Montserrat Ordóñez (ed.), *La vorágine: textos críticos* (Bogotá: Alianza Editorial Colombiana, 1987), pp. 437–52.

Müller-Bergh, Klaus, *Alejo Carpentier: estudio biográfico-crítico* (New York: Las Americas, 1972).

Mulvey, Christopher, *Anglo-American Landscapes: A Study of Nineteenth-century Anglo-American Travel Literature* (Cambridge: Cambridge University Press, 1983).

Nash, Roderick, *Wilderness and the American Mind*, rev. edn (New Haven: Yale University Press, 1973).

Neale-Silva, Eduardo, 'The Factual Bases of *La vorágine*', *PMLA*, 54 (1939), pp. 316–31.

——, *Horizonte humano: vida de José Eustasio Rivera* (Madison: University of Wisconsin Press, 1960).

Ngugi wa Thiong'o, *Decolonising the Mind: The Politics of Language in African Literature* (London: Currey, 1986).

Oelschlaeger, Max, *The Idea of Wilderness: From Prehistory to the Age of Ecology* (New Haven: Yale University Press, 1991).

Olivera, Otto, 'El romanticismo de *La vorágine*', in Montserrat Ordóñez (ed.), *La vorágine: textos críticos* (Bogotá: Alianza Editorial Colombiana, 1987), pp. 259–67.

Ordóñez, Montserrat, 'Introduction', in José Eustasio Rivera, *La vorágine*, ed. Monserrat Ordóñez (Madrid: Cátedra, 1998).

——, (ed.), *La vorágine: textos críticos* (Bogotá: Alianza Editorial Colombiana, 1987).

Outram, Dorinda, *The Enlightenment* (Cambridge: Cambridge University Press, 1995).

Ovid, *Metamorphoses*, trans. A. D. Melville (Oxford: Oxford University Press, 1987).

Pagden, Anthony, *The Fall of Natural Man: The American Indian and the Origins of Comparative Ethnology* (Cambridge: Cambridge University Press, 1982).

——, *European Encounters with the New World: From Renaissance to Romanticism* (New Haven: Yale University Press, 1993).

——, 'Shifting Antinomies: European Representations of the American Indian since Columbus', in Deborah L. Madsen (ed.), *Visions of America Since 1492* (London: Leicester University Press, 1994), pp. 23–34.

Parker, Michael, and Roger Starkey, 'Introduction', in Michael Parker and Roger Starkey (eds.), *Postcolonial Literatures: Achebe, Ngugi, Desai, Walcott* (Basingstoke: Macmillan, 1995), pp. 1–30.

Pérez Firmat, Gustavo, *The Cuban Condition: Translation and Identity in Modern Cuban Literature* (Cambridge: Cambridge University Press, 1989).

Pérus, Françoise, 'Universalidad del regionalismo: *Canaima* de Rómulo Gallegos', in Rómulo Gallegos, *Canaima: edición crítica*, ed. Charles Minguet (Madrid: Archivos, CSIC, 1991), pp. 417–72.

Pizarro, Ana, 'Imaginario y discurso: La amazonía', *Revista de Crítica Literaria Latino-americana*, 61 (2005), pp. 59–74.

Poignant, Roselyn, *Professional Savages: Captive Lives and Western Spectacle* (New Haven: Yale University Press, 2004).

Porras, María del Carmen, 'Entre los peligros de la desmesura y las limitaciones de la normalidad: *Canaima* de Rómulo Gallegos', *Alpha*, 18 (2002), pp. 43–62.

Porter, Dennis, *Haunted Journeys: Desire and Transgression in European Travel Writing* (Princeton: Princeton University Press, 1991).

Potelet, Janine, '*Canaima*, novela del Indio Caribe', in Rómulo Gallegos, *Canaima: edición crítica*, ed. Charles Minguet (Madrid: Archivos, CSIC, 1991), pp. 377–416.

Pratt, Mary Louise, *Imperial Eyes: Travel Writing and Transculturation* (London: Routledge, 1992).

Price, Sally, *Primitive Art in Civilized Places* (Chicago: University of Chicago Press, 1989).

Prieto, René, *Miguel Angel Asturias's Archaeology of Return* (Cambridge: Cambridge University Press, 1993).

——, 'The Literature of *Indigenismo*', in Roberto González Echevarría and Enrique Pupo-Walker (eds.), *The Cambridge History of Latin American Literature*, 3 vols (Cambridge: Cambridge University Press, 1996), II, pp. 138–63.

Quiroga, Horacio, *Cuentos de la selva* [1918], ed. Leonor Fleming (Madrid: Cátedra, 2001).

Rasch Isla, Miguel, 'Cómo escribió Rivera *La vorágine*', in Montserrat Ordóñez (ed.), *La vorágine: textos críticos* (Bogotá: Alianza Editorial Colombiana, 1987), pp. 83–88.

Rawson, Claude, '"Indians" and Irish: Montaigne, Swift, and the Cannibal Question', *Modern Language Quarterly*, 53 (1992), pp. 299–363.

Relph, E., *Place and Placelessness* (London: Pion, 1976).

Rider Haggard, H., *King Solomon's Mines* [1885] (Harmondsworth: Penguin, 1994).

——, *She* [1887], ed. Patrick Brantlinger (London: Penguin, 2001).

Roberts, Morley, *W. H. Hudson: A Portrait* (London: Eveleigh Nash & Grayson, 1924).

Rivera, José Eustasio, *La vorágine* (Bogotá: Editorial Cromos, 1924).

——, *La vorágine*, 3rd edn (Bogotá: Minerva, 1926).

——, *La vorágine*, 5th edn (Nueva York: Editorial Andes, 1928).

——, *Tierra de promisión* [1921] (Bogotá: Imprenta Nacional, 1955).

——, *La vorágine*, ed. Montserrat Ordóñez (Madrid: Cátedra, 1998).

Rocha, Joaquin, *Memorandum de viaje* (Bogotá: Editorial El Mercurio, 1905).

Rodríguez, Ileana, 'Naturaleza/nación: lo salvaje civil. Escribiendo Amazonía', *Revista de Crítica Literaria Latinoamericana*, 45 (1997), pp. 27–42.

Rolston III, Holmes, 'Aesthetic Experience in Forests', *The Journal of Aesthetics and Art Criticism*, 56 (1998), pp. 157–66.

Rosaldo, Renato, *Culture and Truth: The Remaking of Social Analysis* (London: Routledge, 1993).

Rose, Margaret A., *Parody: Ancient, Modern, and Post-Modern* (Cambridge: Cambridge University Press, 1993).

Rousseau, Jean-Jacques, *The Confessions*, trans. J. M. Cohen (New York: Penguin, 1953).

——, *The Discourses and Other Early Political Writings*, ed. and trans. Victor Gourevitch (Cambridge: Cambridge University Press, 2003).

Rubiés, Joan-Pau, 'Travel Writing and Ethnography', in Peter Hulme and Tim Youngs (eds.), *The Cambridge Companion to Travel Writing* (Cambridge: Cambridge University Press, 2002), pp. 242–60.

Sá, Lucia, *Rain Forest Literatures: Amazonian Texts and Latin American Culture* (Minneapolis: University of Minnesota Press, 2004).

Said, Edward, *Culture and Imperialism* (London: Vintage, 1994).

——, *Orientalism: Western Conceptions of the Orient* [1978], with a new afterword (London: Penguin, 1995).

Santander T., Carlos, 'Lo maravilloso en la obra de Alejo Carpentier', in Helmy F. Giacoman (ed.), *Homenaje a Alejo Carpentier: Variaciones interpretativas en torno a su obra* (New York: Las Americas, 1970), pp. 99–144.

Santayana, George, *The Sense of Beauty: Being the Outlines of Aesthetic Theory*, ed. William G. Holzberger and Herman J. Saatkamp, Jr., The Works of George Santayana (Cambridge, MA: MIT Press, 1981), II.

Sarmiento, Domingo F., *Facundo: civilización y barbarie* [1845] (México: Editorial Porrúa, 1998).

Seed, Patricia, 'Colonial and Postcolonial Discourse', *Latin American Research Review*, 26.3 (1991), pp. 181–200.

Serje, Margarita, *El revés de la nación: territorios salvajes, fronteras y tierras de nadie* (Bogotá: Ediciones Uniandes, 2005).

Shakespeare, William, *King Lear*, ed. Kenneth Muir (London: Methuen, 1986).

Shaw, Donald L., *Alejo Carpentier* (Boston: Twayne, 1985).

Shelley, Percy Bysshe, *Shelley's Poetry and Prose*, ed. Donald H. Reiman and Sharon B. Powers (New York: Norton, 1977).

Slater, Candace, *Entangled Edens: Visions of the Amazon* (Berkeley: University of California, 2002).

Smith, Jonathan, 'The Slightly Different Thing that is Said: Writing the Aesthetic Experience', in Trevor J. Barnes and James S. Duncan (eds.), *Writing Worlds: Discourse, Text and Metaphor in the Representation of Landscape* (London: Routledge, 1992), pp. 73–85.

Sommer, Doris, *Foundational Fictions: The National Romances of Latin America* (Berkeley: University of California Press, 1991).

——, *Proceed with Caution, when Engaged by Minority Writing in the Americas* (Cambridge, MA: Harvard University Press, 1999).

Soper, Kate, *What is Nature?: Culture, Politics and the Non-Human* (Oxford: Blackwell, 1995).

Spruce, Richard, *Notes of a Botanist on the Amazon and Andes*, ed. Alfred Russel Wallace, 2 vols (London: Macmillan, 1908).

Spurr, David, *The Rhetoric of Empire: Colonial Discourse in Journalism, Travel Writing, and Imperial Administration* (Durham, NC: Duke University Press, 1993).

Stabb, Martin S., *In Quest of Identity: Patterns in the Spanish American Essay of Ideas, 1890–1960* (Chapel Hill: University of North Carolina Press, 1967).

Steiner, George, *After Babel: Aspects of Language and Translation* (London: Oxford University Press, 1975).

Stepan, Nancy Leys, 'Biological Degeneration: Races and Proper Places', in J. Edward Chamberlain and Sandra L. Gilman (eds.), *The Dark Side of Progress* (New York: Columbia University Press, 1985), pp. 97–120.

——, *'The Hour of Eugenics': Race, Gender, and Nation in Latin America* (Ithaca: Cornell University Press, 1991).

——, *Picturing Tropical Nature* (London: Reaktion Books, 2001).

Stevens, Evelyn P., '*Marianismo*: The Other Face of *Machismo* in Latin America', in Ann Pescatello (ed), *Female and Male in Latin America: Essays* (Pittsburgh: University of Pittsburgh Press, 1973), pp. 89–101.

Sturtevant, William C., 'First Visual Images of Native America', in Fredi Chiappelli (ed.), *First Images of America: The Impact of the New World on the Old*, 2 vols (Berkeley: University of California Press, 1976), I, pp. 417–54.

Suárez-Araúz, Nicomedes, *Literary Amazonia: Modern Writing by Amazonian Authors* (Gainesville: University Press of Florida, 2004).

Subero, Efraín, 'Génesis de *Canaima*', in Rómulo Gallegos, *Canaima: edición crítica*, ed. Charles Minguet (Madrid: Archivos, CSIC, 1991), pp. 309–16.

Swift, Jonathan, *Gulliver's Travels* [1726] (London: Penguin, 1994).

Taussig, Michael, *Shamanism, Colonialism, and the Wild Man: A Study in Terror and Healing* (Chicago: University of Chicago Press, 1991).

Tedlock, Denis (trans.), *Popol Vuh: The Mayan book of the Dawn of Life*, rev. edn (New York: Simon & Schuster, 1996).

Thoreau, Henry David, *The Portable Thoreau*, ed. Carl Bode (Harmondsworth: Penguin, 1982).

Tiffin, Helen, 'Post-Colonial Literatures and Counter Discourse', in Bill Ashcroft, Gareth Griffiths, and Helen Tiffin (eds.), *The Post-Colonial Studies Reader* (London: Routledge, 1997), pp. 95–98.

Todorov, Tzvetan, *The Conquest of America: The Question of the Other*, trans. Richard Howard (New York: Harper & Row, 1984).

Tomlinson, Ruth, *W. H. Hudson: A Biography* (London: Faber and Faber, 1982).

Torgovnick, Marianna, *Gone Primitive: Savage Intellects, Modern Lives* (Chicago: University of Chicago Press, 1990).

Trigo, Benigno, *Subjects of Crisis: Race and Gender as Disease in Latin America* (Hanover, NH: Wesleyan University Press, 2000).

Tuan, Yi-Fu, *Topophilia: A Study of Environmental Perception, Attitudes, and Values* (Englewood Cliffs: Prentice Hall, 1974).

Unruh, Vicky, *Latin American Vanguards: The Art of Contentious Encounters* (Berkeley: University of California Press, 1994).

Up de Graff, F. W., *Head Hunters of the Amazon; Seven Years of Exploration and Adventure*, ed. R. B. Cunninghame Graham (London: Jenkins, 1923).

Uribe Piedrahita, César, *Toá y Mancha de aceite*, ed. J. G. Cobo Borda (Bogotá: Instituto Colombiano de Cultura, 1979).

Valente, José Angel, 'La naturaleza y el hombre en *La vorágine*, de José Eustasio Rivera', *Cuadernos Hispanoamericanos*, 24.67 (1955), pp. 102–08.

Van den Berg, J. H., *The Phenomenological Approach to Psychiatry: An Introduction to Recent Phenomenological Psychopathology* (Springfield, IL: Thomas, 1955).

Vargas Llosa, Mario, *La casa verde* [1965] (Barcelona: Seix Barral, 1967).

——, 'Primitives and Creators', *TLS*, 14 November 1968.

——, *La utopía arcaica: José María Arguedas y las ficciones del indigenismo* (México: Fondo de Cultura Económica, 1996).

——, *El hablador* [1987] (Barcelona: Seix Barral, 1997).

Vaughan, Alden T., *Transatlantic Encounters: American Indians in Britain, 1500–1776* (Cambridge: Cambridge University Press, 2006).

Vidal, Hernán, 'The Concept of Colonial and Postcolonial Discourse. A Perspective from Literary Criticism', *Latin American Research Review*, 28.3 (1993), pp. 113–119.

Villanueva-Collado, Alfredo, 'El macho, la historia y la otredad: *Canaima*, de Rómulo Gallegos', *Alba de America: Revista Literaria*, 13 (1995), pp. 105–13.

Virgillo, Carmelo, 'Primitivism in Latin American Fiction', in A. Owen Aldridge (ed.), *The Ibero-American Enlightenment* (Urbana: University of Illinois Press, 1971).

Wakefield, Steve, *Carpentier's Baroque Fiction: Returning Medusa's Gaze* (Woodbridge: Tamesis, 2004).

Webb, Barbara J., *Myth and History in Caribbean Fiction: Alejo Carpentier, Wilson Harris, and Edouard Glissant* (Amherst: University of Massachusetts Press, 1992).

White, Hayden, *Tropics of Discourse: Essays in Cultural Criticism* (Baltimore: Johns Hopkins University Press, 1978).

Whitehead, Neil L., 'South America/Amazonia: The Forest of Marvels', in Peter Hulme and Tim Youngs (eds.), *The Cambridge Companion to Travel Writing* (Cambridge: Cambridge University Press, 2002), pp. 122–38.

Williams, Raymond, *Keywords: A Vocabulary of Culture and Society*, rev. edn (London: Fontana Press, 1988).

Williams, Raymond L., 'La figura del autor y del escritor en *La vorágine*', *Discurso Literario*, 4 (1987), pp. 535–51.

Wilson, Jason, *W. H. Hudson: The Colonial's Revenge* (London: University of London Institute of Latin American Studies, 1981).

Woodroffe, Joseph F., *The Upper Reaches of the Amazon* (London: Methuen, 1914).

Wyers, Frances, 'Carpentier's *Los pasos perdidos*: Heart of Lightness, Heart of Darkness', *Revista Hispánica Moderna*, 45 (1992), pp. 84–95.

Wylie, Lesley, 'Hearts of Darkness: The Celebration of Otherness in the Latin American *novela de la selva*', *Romance Studies*, 23. 2 (2005), pp. 105–16.

——, 'Colonial Tropes and Postcolonial Tricks: Rewriting the Tropics in the *novela de la selva*', *Modern Language Review*, 101. 3 (2006), pp. 728–42.

Zamora, Lois Parkinson, *The Usable Past: The Imagination of History in Recent Fiction of the Americas* (Cambridge: Cambridge University Press, 1997).

Index